D1124403

THE MITRED EARL

The odd behaviour of the Hervey family in the eighteenth century made people say that when God created the world he made men, women and Herveys. By far the most eccentric of them was Frederick Hervey, 4th Earl of Bristol and Bishop of Derry. Traveller, politician, scholar, collector and the subject of a series of amorous adventures, he was a continuous source of amazement to his contemporaries. Horace Walpole condemned his profligate folly, John Wesley praised his plenteous good works, and George II denounced him as 'that wicked prelate'.

Hervey was known to his contemporaries as the 'edifying bishop', not through any apostolic zeal but on account of the number of great houses he built. Of the two that he built in Ireland, one was later pulled down and the other, Downhill, is now a ruin, although the Bishop's charming Mussenden Temple survives in the care of the National Trust. However, it is the great house at Ickworth near Bury St Edmunds in Suffolk, with its vast central rotunda, which remains as Hervey's principal memorial, again in the care of the National Trust.

As a traveller Hervey spent money lavishly and startled foreigners by his extraordinary behaviour and peculiar manner of dress – the many Bristol hotels on the Continent are named after him. In politics he was a staunch Whig, and — though an Anglican bishop — he bravely defended the rights of Catholics and Presbyterians in Ireland, joining vigorously in the movement for emancipation and reform. His political intrigues in Europe at the time of the French Revolution landed him for a brief spell in prison but failed to suppress his zest for life and adventure.

Hervey was a man with ideas well in advance of his times both in politics and connoisseurship, but his influence was undermined by the extraordinary eccentricties of his life. He spent his last years in restless travel, buying works of art for the mansion he was building at Ickworth, and in plotting to retrieve his collection when it was impounded by the revolutionary French. He died in circumstances no less odd, suddenly on the road between Albano and Rome on 8 July 1803.

Brian Fothergill was born in 1921 and educated at Wycliffe and King's College, London. After war service with the Intelligence Corps, he taught for a while before becoming a professional writer in 1958. Specializing chiefly in eighteenth-century biography, his books include lives of the last Stuart pretender Cardinal York, Sir William Hamilton and William Beckford as well as a study of Horace Walpole and his circle. He received the Heinemann award in 1969 and again in 1980, and the Silver Pen Prize in 1970. He is a Fellow of the Society of Antiquaries and a Vice-President and Chairman of the Council of the Royal Society of Literature.

Titles in the National Trust Classics series:

BATH by Edith Sitwell
THE EARLS OF CREATION by James Lees-Milne
FELBRIGG, THE STORY OF A HOUSE by R.W. Ketton-Cremer
FIRST AND LAST LOVES by John Betjeman
GHASTLY GOOD TASTE by John Betjeman
THE HOUSEKEEPING BOOK OF SUSANNA WHATMAN by Susanna Whatman
IN A GLOUCESTERSHIRE GARDEN by Canon Ellacombe
MADE IN ENGLAND by Dorothy Hartley
THE RULE OF TASTE by John Steegman
RUSTIC ADORNMENTS FOR HOMES OF TASTE by Shirley Hibberd
VICTORIAN TASTE by John Steegman
THE WILD GARDEN by William Robinson
UPPARK AND ITS PEOPLE by Margaret Meade-Fetherstonhaugh and Oliver Warner
GALLIPOT EYES by Elspeth Huxley
A HAMPSHIRE MANOR by Ralph Dutton
POT-POURRI FROM A SURREY GARDEN by Mrs C.W. Earle
THE SEVEN LAMPS OF ARCHITECTURE by John Ruskin

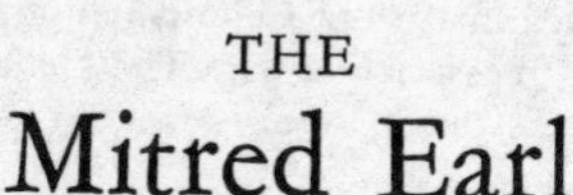

THE Mitred Earl

An Eighteenth-Century Eccentric

BRIAN FOTHERGILL

CENTURY
London Melbourne Auckland Johannesburg

First published in 1974 by Faber and Faber

This edition first published in 1988 by Century, an imprint of Century Hutchinson Ltd, in association with The National Trust for Places of Historic Interest or Natural Beauty, 36 Queen Anne's Gate, London SW1H 9AS

Century Hutchinson Ltd, Brookmount House, 62–65 Chandos Place, London WC2N 4NW

Century Hutchinson Australia Pty Ltd,
PO Box 496, 16–22 Church Street, Hawthorn, Melbourne,
Victoria 3122, Australia

Century Hutchinson Group New Zealand Limited,
PO Box 40–086, Glenfield, Auckland 10, New Zealand

Century Hutchinson South Africa (Pty) Ltd,
PO Box 337, Bergvlei, 2012 South Africa

Cover illustrations of Frederick Hervey and Ickworth
by courtesy of the National Trust

British Library Cataloguing in Publication Data

Fothergill, Brian
The mitred earl : an eighteenth-century
eccentric
1. Church of Ireland. Bristol, Frederick
Augustus Hervey – Earl of – Biographies
I. Title
283.'.092'4

ISBN 0-7126-2437-6

Printed in Great Britain by
Richard Clay (The Chaucer Press) Ltd, Bungay, Suffolk.

Published in association with The National Trust, this series is devoted to reprinting books on the artistic, architectural, social and cultural heritage of Britain. The imprint covers buildings and monuments, arts and crafts, gardening and landscape in a variety of literary forms, including histories, memoirs, biographies and letters.

The Century Classics also include the Travellers, Seafarers and Lives and Letters series.

Contents

Acknowledgements

I must thank Mr. Angus Davidson who first suggested to me the idea of writing a biography of the Earl-Bishop of Derry and who has helped me in many ways; also Count Charles de Salis who kindly allowed me to see copies of letters from Lord Bristol written to members of his family. I am grateful to Mr. Edward T. Joy who was most helpful to me at Ickworth and Mr. Douglas Sellick who has given me invaluable assistance in selecting the illustrations. Thanks are also due for help or advice to Miss T. Creyke-Clark, the Knight of Glin, Mr. Spike Hughes and Mr. Raleigh Trevelyan.

I

Men, Women, and Herveys

I

On a January day in the year 1768 an unusual scene might have been observed in the grounds of the palace of the Bishop of Cloyne. Perhaps to keep themselves warm in what must surely have been cold weather, or possibly just from sheer high spirits, a group of young men were engaged in a jumping competition. There is nothing particularly surprising in this, except for the fact that the group consisted of clergymen and that they were led in their game by the Bishop himself, who was still some years short of his fortieth birthday. As his turn came round and he got ready to leap, their frolics were interrupted by the arrival of a messenger from Dublin Castle. 'I will jump no more,' declared the Bishop after reading what the messenger had brought him: 'I have beaten you all, for I have jumped from Cloyne to Derry.' It was a leap indeed, not only from the little town of Cloyne not far distant from Cork in southern Ireland to Londonderry in the extreme north, but also from one of the more obscure to the wealthiest diocese in all Ireland.

Though various versions of this story exist there is, alas, no conclusive evidence that the episode ever took place at all. This is unfortunate, for the remark as well as the action is so highly characteristic of the eccentric and boisterous personality of the central figure. Frederick Hervey, later to be fourth Earl of Bristol as well as forty-eighth Bishop of Derry, belonged to that family springing from Ickworth, near Bury St. Edmunds in Suffolk, of whom it was said that when God created the human race he made men, women, and Herveys, for such was the fame of their eccentric behaviour. The remark was too good to be claimed by any one person and has been attributed variously to Lord Chesterfield, Lady Townshend, Lady Mary Wortley Montagu, and even to Voltaire himself. If originally made of an earlier generation of the family it was to find full expression and justification in the life and career of the Earl-Bishop of Derry. In the words of his contemporary and political rival Lord Charlemont: 'His family was indeed famous for talents, equally so for eccentricity, and the eccentricity of the whole race shone out and seemed to be concentrated in him.'[1]

The Herveys were a family of strong Whig principles. The Bishop's grandfather had been Member of Parliament for Bury St. Edmunds in 1694 and was raised to the peerage as Lord Hervey of Ickworth in 1703. With the death of Queen Anne he had shown no tendency to flirt with the Pretender but had declared his full support for the principles of the Revolution and the Hanoverian succession. If the new monarch lacked English he did not lack gratitude (or, at least, prudence) and in October 1714 Lord Hervey was advanced in the peerage as Earl of Bristol.

It was this peer's eldest son who was the Bishop's father. He was the Lord Hervey celebrated for his entertaining and unfettered memoirs of the Court of King George II and Queen Caroline and also as the victim of Pope's biting satire where, under the guise of Sporus, his principles, morals, deportment and diet even, had been mercilessly exposed to ridicule:

Amphibious thing! that acting either part,
The trifling head, or the corrupted heart!
Fop at the toilet, flatterer at the board,
Now trips a lady, and now struts a lord . . .

In spite of the poet's innuendo Hervey had managed to enjoy the favours of a mistress (the paternity of whose child he was to dispute with the heir to the throne), and in 1720 to have married for love the charming and clever Molly Lepel, as praised by Pope as her husband had been vilified and the subject of the only verses written in English to have survived from the pen of Voltaire. Eight children were the fruit of this union, four boys and four girls; not altogether a bad achievement for

that thing of silk,
Sporus, that mere white curd of ass's milk.

Frederick[2] was their third son and was born on Saturday, 1 August 1730. His name derived from no less a person than his father's future rival in love, Frederick, Prince of Wales, who stood sponsor at his christening on September 3. His other sponsors, hardly less august, were all of ducal rank: Charles, second Duke of Richmond, and Henrietta, Countess of Godolphin, who was also Duchess of Marlborough in her own right.

In such splendid company was Frederick Hervey made a Christian though the strength and even the sincerity of his religious convictions were later sometimes to be called in question – not least after he had become a bishop of the established Church of Ireland. Perhaps it should be stated at once that it was his fame for building palatial country houses for his own occupation and enjoyment, rather than for any noticeable apostolic zeal, that caused him later to be known as 'the edifying bishop'.

He was fortunate in his education. At the age of twelve he entered Westminster School which at that period was, by the brutal standards of the day, a place of some culture and scholastic distinction. It was here that he met and formed a lifelong attachment to William Hamilton, later British Minister to the Court of Naples and ultimately husband of the notorious Emma Hart. With Hamilton, even at this early age, he shared an enthusiasm for art and antiquity. They were destined to die in the same year (as both had been born in 1730) and their friendship survived to the end. It was one of the happier and least complicated relationships of his life.

Eighteen months after entering Westminster he lost his father, Lord Hervey, who died in July 1743. By his father's will Frederick was left £100 a year for his education and maintenance and an annuity of '£200 a year clear' upon the death of his grandfather Lord Bristol, an event which did not occur for nearly eight years. It was hardly a princely income to look forward to, even by the money values of the day, but as much as could be expected for a younger son. Upon becoming a widow his mother retired to Ickworth where she spent most of her time in her father-in-law's house, himself by then for the second time a widower and in his late seventies. It was from here, a year later, that she wrote to her son's tutor: 'I am extremely pleased with all you say of Frederick for I value your judgement. He has certainly very good parts and great application, and will, I am persuaded, make a considerable figure in the world. I have heard from him of late pretty often; he is a very agreeable and entertaining correspondent. His scheme of study and travelling as you relate it to me seems a very good one.' So the young boy, later so famous for his peregrinations, was already turning his mind towards travel.

From Westminster Frederick went on to Cambridge, entering Corpus Christi College on 10 November 1747. As at this time his interests lay in the direction of the law (or did so when he thought of a career, for already his real tastes were for art, history, and antiquarian pursuits) he was the following February also admitted to Lincoln's Inn; though here he seems chiefly to be remembered as the author of a satire against card-playing called *The Female Drum, or the Origin of Cards*, rather than for any hot pursuit of the principles of jurisprudence.

At Cambridge, however, he soon made his mark. 'His good sense, great good-nature and affability,' according to the antiquary William Cole, 'gained him the love and esteem of all who knew him; and his sprightliness, wit, vivacity, ingenuity and learning proved him to be a genuine Hervey, and the son of my Lord Privy Seal.'[3] Frederick's later life was to prove that this was not just sycophantic praise offered to an influential sprig of the nobility; certainly good nature, sprightliness (often at the cost of episcopal dignity), wit and vivacity were to be attributed to him through life. Learning seemed to come easily to him, though often with more enthusiasm than discipline. He had a particular gift for foreign languages, being later, according to Martin Sherlock, the master of five, while Arthur Young more sweepingly claimed that he 'spoke all modern languages fluently, and had an uncommon vein of pleasantry and wit which he greatly exerted, and without reserve, when in the company of a few select friends'.[4] But the acquisition of knowledge was always achieved with a characteristic lightness of touch. 'I have applied myself so close to recover Hebrew and Italian (not that I propose being either circumcis'd or castrated)', he wrote once from abroad, 'that I have had little time to write mere English'. He seems to have been equally at home in English, French, and Italian, and in his letters he often jumped inconsequently from one language to another.

In January 1751 his grandfather died at the age of eighty-five. He had had twenty children and had survived fourteen of them and was succeeded as second Earl of Bristol by his grandson George, Frederick's eldest brother. In the same year Frederick himself came down from Cambridge without taking a degree. Learning no doubt became the brother of an earl but examinations were for lesser men. Three years later he took his degree by right as a nobleman's son.

2

The problem of finding employment was always a difficult one for the younger sons of noble houses in the eighteenth century; that is, if they did not have enough money on their own account to do what was most expected of them, which was to do nothing at all. One way of solving the problem was to marry an heiress. It was often done; it was quite accepted – even encouraged – by society; and the marriages were usually happy. It was a course Frederick Hervey might very well have chosen, but instead, while only a year down from Cambridge, he elected to marry for love a girl who brought him no more than £3,000 as dowry. They were married on 10 August 1752, the bridegroom being twenty-two and the bride nineteen. His family disapproved, so did hers; only his elder sister Lepel and her husband Constantine Phipps, later Lord Mulgrave, seem to have accepted the young couple.

It was not entirely surprising that the Hervey family looked askance at the match. The bride, Elizabeth, was a daughter of the late Sir Jermyn Davers of Rushbrook Hall, Suffolk, by his wife Margaretta, who had lived with him for ten years before they had decided to get married in the year 1729. Of their numerous family some were born before, some after, this timely event. In the simple environment of rural Suffolk such a scandal was not quickly forgotten. But this was not all: a political barrier also separated the two families. The Daverses were Tories and had opposing interests to the Whig Herveys in the borough of Bury St. Edmunds. It was all most unfortunate.

The Herveys were the first to relent, won over, perhaps, by the quiet charm and good sense of Elizabeth, who very clearly lived up to her pet name of 'Excellent'. Frederick's mother was in no position to object to a love match; she had married for love herself. Lady Davers was more adamant, though hardly able to point as an example to her own past history. She was now a formidable dowager and did not lift her ban until some fifteen months after the marriage, by which time a daughter had made her appearance, to be followed in due course by two more girls and four sons. The couple settled first near Peterborough and later at Horrenger, close to Ickworth. They presented a charming picture of domestic bliss.

All for the present went well; all, that is, except for the problem of employment. Hervey's interest in the law was beginning to flag (it was, he considered, a 'plodding profession') and there seemed little chance just then of a comfortable 'place' or sinecure under government being found for him. He began to look elsewhere. His younger brother William, who had always been destined for the Church, suddenly announced his intention of joining the Army. It was this change of plan in another member of the family that turned Frederick's thoughts in the direction of an ecclesiastical career for himself. On 29 June 1754, he told his brother-in-law Phipps of William's decision, and added: 'Since he has resolv'd not to be a clergyman I think I have determined to become one – my Inclination, my interest, and what tho' last mentioned yet first consider'd, Mrs. Hervey's desire, all unite and have all been since strengthen'd by my brother's [Lord Bristol's] approbation, so that nothing now remains to complete my scheme, but some preparation and the time to execute it.' As a first step in this direction he availed himself of his privilege as a peer's son to take his master's degree at Cambridge without examination.

What form his other preparation took does not transpire. He had shown an interest in theological reading for some time past. Writing to Phipps in April 1753, he told him that he had been buying theological books though 'that science is at a poor ebb at present'. He was made deacon by Dr. Mawson, Bishop of Ely, on 24 August 1754, and ordained priest on January 26 the following year. He continued to live in the neighbourhood of the family estate at Bury St. Edmunds; whatever else his motives may have been in taking Holy Orders he does not appear ever to have contemplated parochial work. The clerical profession at this period was considered very much like any other, and one of the few in which a gentleman could decently employ himself. Ideas of any special vocation belong to earlier and later periods; at the time of Hervey's ordination the notion of a divine call would have come under the general disapproval in which all manifestations of 'enthusiasm' were held. It was only five years since Horace Walpole had recalled seeing Dr. Blackburne, Archbishop of York, at dinner where 'his mistress, Mrs. Curwys, sat at the head of the table, and Hayter, his natural son by another woman, and very much like him, at the bottom, as Chaplain.'

The next decade, in fact, was to see little advance in Hervey's fortunes. As the brother of an earl he naturally looked towards his elder brother for patronage but at this period Lord Bristol, a man of delicate health, lived mainly abroad. In 1755 he had been appointed British Minister at Turin, being promoted two years later to be Ambassador to the Court of Spain. Such offices as came Frederick's way were civil ones. In 1756 he obtained the post of Clerk of the Privy Seal, becoming Principal Clerk five years later. This was a lay office and he owed it, very probably, to the fact that his father had, in his day, been Lord Privy Seal. It was the custom for the holders of these posts to draw the salary and appoint a deputy, on a considerably inferior stipend, to perform the duties. In this case the post was not lucrative and Hervey's position was very far from being affluent.

Meanwhile his family increased. In October 1755 a son, christened George, was born. This child did not reach manhood but was destined to die at Spa in Germany at the age of nine. Another son, John Augustus, was born on 1 January 1757, and a second daughter, Elizabeth Christiana (later the celebrated Lady Elizabeth Foster) made her appearance in May 1758. Yet another son, who died in infancy, made his brief entrance on the scene in 1761, after which Frederick's 'Excellent' had a few years respite before her last two children, Louisa and Frederick William, were born in 1767 and 1769 respectively. With each new arrival Hervey's need for a solid preferment in the Church became more pressing.

In such circumstances the news of the death of some well-endowed dignitary of the Church, with the consequent vacancy of his office, can hardly have been less than welcome. Such news, alas, could not always be relied upon. When Hervey applied in June 1760, for the deanery of Bristol, the Duke of Newcastle felt obliged to reply that the present Dean was 'in extreme good health on Friday last . . .' and attempts to obtain the deanery of Norwich or the mastership of Magdalene College, Cambridge, fared no better. By 1763 Hervey, for all his aristocratic connections, could claim no more impressive ecclesiastical dignity than Chaplain to King George III.

Financial troubles, indeed, seem to have dogged Hervey at this period of his life. To his sister Lepel he wrote in May 1760: 'I have long solicited Sir R. Davers to pay Mrs. Hervey's fortune, but all to no purpose, till I did more than sollicit about last Christmas, when he and his Attorney promised to let me have what I wanted almost immediately, but after various delays, I am now put off till Michaelmas . . . but my difficulty now is to get the money a quarter of a year sooner, and as you mention'd sometime ago your being oblig'd to borrow money to pay the Crown fine, I am in hopes you might borrow the additional sum that I want and let me stand accountable to you for it . . .'

Troubles in his own family may well have accounted for Sir Robert's failure to pay his sister's dowry with the promptness expected by her exigent husband. In the previous year his brother Henry Davers, a naval officer, had shot himself on board ship for no known reason. It was the first of a series of tragedies that were to afflict poor 'Excellent's' family in the next few years. About the time that Hervey was writing to his sister Lepel, Sir Robert let Rushbrook to the Duke of Cleveland and sailed for America. In 1763 news reached home that he had been attacked and killed by Indians in the region of Lake Huron. Tragedy did not end there, however, for in 1766 Thomas, the youngest of the family and a clergyman, also shot himself in the greenhouse of his mother's house during a visit to her at Bury St. Edmunds. The reason for these two suicides remains obscure, though in the later case it was said that Thomas Davers 'had been under a discontent for some time'.

Just before this sad event Frederick and Elizabeth Hervey set out on their first continental journey. They visited Brussels, Geneva, Naples, Rome, Florence, Venice, Padua, and even Corsica, where Frederick was received by the patriotic General Pasquale de Paoli. It was an itinerary that was to become very familiar in Frederick's life. Indeed, after succeeding to the earldom his fame as a traveller no less than his reputation as a munificent patron was to win him such renown that his name alone would succeed in recommending an inn or hostelry if it could be suggested to the cautious visitor that Lord Bristol himself had once put up there. So it was that a series of Bristol hotels sprang into being all over Europe after his death even though, as was quite often the case, they were in places he had never actually visited during his lifetime.

Of his first continental journey, saddened by the death of their eldest son at Spa, only two episodes need concern us. From Zurich Hervey made the pilgrimage to Ferney to pay his respects to Voltaire. In showing his estate to this clergyman, son of the woman to whom he had once addressed the lines

Hervey, would you know the passion
You have kindled in my breast?

the patriarch of Ferney, now aged seventy-one, indicated the church and the theatre he had recently had built and asked the question: '*Où jouet t'on la plus grande farce?*' Hervey studied the two buildings and replied: '*C'est selon les auteurs.*'

The second episode occurred in Naples where the Herveys found themselves in the spring of 1766. Here they were the guests of Frederick's old schoolfellow William Hamilton who had been British Minister to the King of the Two Sicilies for the past two years. It was the period of his first marriage to the quiet and charming Catherine Barlow, and many years before the beautiful but predatory Emma Hart appeared on the scene.

Hamilton had already become fascinated by the volcano which was his close neighbour and upon whose activities he would soon become a leading authority. On this occasion Vesuvius obligingly put on a dramatic display for the benefit of his guests, though when climbing to the crater Hervey, lacking his friend's skill in anticipating the volcano's fury, almost came to grief. To his daughter Mary, home in England, he wrote describing his adventure: 'At last after about an hour's fatigue we reach'd the summit, where we found a great hollow of about forty feet and half a mile round: at the bottom of this were two large mouths from whence the mountain frequently threw up two or three hundred red hot stones some as big as your head, and some considerably larger. One of these struck me on the right arm, and without giving me much pain at the time made a wound about 2 inches deep, tore my coat all to shreads, and by a great effusion of blood alarm'd my companions more than myself. In a few days it became very painfull, then dangerous, and so continued to confine me to my bed and my room for near five weeks.'

If Hervey, as he lay ill in Naples, was troubled by thoughts of his still unsettled future and blamed the brother who so inconsiderately took posts abroad far from news of vacant prebends or dying deans, so useless to a younger brother very much in need of influence in high places, he need have worried no longer. On 26 August 1766, Lord Bristol was offered the Lord Lieutenancy of Ireland which he accepted the following day. As an earnest of better things to come he immediately appointed his brother to the post of First Chaplain. Cured of his wounded arm and in great hopes for the future, Hervey returned home by way of Verona, Trent, and the Swiss cantons.

3

Lord Bristol resigned his office within a year of his appointment and never set foot in Ireland; but he lost no time in promoting the interests of his younger brother. Lord Chatham headed the Ministry and his support for Frederick's nomination to the first vacant bishopric in Ireland was gained without trouble. It was Lord Bristol's ambition to promote his brother to the See of Derry for it was the richest in Ireland, but the reigning prelate, Dr. William Barnard, though despaired of by his doctors, showed no signs of dying in order to oblige the Lord Lieutenant. The Bishop of Cloyne displayed more tact and conveniently expired in January 1767, whereupon Lord Bristol immediately pressed his brother's claims upon the King's attention. 'Remember you are engaged to me for the first bishopric,' the King declared, but added: 'I desire my recommendation may take place and that your brother shall be the new bishop.' When Bristol expressed his thanks (as he afterwards told Lord Chatham) George III replied: 'I am as well pleased as yourself with his being a bishop.'

Apart from once having been ruled by the great philosopher George Berkeley, the diocese of Cloyne, remote and rather obscure, can have had no great merit in the eyes of Frederick Hervey except its vacancy. It was a convenient stepping-stone and he was quite ready to fill this vacancy until another and better one presented itself. There never seems to have been very much doubt that he would go on to Derry as soon as Dr. Barnard did what was expected of him and departed this world for a better one. If there was any doubt it was quickly expelled in the October following his consecration when Hervey was sworn a member of the Irish Privy Council, an honour usually confined to the Archbishops of Armagh and Dublin and the Bishop of Meath.

The consecration itself took place in Christ Church Cathedral, Dublin, on 31 May 1767. The service was conducted by the Archbishop assisted by the Bishops of Meath and Ferns. Early next month the new Bishop was back in London on a brief visit where he met the poet Gray whom he had known well at Cambridge. 'I have seen his Lordship of Cloyne often', wrote Gray. 'He is very jolly, and we devoured four raspberry puffs together in Cranbourne Alley; but he is gone, and Heaven knows when we shall eat any more.' Hervey seems to have carried his new dignity with an easy grace.

When Frederick Hervey crossed the sea for his consecration as Bishop of Cloyne he was making his first visit to the country with which, despite all the years he was to spend on the continent of Europe, he was to be so closely associated until his death. Ireland, Italy, and Germany, almost more than his native England, were now to form the setting in which the scenes of his extravagant existence were to be acted out. He was to identify himself entirely with the aspirations of Irish nationalism which were beginning to manifest themselves among the upper-middle classes of the Protestant establishment, and show himself a staunch friend to the suppressed Catholic majority as well as to the Presbyterian element in the north. It was a curious role for a Church of Ireland bishop and was to lose him the goodwill of the Monarch who had expressed such pleasure at his appointment.

Hervey was at Cloyne for less than a year. In January 1768 Dr. Barnard at last died and Hervey's appointment to the coveted See of Derry was announced the following month. The letters patent for his translation were dated 18 February, two days after the degree of Doctor of Divinity had been conferred on him by Trinity College, Dublin.

Some idea of the value of his new diocese can be gained from Litton Falkiner's *Studies in Irish History and Biography*. 'The emoluments of the bishopric', he writes, 'which at the date of his appointment amounted to £7,000, rose ultimately, under the skilful management of its new occupant, to a princely revenue not far short of £20,000 a year. Attached to the bishopric were 70,000 acres of land, and for the renewal fines on the leases of the diocesan estate the Bishop received immense sums, which he spent with lavish profusion.'[5] No wonder the new Bishop could write somewhat complacently to the French scientist D'Anville '*Je suis Evêque de cent-vingt et quatre-mille livres de rentes.*' If the sum was a little exaggerated at the time (for the letter was written only two months after his appointment) it was a pardonable hyperbole in one who had just leapt so satisfactorily from Cloyne to Derry.

It is quite true that the new Bishop spent his money 'with lavish profusion'. If he lived like a *grand seigneur* it was partly because he was expected to do so, though there was no denying that he enjoyed the role and played it with aplomb. Vast sums were to go into his building schemes, which included repairs and restoration to his Cathedral, a bridge to span the river Foyle at Derry, and the erection of spires on churches which lacked this elegant and symbolic embellishment (especially when the result improved the view from one of his houses). As well as the creation of palatial residences for himself, he laid down roads at his own expense and encouraged the development of coal-mining in his diocese. He was, in fact, a whirlwind of reforming energy.

One of his early acts was to make a visitation of his entire diocese, visiting each parish and assuring himself that every parson was adequately housed. He also made a levy on every living (including his own which he valued at £6,000 a year) to raise a fund for the support of superannuated curates. Some of these reforms were received with mixed feelings; but one, at least, had the enthusiastic support of his Irish clergy. This was his resolution never to appoint an Englishman to an Irish benefice. It was acts such as this, according to William Cole, that 'rendered him the idol of his people and had a wonderful effect in conciliating the natives of that kingdom, who were not apt to be over-fond of the English Clergy'.

This action came at a time when the richer Irish livings were regularly plundered for the benefit of the nominees of people of political influence in England. Indeed, in his own earlier days, he had tried unsuccessfully to secure a rich benefice near Cork; and this, together with the fact that he notoriously owed his own present office as an Englishman to the patronage of his brother when Lord Lieutenant, struck a note of effrontery of a type he was often to cultivate. He was not a man, however, to consider his own position as being vulnerable. The reform was well meant and he kept to it. Derry showed its appreciation: he was voted the freedom of the city and this honour, never previously given to its bishop, was conferred on him in December 1768.

These manifestations of enlightenment were in the best Whig tradition. Though he often abandoned his diocese for long periods (ultimately spending a period of eleven consecutive years away from Ireland, an absence which his death alone prevented from being even longer) Hervey continued to administer it in what he considered to be its best interests as well as his own. But some of the methods he used must more often have startled rather than edified the more timid or conservative of his ecclesiastical subjects.

On one occasion when a particularly rich living had fallen vacant he invited the fattest of his clergy and entertained them with a splendid dinner. As they rose heavily from the table he proposed that they should run a race and that the winner should have the living as his prize. Greed contending with consternation the fat clerics were sent panting and purple-faced on their way, but the Bishop had so planned it that the course took them across a stretch of boggy ground where they were all left floundering and gasping in the mud, quite incapable of continuing. None reached the winning-post. The living was bestowed elsewhere and the Bishop, though hardly his exhausted and humiliated guests, found the evening highly diverting.

Arranging races seemed to appeal to him. He once invited some of his clergy to meet a group of Presbyterian ministers. After dinner he took them for a walk by the shore where, as previously arranged, his grooms had assembled the best horses from his stables all saddled and ready. The Bishop now suggested a sort of oecumenical sweepstake with the Presbyterian ministers racing against the more bulky representatives of the Established Church. The challenge could hardly be refused and the disciples of Calvin, lean and austere, were easy winners. If the Bishop intended to draw a moral from this contest it must remain an obscure one and was no doubt lost on his own clergy.

From all this it will be seen that a cruel note ran through the Bishop's humour and that he had a very complete lack of consideration for the dignity of others. It can have been no great consolation for his victims to know that he rarely stood on dignity himself. His virtues were many, as were listed in his student days; they remained very much the same through life and were dominated by a single-minded enthusiasm for life itself. There was something almost pagan in such an appetite for living, certainly something not immediately or usually associated with the episcopate. But he was essentially self-centred and cared very little whose feelings he hurt. To those who saw only this side of his character it was often debated whether the Bishop of Derry was a Christian at all – though the traveller John Morritt (to whom Scott dedicated *Rokeby*) altogether went too far in seeing him as having 'all the vices and follies of youth, a drunkard and an atheist though a bishop'.

Hervey's behaviour, none the less, sometimes encouraged the spread of such ideas.

4

In April 1770 Hervey received a second doctorate of Divinity, this time from Oxford. He now held degrees at both English universities as well as at Trinity College, Dublin, despite his aristocratic disdain or indifference for examinations. Almost immediately after receiving his Oxford degree he went abroad once more, taking with him his eldest surviving son, John Augustus. Though only thirteen years old this boy had already started his career in the Navy as a midshipman; the present trip was to be his 'Grand Tour'. Elizabeth Hervey (whom we no longer hear of being referred to as 'Excellent') remained in England with the younger children at Bury St. Edmunds. Ireland, for the time being, was abandoned.

Hervey was abroad from April 1770 until October 1772, leaving his diocese to look after itself; a fact which very much annoyed George III when complaints of the Bishop's long absence reached his ears. In later years when the Bishop's political activities were so much at variance with royal policy the situation was to be reversed, and it would be news of the return to his diocese of 'this wicked Prelate' (as the King came to call him) rather than his then welcome absences from it that would cause the greatest royal indignation.

The Bishop went on horseback more often than by carriage and travelled at speed. He covered great distances and darted about so quickly that it is often difficult to pin him down to any one place at any particular time. He took an artist with him to draw notable scenes or sites of geological interest but could not wait until the sketches were completed so that often artist and patron lost each other for days and weeks on end. During these two years we find him at Geneva, Great St. Bernard, Rome, Trieste, Spalato, Vienna, Verona, Padua, Toulouse, Clermont, Lyons, Rouen; always on the move, pausing only for the briefest rest, passing through Verona 'like a flash of lightning' but missing nothing that interested him and always eager for more. Only illness could halt or slow down this feverish progress from place to place, for nothing else could exhaust so indefatigable a traveller.

It was at the famous monastery of Great St. Bernard that an episode took place which was to become the subject of one of the Bishop's favourite anecdotes. He was to tell the story years later to Emma Hamilton and it appeared in the volume published in the year of her death as the *Memoirs of Lady Hamilton*. Arriving at the monastery while the monks were at dinner 'he found the convent door shut and, on knocking, the porter told him that no one was permitted to enter while the monks were at their meals: upon this he gave the porter a letter to the Abbot from a neighbouring bishop, who had sent this recommendation, in which the bishop called him his brother the Bishop of Derry. Immediately after the letter was delivered the door flew open and the whole convent on their knees, met his Lordship, craving his blessing; which he, without any ceremony, delivered to them as he passed along. The good brotherhood were wholly ignorant where Derry was situated; and relying upon the testimonial which he brought, they of course took him for a Catholic bishop. Without attempting to undeceive them his Lordship blessed them all, throwing out his benedictions very gravely with his hands. When the monks became better informed of his character they had no doubt a very different opinion of the efficacy of his benedictions.'[6]

The monks would have been all the more alarmed had they known that the Bishop had very recently been the guest of Voltaire at Ferney, and that the old philosopher, hearing that he was on his way to Rome, had asked him to bring back the ears of the Grand Inquisitor. It should not have surprised Hervey when he next visited the monastery that he was met with scant hospitality, complaining in their visitors' book that he left 'more loaded with compliments than food', and after seeing two friars with their paunches as full as their wallets was reminded forcibly of the text: 'He hath filled the hungry with good things, but the rich He hath sent empty away.'

The Bishop, who on his later journeys abroad was chiefly concerned in collecting pictures, statues, and other *objets d'art,* was at this period mainly interested in geology. His ascent of Vesuvius four years previously had kindled this interest which was further stimulated by the fact of his having in his Irish diocese the curious formation of basaltine rocks known as the Giant's Causeway. He was now in search of similar geological formations in other parts of Europe. To make sketches of these he at first employed Michael Shanahan (who was afterwards to do more important work for him as an architect) and later on an Italian artist named Bitio, a native of Belluno, who returned with him to Ireland. It was on these expeditions that the Bishop met John Strange, a Fellow of the Royal Society and later to be British Envoy to the Venetian Republic, who was to remain his friend and correspondent for many years.

Hervey summarized his discoveries in a letter to his nephew Constantine Phipps (his sister Lepel's son) after his return to Ireland. 'You have doubtless heard much of our Giant's Causeway,' he wrote. 'Till lately it has been reckon'd single of its kind, but I have lately discover'd such varieties of the same sort both in France and Italy, and accompanied with such peculiarities of soil as can no longer leave the origin of this strange phenomenon a Problem. The entire little district of Velay in France is compos'd of it; the villages, the Castle and farm houses are built of these materials which are a true Basaltine Stone, and every Isolated and Conical hill is compos'd of it: at the back of Clermont in Auvergne, a country strongly convuls'd and almost shatter'd by volcanos in the time of Sidonius Apollinaris, Bishop of Clermont, A.D. 450. There is among many other isolated mountains full of craters and covered to this day with cinders, lava and pumice-stone, one in particular compos'd entirely of these Polygon Basaltes which in such a situation leaves their origin unquestionable – to confirm this one need but observe the shooting of salts in any chymical experiments or the formation of sugar-candy in a sugar-house, to be convinced that these columns have likewise been in a state of Fusion, and owe their figure to the action of Fire – all this country of Ireland has in some remote age been equally agitated by subterranean fires and the numerous sugar loaf'd and isolated hills, full of Lava and Pumice-stone with Chrystal and Vitrifications, are strong proof of it – but when I see many of the same hills as full of marine bodies partly calcin'd and partly uncalcin'd mix'd with the same Volcantic matter, I cannot hesitate in supposing the whole mass thrown up like the Islands near Santorini in the Archipelago at the beginning of this century, like Thera and Therasia in the same Sea at the time of Pliny, and like Delos and Rhodes itself long before his time, by fire under the sea.'

Hervey broke off his geological field-work in order to visit Rome, where he arrived early in 1771. It was on this visit that he first caused comment by appearing in the Papal city in what has been described as 'the dress of an English bishop'. If by this is merely meant the black frock and short cassock or 'apron' then already familiar in England it would hardly have caused much of a stir in the ecclesiastical atmosphere of Rome. It seems unlikely, on the other hand, that Hervey would have had occasion to appear (even if he had wished to) in his rochet and lawn sleeves. Probably what really startled the Romans, as it was to startle many others, was the very curious mode of dress which Hervey began to adopt after becoming a bishop in which the colour puce often predominated. Many years later Lord Cloncurry recalled how he had seen 'the eccentric Earl-Bishop ride about the streets of Rome dressed in red plush breeches and a broad brimmed white or straw hat, and was often asked if that was the canonical costume of an Irish prelate'.[7]

While he was in Rome Hervey made tentative approaches to the Holy See on the question of the Irish Roman Catholics whose lot he very sincerely wished to improve. His hope was to find some plan or scheme whereby the Catholic clergy in Ireland could subscribe to the oath of allegiance to George III without doing violence to their consciences as priests. He envisaged a situation developing in Ireland similar to that urged by the Gallican party in France, who made a distinction between the spiritual and the temporal jurisdictions of the Pope, holding that the latter stopped short at the frontier of the French King's dominions and that only the former was of universal application. It was not a plan that was likely to appeal to the Roman Pontiff or to his advisers. Rome had always strenuously resisted the claims of the Gallican party and was even now condemning a movement in Germany and Austria where similar ideas were emerging under the name of Febronianism.

In spite of this unfavourable atmosphere Hervey had one or two audiences with the Pope. The Franciscan Ganganelli, who had been elected in May 1769 as Clement XIV, was at this time hard pressed. His election had been secured by the diplomacy of Cardinal de Bernis (later a close friend of Hervey's and French Ambassador at the Vatican) as the candidate of the Bourbon Courts and Portugal in their campaign for the suppression of the Jesuits. Now desperately trying to escape the consequences of a compact that went against his conscience the Pope was looking for friends where he could find them, and the ear he gave to Hervey's proposals arose probably much more from a desire to placate England than to accede to any of the suggestions made by the eccentric Protestant bishop. Nothing came of the meetings, though Hervey was later to return to the charge.

We next find him in Trieste, which he reached in May 1771, having sent his son to Venice where he was taken care of by John Strange and his wife. To Strange the Bishop declared that Rome had become a place he was 'heartily sick of and would not go twenty miles to visit' except on his son's account 'who has a real relish for architecture'. In fact he was to visit Rome many times again and seems to have been particularly fond of it; his present distaste was no doubt due to the failure of his talks with the Pope.

It was pleasant to turn from the tortuous diplomacy of the Vatican to meanderings of another sort. 'I have visited almost every subterraneous river in Istria and its neighbourhood,' he wrote to Strange, 'so that I should in consequence not have the least difficulty in believing that Alpheus might sink in Peloponnesus, and rise again in Sicily; for that part of the Ionian Sea is 300 feet deep – yet this is the dive made by the Lemme, which rises near Fiume, plunges into the Gulf of Pisino and appears again in a large bay between Ossero and Rovigno, about five miles circuit, and sometimes drowning the villages in the neighbourhood, for I *saw* the marks of its elevation last winter, 18 feet within the walls of my bed-chamber – it quickly takes its progress underground, reappears near old Naupactus and Upper Laybach, flows afterwards into the Savus, thence into the Danube, and so into the Black Sea'.

Always eager to share his experiences he tried to persuade Strange to join him: 'I wonder how so eager a suitor of Nature as you can so long interrupt your Courtship, or fancy that you can either win or woo her within the blank walls of your closet. Come forth then my dear friend, leave your books and Sibyll's leaves, and open the great volume of Nature. There let us read together the principal and leading facts of her history unbiassed by any system and unawed by any authority.' Strange, however, remained in Venice and Hervey had to make do with the company of the Abbé Fortis as he continued his journey to Dalmatia.

Having exercised his talents for intrigue in Rome and his enthusiasm for nature in Italy and Istria it was now, in Dalmatia, the turn of architecture. On 26 July Hervey and the learned Abbé who was now his companion reached Spalato (the modern Split), the town built entirely within the ruined remains of Diocletian's vast palace.

It is most unfortunate that no account of the Bishop's visit to Spalato has survived to record his reaction to this great ruin which not very long before had had so profound an effect upon Robert Adam. Through Adam the influence of these remains of antiquity was to be felt in contemporary architecture and interior decoration. The Bishop, on his return to Ireland, was to embark upon his long career of building, and neo-classical themes were to dominate his architectural taste in almost everything he built except for the spire to Derry Cathedral and similar embellishments to other churches. It is not even clear whether Shanahan was with him on this occasion, but the house that Hervey began soon afterwards at Downhill (now itself a ruin) shows the influence both of Adam and of Charles Cameron and it is not impossible to suppose that the Bishop returned from Spalato with strong ideas of his own on the subject of architecture both ancient and contemporary.

From Dalmatia Hervey returned to Italy, but being the restless traveller he was he decided to make the journey by way of

Vienna, which was hardly the most direct route. Even his constitution could not stand up to such constant movement and by the autumn, which found him in north Italy once more, he had fallen seriously ill.

Most of the winter was spent in Padua in indifferent health. At the height of his illness Count de Salis, whose acquaintance the Bishop had made on his journey out, kindly sent his personal physician to attend to the invalid. For this he received little gratitude. '*Je vous écris dans l'étal de faiblesse la plus déplorable que vous puissiez vous imaginer,*' the sick man wrote. '*Je vous renvoye votre médecin comme le Duc de Buckingham renvoya le fameux poete Dryden qui venait de faire une satyre des plus piquantes contre lui – il lui donna une bourse de quinées pour ses bons vers, et vingt coups de bâton pour la satyre renfermaient. Voilà le cas de votre médecin, il m'a surement sauve la vie, je crains qu'il m'a aussi surement ruiné la Santé.*' It is only fair to say that this somewhat unflattering opinion was revised when the patient was in better health. 'With regard to Doctor Balerini,' the Bishop later wrote, 'I am now convinced of his judicious treatment of me and that instead of having purged me too much I unfortunately prevented him from doing so sufficiently' – and he sent him a purse of fifty pounds.[8]

On his journey home, which took him through France, Hervey went out of his way to show a sympathetic interest in the affairs of Irish Roman Catholics who at that time could only be educated for the priesthood outside their native country. At Toulouse he visited the Irish College where he showed a little more susceptibility for the religious feelings of its inmates than he had displayed to the monks of Great St. Bernard on his journey out.

At a dinner given in his honour by the professors of the college he told them of his concern that they should have to spend the most valuable part of their lives abroad. For himself, he assured them, he wished that all Catholics could enjoy freedom of conscience, but he could not see how this could come about in Ireland unless they could give their native sovereign the same allegiance that they were able to show to the foreign monarchs in whose lands their colleges were situated. His frank manner and obvious sincerity quickly reassured the exiles; a lengthy discussion followed and the Irish fathers (in the words of a contemporary report) declared 'their hearty abhorrence of the opinions imputed to them of holding no faith with heretics, and of being prepared, at every intimation of their religious superiors, to trample upon the aweful obligations of an oath'.

Hervey was able to give another example of his tolerant attitude and interest in his fellow Christians of another denomination when he reached Rouen on the final stage of his homeward journey, for here he stayed at the palace of the Archbishop and, as in Rome, 'appeared constantly in the habit in which a bishop would travel in England'. His host was Dominique (later Cardinal) de la Rochefoucauld, a champion of the rights of the Gallican Church and a person likely to sympathize at many points with the religious views of his guest. He was also called upon to show a certain degree of tolerance himself, at least as a host, for we are told that the Bishop of Derry spent several weeks under the archiepiscopal roof.

5

Back in Ireland the Bishop continued his geological researches while Bitio, transported from his native Veneto to the bleaker prospects of County Antrim, was kept busy with his pencil and sketch-book. As a result of Hervey's detailed exploration of the rocky coast further formations similar in structure to the Giant's Causeway were discovered at Bengore.

Volcanic remains, however, though decidedly fascinating and important, form no part of the office and work of a bishop, and some at least of Hervey's time was given over to the affairs of his diocese. At this period he launched a scheme for a thorough reform of the tithe system, a burden even more unpopular in Ireland than it was in England, for while the English farmer was as likely as not a member of the Established Church his tithe went to support, in Ireland he was very much more likely to be a Roman Catholic or (especially in the Derry diocese) a Presbyterian.

Hervey's plan was simple and might well have been effective had it ever come into force. He proposed that each incumbent should exchange his tithe for land to the same value. To ensure a fair exchange the value should in each case be confirmed by a jury convened by the local sheriff. As this practice was usual in exchanges of land there seems to be no reason why the scheme should not have worked to the advantage of both farmer and parson. The bench of bishops agreed that the experiment should be tried out in the diocese of Derry, but somehow the plan fell through. 'Illness and other circumstances' are somewhat vaguely given as the reasons why Hervey never implicated his own reform. Perhaps among the 'other circumstances' must be counted the very extensive and not always strictly scrupulous operations he was conducting on his own account to increase the revenues of his episcopal estates.

More to Hervey's credit, though disappointing to him in the result, were his efforts on behalf of the Roman Catholic community. In July 1774 the Royal Assent was given to an Act which embodied many of the proposals with regard to the oath of allegiance which he had urged in his negotiations in Rome and discussed with the Irish fathers at Toulouse. By the terms of this Act Catholics could take an oath before a Justice of the Peace attesting their loyalty to George III at the same time renouncing any allegiance to the exiled Stuarts and repudiating the opinion that heretics might lawfully be murdered. At the same time they were required to deny that the Pope had any temporal or civil jurisdiction directly or indirectly within the realm.

The Bishop had worked hard for the passage of this Bill since his return from the Continent, and had discussed the form of the oath with the Roman Catholic Archbishop of Dublin who had considered it acceptable to all Catholics 'except for those trained by the Jesuits'.[9] His talks in Rome and his often expressed sympathy with the plight of Catholics had all been directed to this end. But the Act when passed, though it made no mention of the spiritual jurisdiction of the Pope, did not meet with approval in Rome, and no encouragement came from that quarter to assist Catholics in taking advantage of the new law. Hervey showed his disappointment in a letter to Strange: 'I carried my point for the Roman Catholics last Session, and got an Act passed enabling them to take Oaths of Allegiance without blending them with the Oath of Supremacy, and tho' the bill passed in concert with themselves, not one has had courage or honesty enough to avail himself of it, and thus they preclude themselves from all further indulgence.' This disillusion with the Court of Rome was later expressed in more trenchant terms:

'Rather than permit an abridgment of her privileges Rome would forgo a Toleration of her religion.'

Though he continued his struggle to improve the conditions of Catholics in civil matters (in this he was far in advance of contemporary 'establishment' opinion either in Ireland or England) he was hampered by his inability to appreciate the Catholic point of view on questions of religion and conscience. It was characteristic of this blindness that he should think the Irish Catholics, with their long history of persecution and suppression, could be capable of adopting an attitude of intransigence in the face of the expressed wishes of the Holy See in this or in other matters; or that there could be a parallel between the oppressed hierarchy of the Irish Church and the privileged, Gallican-minded prelates of the Church of France. As a Whig and (very probably) a deist he had little patience with the religious scruples of those who, in his opinion, were led by superstition rather than by reason. He expected those whom he wished to help to have the same high-handed and often cavalier attitude to authority that he had himself; that they failed to adopt such an attitude caused him surprise and irritation.

The question of Hervey's own religious beliefs remains something of an enigma. In his later years he certainly gives the impression of being a free-thinker; an impression which derived from his very unguarded manner of speech and also from a certain desire to shock or scandalize, especially when confronted with people whom he found either dull or pompous. Emma Hamilton, who knew him well, held the opinion that 'though an ecclesiastic of such high station in the Church, the bishop was an avowed sceptic in religion, the doctrines and institutions of which he would not scruple to ridicule in the company of women, treating even the immortality of the soul as an article of doubt and indifference.'[10]

Certainly Emma brought out the worst in him, as she did in most men, but others shared her view. The Countess Lichtenau (who, as we shall see, knew him as well as Emma did) declared roundly that the Bishop of Derry 'professed no religion although he had strong innate principles'. Lord Charlemont condemned him as a blasphemer and a deist, but Charlemont was his political rival and had no reason to love or praise him. Against these adverse judgements must be set the opinion of John Wesley, who met the Bishop in 1773 and again in 1775. After hearing him preach 'a useful sermon' on the Holy Ghost the evangelist noted in his diary: 'He is both a good writer and a good speaker. And he celebrated the Lord's Supper with admirable solemnity.' Some days later after dining at Hervey's table he recorded: 'The Bishop is entirely easy and unaffected in his whole behaviour, exemplary in all parts of worship, plenteous in good works.'[11]

Though Hervey was very free and often bawdy in his talk he never seems to have offended (except by absence) in the actual exercise of his office. Indeed in his episcopal capacity he could occasionally show more tact and imagination than was the case in some of his private dealings. A story is told of a confirmation service at which he presided. As he was about to administer the Sacrament to a young girl her old grandfather came forward and tried to lay his hands on the child's head at the same time as the Bishop. When a chaplain attempted to intervene Hervey prevented him. 'Mine is the benediction of office,' he said, 'his the benediction of love.'[12]

It does seem, however, that Hervey's religious convictions (whatever they may have been) became less strong as he grew older. As the friend of Voltaire, the student of geology at a time when official Christianity frowned upon any scientific speculation that might challenge a strictly fundamentalist interpretation of Holy Scripture, as a Whig magnate in a bishop's apron, he at no time aspired to a public reputation for piety; and to the narrowly orthodox a man whom Jeremy Bentham could describe as 'a most excellent companion, pleasant, intelligent, well read and well bred, liberal-minded to the last degree, has been everywhere and knows everything', was bound to be suspect.

He never resigned his See though his last eleven years were all spent away from his diocese. His numerous foreign pilgrimages could hardly have been described as being in pursuit of holiness. A man who spends so much of his time in collecting works of art to fill the great houses he has built for his own pleasure is not usually accused of laying up for himself treasure in heaven. After succeeding to the family honours Hervey remained a bishop but he lived more and more the life of an ordinary (or in his case extraordinary) secular nobleman. Lord Charlemont's assertion that the Bishop of Derry was a deist probably fits as well as any. The more sensational claim that he was an atheist cannot be proved.

6

In March 1775 an event occurred which was greatly to alter Frederick Hervey's future prospects. His eldest brother the Earl of Bristol died at Bath on the eighteenth of the month. By his will he left the Bishop a legacy of £10,000, but it was not this accretion in fortune that so changed his destiny. The Earl had died unmarried and his next brother Augustus, who now succeeded as third Earl, had no legitimate children and such was the complicated state of his private life that it seemed very unlikely that he would ever have any.

He had made a clandestine marriage many years previously to the notorious Elizabeth Chudleigh, but this lady had left him to become mistress to the Duke of Kingston. As her marriage had been contracted in secret she saw it as no obstacle to a second marriage to the Duke, but after his death the bigamy was discovered and the 'Countess-Duchess' (as Horace Walpole called her) narrowly escaped being branded in the hand as an adulteress but contrived none the less to retain the fortune which the Duke had left her. As the new Lord Bristol was thought to have connived at his wife's bigamy he was unable to divorce her. It was a deplorable situation for the brother and sister-in-law of a bishop to find themselves involved in but it had one unexpected advantage from the Bishop's point of view; he was himself now their heir presumptive to the family title and estates.

Hervey seems genuinely to have been fond of his brother George to whom he owed his preferment in the Church, and he sincerely mourned his loss. 'Within the last few days I have lost the kindest and most affectionate brother,' he wrote to John Strange shortly after the news reached him. 'This has blunted in me every sense of pleasure, and left me a mass and lump of inanimate matter. He has testified his kindness for me to the last; but no accession to wealth, especially to one in my situation, can compensate for the loss of a real friend – in my circumstances in life one seeks rather to share the comforts of life than to accumulate them. Neither his honours, nor his rank, nor his property, can make me any amends for losing him. I cannot but regret him as long as I live.'

It was probably his brother's legacy which prompted Hervey to begin his building operations on land nominally the property of his diocese but which, by a skilful manipulation of leases, he had secured to himself and his heirs for a more or less indefinite future. Certainly a year later in the summer of 1776 enough of the house was built for Arthur Young, the traveller and agricultural reformer, to record seeing the shell of it, which he described as already giving evidence that the completed building would 'be a large and convenient edifice when it is finished'. Largeness tended to predominate over convenience in this and the other houses which the Bishop was to build, a fault which no doubt sprang from his professed inability to breathe in small rooms.

Young described the house as standing 'on a bold shore where a tree is a rarity'. This was an understatement; to many people the site chosen by the Bishop made his house at Downhill a folly before it was built. On the extreme northern coast of County Londonderry, not far from Coleraine, the house was situated on an exposed, barren, and windswept cliff with the Atlantic Ocean raging at its foot and so little shelter from the prevailing wind that hardly a tree would grow in its vicinity. But the Bishop had not been entirely capricious in choosing so apparently inhospitable a site; it was the contrast to the languid and enervating environment of his native Ickworth that made him pick on this bracing spot. Some ten years later he wrote to this same Arthur Young: 'A thousand thanks to you, my dear friend, for your recollection of me at so many miles distance . . . but no thanks at all to you for wishing me back to the foggy, ferney atmosphere of Ickworth, in preference to the exhilarating and invigorating air, or rather ether, of the Downhill.'[13] This refreshing climate, he believed, also had a beneficial effect on the gout (or what went by the name of gout) from which he was increasingly to suffer.

The first part of the house to be built consisted of a handsome villa on two floors above a rusticated basement. The south front had rectangular bays at each end and a horseshoe stairway leading to the central front door. The cornice was supported by pilasters arranged in pairs with Corinthian capitals. The house could also be entered on the north side where a projecting bow gave entrance to the hall. This arrangement was made so that visitors could enter the house from either the north or the south according to the state of the wind. When wings were added the north entrance was in a sheltered court-yard. In the years 1784–5 the whole house was faced in freestone, which made the proud Hervey write to his eldest daughter: 'Downhill is greater beauty than ever, the Castle getting a Sourtout of Freestone, with the richest Corinthian Pilasters that could be executed. But you will think your poor Father raving in a feverish delirium.'

The building works were in the hands of Michael Shanahan who had accompanied him on his foreign travels, and whom the Bishop had first employed when he was at Cloyne, for Shanahan was a native of Cork. He was also most probably the architect, though the name of James Wyatt has been suggested in this connection. Shanahan was certainly on friendly terms with both Wyatt and Adam, so it is not surprising that their influence should be visible in his work. Much of the interior decoration was the work of the Italian Placido Columbani whose name has also been suggested as architect. Indeed there seems to have been a sort of conspiracy among subsequent writers to decry the claims of Michael Shanahan as architect of Downhill. Though there may be reasons to think that Wyatt might have designed the original villa (or at least strongly influenced its design) there seems to be little ground for denying that the native architect was at least responsible for the additions that were soon made, extending the house towards the sea in two long parallel wings, the western one containing a gallery for the Bishop's collection of works of art. It is indeed very likely that he was responsible for the whole plan with a good deal of suggestion, encouragement, and not always welcome interruptions from the Bishop.

A feature which was to add a little variety to the desolate landscape of Downhill was the mausoleum which the Bishop began in 1779 in memory of his brother the second Earl. It stood on rising ground to the south of the house in the direction of the road from Downhill to Coleraine. This monument, said to be a copy of the Roman mausoleum at St. Remy in Provence, consisted of a solid rectangular base in the Ionic order over which rose a lighter circular temple of eight Corinthian columns supporting a cupola topped by an urn. Within this elegant temple stood a statue of Lord Bristol with a copy of Magna Carta in his hand. It was the work of John van Nost the younger, a sculptor of Dutch origin who had settled in Dublin in the 1750s, where stood his statues of George II and George III. The memorial to Lord Bristol, the Lord Lieutenant who never set foot in Ireland, withstood the winds of Downhill for another sixty years before falling a victim to the great gale of 1839. The remains of the pedestal can still be seen. Later, as will transpire, the Bishop added another temple on his Downhill estate in honour of a charming young woman.

Downhill was Hervey's favourite residence, for the house he later built at Ballyscullion, though architecturally the more ingenious and original, was not started until the late eighties of the century, a period when the Bishop was spending much of his time abroad, and it was rarely used by him. Ickworth, his last and greatest creation, he was destined never to see completed.

Many years were spent in the improvement of both house and grounds. By 1783 he was able to boast to Arthur Young that he had planted 200,000 trees in the glens round the house and had 'converted sixty acres of moor, by the medium of two hundred spades, into a green carpet sprinkled with white clover'. Two years later, writing to his daughter Mary, he declared with pride that 'Downhill is becoming Elegance itself. 300,000 Trees *without* Doors upon all the banks and upon all the Rocks and almost as many pictures and statues *within* doors count very well. I have had no gout this winter, which I attribute to Musick and Harmony of mind. Everything is redolent of Joy and Youth, and we commonly sit down to table from 20 to 25. We have cold Suppers and a bottle of *Champaign* at each end of the table. The Songsters sing *Ketches* and I go to Bed, which just now invites. . . .'[14]

Much of the internal structure of Downhill as the Bishop conceived it was destroyed in the fire of 1851. Though rebuilt in 1870 the house is now a ruin, so the scheme of decoration of the interior has not survived. One of the principal rooms was the gallery designed to house the ever growing collection of works of art. Situated in the west wing with a large bow on the western wall, the room was lit from both sides by no less than eleven tall windows, an arrangement that must have left very little space for pictures. Beyond this was a smaller room called the New Gallery.

The ceiling of the main gallery was frescoed with a copy by William Pars of Guido Reni's *Aurora*. Here eventually were to hang works by Raphael, Titian, Rembrandt, and other old masters as well as works commissioned from Hervey's contemporaries.

Many years later (in March 1796) Hervey sketched out in a letter to his daughter Elizabeth his idea of how a collection of pictures should be displayed. 'What say you', he asked 'to my idea of a gallery of German painters contrasted with a gallery of Italian painters, from Albert Durer to Angelica Kauffman, and from Cimabue to Pompeio Battoni, each divided by pilasters into their respective school – *Venetian* for colouring, *Bologna* for composition, Florence for designs, Rome for sentiment, and Naples for nothing at all?' As he was to sit to both Kauffmann and Batoni one can imagine this historical procession of pictures ending in splendid portraits of the Bishop himself. Rembrandt and Rubens (especially in his *Descent from the Cross* in Antwerp) he considered jointly as 'the Homer of Painting'. 'Raphael and all Italian painters' he rather surprisingly classified as 'the minor Poets of Painting'. There was, in his estimation, no Shakespeare among the visual artists while 'Michael Angelo is mad, not sublime; ludicrous, not dignified. He is the *Dante* of painters as Dante is the Michael Angelo of poets. The picture of the Last Judgement is so tragicomical 'tis difficult to say which passion it excites most; and St. Barthlemé, all flayed, who holds up his skin as his ticket of admittance into Heaven, is worthy only of *Bartholomew* fair'.[15]

It must be admitted that this forthright if rather eccentric view of art in general and of the great Florentine master in particular was written when its author had been forty days in bed 'reduced to a shadow, yet devouring like a *shark*', his pulse 'of *threads* scarse to be felt', and had Ickworth in mind rather than Downhill; but at least in his historical concept it shows that Hervey had ideas well in advance of the taste of his time, and it was in the gallery at Downhill that he was first able to put his ideas into practice.

It was here also that he was able to indulge his generous instinct for hospitality, keeping open house where people of all creeds and opinions were welcome; where toasts were loudly called for at dinner; and where musical parties were a calming and welcome antidote to the host's somewhat impetuous taste for elaborate practical jokes. He delighted in entertaining the more junior among his clergy who were accommodated in what soon came to be called the curates' corridor, though it must be hoped that it was in some other corridor that the Bishop discovered that one of his lady guests was involved in an amorous liaison, a discovery he made by placing flour outside her bedroom door and tracing the guilty footprints to their source. Life at Downhill could be stimulating and often unpredictable; it was never dull.

II

Travels and Intrigues

I

As well as the beginning of Downhill the year 1776 saw both the Bishop's elder daughters married. Mary, the eldest, became engaged to John Crichton, second Lord Erne (later first Earl) about Christmas-time 1775. 'He is a most unexceptionable man,' Hervey wrote to Strange in Venice, 'who will have about £9,000 a year, possesses a very beautiful seat in our neighbourhood, and is in love with her to the eyes.' It was all a father could wish for and he probably had, unconsciously, shown his own order of priorities; but from Mary Hervey's point of view there was at least one snag: Lord Erne was many years older than she was and had two sons and two daughters by a previous marriage. 'This staggers her', the Bishop declared; but Mary soon became reconciled to the idea of four step-children and they were married the following February.

The beautiful and fascinating Elizabeth was married in December to John Thomas Foster, a member of the Irish Parliament and son of the Rev. Dr. John Foster of County Louth. The two families were well known to each other and the Fosters, father and son, were referred to among the Herveys as 'big F' and 'little f'. It began as a marriage of love in an age of marriages of convenience, very much as the marriage of Elizabeth's father and mother had started. Foster was young, good looking, but of a weak and rather petulant nature; he was to prove himself no match for a Hervey. But first impressions were good. 'I like the young man better than ever,' the Bishop told his daughter Mary, 'and think him peculiarly suited to her.' His opinion, alas, was to prove sadly wrong and the marriage was destined to end in disaster.

With his two daughters settled and his house being built the Bishop felt free to embark upon another long continental journey. Reasons of health were given as the excuse for this second prolonged absence from his diocese which was to last for nearly two and a half years. It is true that he was subject to intermittent attacks of 'gout', a name used to cover a multitude of complaints in the eighteenth century. Whatever was the real cause of these attacks they can hardly be attributed to undue indulgence in food and drink, for Hervey was not a heavy eater or drinker (though his enemies later on accused him of drunkenness) and he took regular exercise on horseback. But his heredity was not good. Neither of his elder brothers survived beyond middle age and his father's notorious use of cosmetics sprang from an attempt to improve a complexion ravaged by the effects of chronic ill-health. Hervey included a 'cure' at the German Spa of Pyrmont (then celebrated for its mineral springs) as part of his itinerary, but the plea of ill-health was probably little more than an excuse to be on his travels again. He was a born traveller; if he needed a cure at all it was from a congenital spirit of restlessness.

On this occasion the Bishop was accompanied by his wife and youngest daughter Louisa, then ten years old. Mary, the newly-wed Lady Erne, also went with them as far as Brussels where her two step-daughters were to be placed in a Convent school. Hervey certainly seems to have been out of sorts to begin with. 'Your father continues to complain and do nothing, but I think a journey will soon put him to right', his wife wrote to their daughter Elizabeth back in Ireland. Mrs. Hervey herself found much to amuse her on her first continental holiday for a dozen years, not least in the conduct of a certain General Hohenhausen ('an Excellence, something *hausen*', as she rather vaguely described him to Elizabeth) whom she encountered in Mannheim. 'He is monstrously partial to the English, laments their present situation, and seems to be a sensible, well-minded man. The conversation turned chiefly on politics, in which, as you may imagine, I took little share; but when he got up to go away, the *ceremonial* was singular enough, with a *permittez moi, Madame, de vous basier la main* (he repeated the *baiser* quick, and I believe as frequent as 20) saying *jusqu'a cent fois*. It was quite new to me, and I was almost ready to laugh, but I can conceive the scene to be sometimes more embarrassing. . . .'[1]

The General had good reason to lament the situation of Great Britain at this juncture in her affairs, deeply embroiled as she was in war on the American continent, while France and Spain threatened at any moment to take up the cause of the American rebels. 'All the letters breathe nothing but war', Hervey was soon to be warning Strange of the news he received from France, and much of his time and energy was to be spent in gathering information about the warlike intentions of Britain's potential enemies.

It was not until they reached Rome, however, that the Bishop began to take alarm at the military preparations he believed to be in train for an assault upon Ireland; in the meantime he was intent on enjoying life in Germany. At Pyrmont, in the territory of the Prince of Waldeck, Mrs. Hervey reported to Lady Erne that her husband was finding the waters highly beneficial 'which would be still greater if the weather were not worse than ever you saw it, even in Derry, constant rain, dirt and puddle, yet in spite of all he is well and cheerful and the gouty pains fly before them.' The Bishop was obviously beginning to discover his zest for life again. 'The lounging life agrees with him also,' his wife continues, 'and he finds great amusement from the company being quite new to him.' Shortly afterwards she was able to write: 'Your father's gout is drove away, he is the life of the company.'

The company which found itself so ready to be diverted by the whimsical Bishop of Derry was typical of the Germany of the *ancien régime* whose agreeable existence had little more than ten years to run before the events in Paris of 1789 would shatter even the Bishop's much publicized reputation for radical thought. There was Augusta, Hereditary Princess of Brunswick and sister to George III ('We dine with her quite *en famille*', Mrs. Hervey explained), two princes of Mecklenburg-Strelitz, brothers of the Queen of England, the Prince of Waldeck himself ('vastly obliging too'), and Prince Augustus of Saxe-Gotha ('We have taken violently to each other') who was to be a travelling companion of the Herveys on their journey into Italy. It was a 'motley society of princes, peers and citizens' as Hervey told his daughter Elizabeth, adding characteristically: 'Among this crowd are expatriated Prime Ministers, exhausted ministers of the gospel, Lutherans, Calvinists, Hernhuters, Jews, Greeks, etc., who altogether form a good savoury oglia of society, especially as one can pick out of the dish such pieces as are too luscious or too hard for one's stomach, or even such as do not suit one's palate. As to the place, it is magical. . . .' But magical or not they could not remain there for ever: 'From hence into dear Italy once more.'

No journey, however, could be absolutely direct when the Bishop of Derry was in charge. Before 'long-wished-for Verona' was reached visits had to be made to Mayence, Mannheim, and Stuttgart. In the latter city the Duke of Würtemberg showed Hervey the academy he had founded where three hundred boys and youths aged from seven to twenty received a strict but liberal education. The Bishop was not entirely easy about the severe regimentation of the system and the fear in which the Duke was held ('Their dread of him was shocking, though he seemed to do everything to familiarize them with him'), but his own liberal views on education could not but approve the general result. 'Lads of every nation, every religion, every age, and even every rank are here admitted – from the sons of common soldiers up to Barons and Counts', he reported to his daughter Elizabeth. 'Each follows his genius. We saw rooms for painting, sculpture, drawing, music, Latin, Greek, Hebrew, etc., etc. This is the true secret of education and it succeeds accordingly. Different geniuses have ripened at different ages, and some premature ones have been blighted when least expected. Those who, after every trial, have shown no talent at all become good dunces; this event never fails. The Duke feeds, clothes and lodges every one. None is allowed to receive money even from his parents, nor on any pretence to transgress the bounds of the College without an Inspector. Each lies in a separate bed, and fifty of them sleep so cleanly in one room that the air is as pure within as without. I did not think so perfect a system of education existed anywhere.'[2]

It was September before the party crossed the Alps and began the descent into Italy. From Verona Lady Erne was informed by her mother that the Bishop was in his element in the perilous mountain passes and even she herself was not too much alarmed 'tho' the weakness of my Frame does not support objects of terror, and my long journey, the heat, the buggs, etc. and sometimes bad Beds had robb'd me of some advantages which I had on leaving Pyrmont.' The lodgings that Hervey had hoped to occupy in Verona were in the charge of a new innkeeper who proved sullen and impertinent and their rooms were above the stables where 'Louisa is confin'd all day in the stink.' It is no surprise to find poor Mrs. Hervey writing that she is ready to decamp – one only wonders whether this particular host was later to transform his disagreeable establishment into a 'Hotel

Bristol'. They moved as soon as they could to Valdagno, another spa, where Mrs. Hervey revived her sinking spirits with a twenty-day course of the waters. Hervey considered ten days sufficient for himself, being, in his wife's words, 'so perfectly free from all complaints that he did not require it'. Instead he 'rov'd about the mountains' with Bitio, who had now joined the party, and 'got two or three fine drawings'.

The travellers continued their journey via Vicenza and Padua to Bologna which Mrs. Hervey found 'still a kind of republic tho' under the Pope's dominion', and where she watched the election of a Gonfalonier or Chief Magistrate. The Bishop, not finding these antiquated ceremonies much to his taste, passed his time in the neighbouring mountains.

In Florence they found their friend Sir Horace Mann 'a good deal broke but amiable as ever'. The old diplomat was in his mid seventies and had been British Minister to the Court of Tuscany since 1740. Horace Walpole's lifelong friend and correspondent, he was the recipient and disseminator of all the gossip of Europe. Among his other duties it was his business to keep an eye on the dilapidated court of the Stuart Pretender. Neither Hervey nor his wife seemed curious to see this sad figure, long past his days as 'Bonnie Prince Charlie' but now the jealous and rather bibulous husband of a wife thirty years his junior. The Bishop was more interested to meet the poet Count Vittorio Alfieri who was later to cuckold the unfortunate Prince and run off with his wife. Alfieri gave him introductions for a brief visit to Siena while Mrs. Hervey passed her time with the English colony in Florence. Before leaving they were to pass an evening with the Grand Duke Leopold (later the Emperor Leopold II) and his Grand Duchess, an occasion which passed off 'totally without form'.

Rome was reached by the middle of November. Six years before Hervey had told John Strange that he was heartily sick of the place; as his party (which still included Prince Augustus of Saxe-Gotha) settled down in their lodgings he now wrote to the same correspondent in a burst of enthusiasm: 'Rome contains everything that can amuse, interest or instruct the mind.'

Here his passion for art and intrigue was to have full scope while he was to enjoy the social life of the Eternal City in the exclusive circle of the Cardinal de Bernis. Bernis, as ambassador of Louis XVI, was famous for the splendour of his hospitality and to Hervey he soon became 'my Cardinal', but Mrs. Hervey did not join her husband at the Cardinal's entertainments. Whether it was ill-health (and her health seems generally to have been poor at this time) or her anomalous position in the Papal capital as a bishop's wife that prevented her from doing so does not transpire. Later she expressed regret at not having known the Cardinal, which might suggest that Hervey purposely excluded her from these gatherings (which were by no means exclusively masculine) but her own reticence on the subject leaves it a question for speculation. Mrs. Hervey seems to have been a little bored in Rome; there are indications that her patience was often put to the test by her husband's selfishness and unpredictable conduct. When she writes home to her eldest daughter that 'your father continues to amuse himself', there is a hint that perhaps she was not quite in the same happy state herself.

The Bishop's own account of his amusements (written to Lady Erne because 'your Mother, dear Mary, has a snivelling cold which prevents her writing') shows us very pleasantly his manner of life in Rome. 'Every Wednesday I dine with my Cardinal and nobody else gives any dinners except in the Carnevale. The conversations here are highly amusing, such is the equal mixture of cards and company. At one house we have a weekly concert accompanied with some tolerable voices; billiards are a favourite amusement in the evening, and the Gazettes are open to everyone. The English are upon the best footing, and of course well receiv'd everywhere. Their apartments of reception are splendid beyond description and whatever magnificence can be deriv'd from Pictures, Gilding, Glasses, lights and multiplicity of servants is all here exhibited – the morning especially is pass'd most deliciously – here is an incredible variety of admirable artists of every kind, so that one enjoys not only sculpture, painting and musick in the highest degree, but also sculptors, painters and musicians. 'Tis likewise difficult to say which pleases one most, the magnificence of ancient or the elegance of modern Rome; for my own part I have been singularly fortunate – several ancient rooms have been unearth'd since my arrival – the paintings were in fresco and almost as perfect as at first – the secret was soon found of detaching the painted stucco from the walls, and I have bought three complete rooms, with which to adorn the

Downhill and *le rendre un morceau unique*. The Pope has granted me a permission to take a model from the Apollo Belvedere – a favour rarely granted but to crown-heads. I suppose his Holiness is so accustom'd to consider mitred ones on a footing with them that in my case he made no distinction, and I will venture to say that few heretics are on as good a footing with him. I cannot resist the temptation of being extravagant here especially when it is with a view of beautifying dear Ireland.'

It is clear that the Bishop's health, so sluggish in Germany, was now fully restored. 'My rides in a morning', his letter continues, 'are of five and six hours among tombs of Heros, the Palaces of Emperors and spoils of the Universe, for miles together you discover Aqueducts, temples, Pillars, etc. all that can recall the idea of great men and great works; and when one returns, the view of Rome from whence all originated, and to which all tended, fills the eye with all that is magnificent and the mind with all that is aweful . . .'. Rome had effected a cure of quite a surprising kind. 'I never saw anything like your Father's spirits,' his wife wrote early in the next year after three months in the city, 'he jumps about the room like a Boy when we are quite alone, and protests that he feels like five and twenty.'

The Bishop himself was writing to his daughter Elizabeth asking her to send him enough poplin to make two suits of clothes, one of which was to be 'of a puce colour'.[3] ''Tis incredible how pleasantly I pass my time here both within the town and without,' he told her, 'and how agreeably the first nobility receive strangers. Your mother begins now to mix a little more, and I hope will gain both health and spirits by it: but she dares not attack palaces or antiquities, both on account of the fatigue and the damp. I am impenetrable to both, and have besides painters working in my room all the day. 'Tis really a life of Paradise.'

It was on this visit to Rome that Hervey sat for his portrait to Pompeo Batoni. He had been reluctant to sit (there were so many other exciting things to occupy his time) but his wife managed to persuade him that the picture would become a valuable possession in his family, and so that he would not be bored the ever accommodating Prince of Saxe-Gotha agreed to sit with him in the studio to keep his spirits up. Batoni had secured his position as the most fashionable portrait painter in Rome in 1769 when he had painted his charming portrait of the two imperial brothers, Joseph II and the Grand Duke Leopold, standing hand in hand in a setting of classical architecture. The picture which he now completed shows the forty-eight-year-old Bishop looking remarkably youthful in his lawn sleeves standing at a writing table with a view of Derry Cathedral (showing the new spire) visible in the background. It was considered by Mrs. Hervey to be 'a striking and pleasing likeness'.

2

In the spring and early summer of 1778 the Bishop began to grow more apprehensive over the dangers of war. Some officers of Dillon's Regiment (an Irish regiment in the service of the French crown) were in Rome when the news of their recall to France made Hervey certain that an invasion of Ireland was being planned. Indeed it became something of a joke between the Bishop and Colonel Dillon when they met in Roman society. 'The Colonel promises to be careful of the Palace,' Mrs. Hervey told her daughter Elizabeth, 'your father to be *indulgent to the prisoners*.'

But to Hervey the situation appeared serious enough despite his jokes with the colonel. He realized more than ever that the cruel and repressive treatment of the Irish Catholics by successive English governments and by the Protestant ascendancy in Ireland itself had only succeeded in making the country an ideal place for a successful French invasion. In May he, too, wrote to Elizabeth a letter which was probably intended equally for the eye of her husband Foster as a member of the Irish Commons.

'The regiments in [the French] service are already quartered on the coast and ready to be embarked,' he wrote, 'and the officers belonging to those regiments who had made an excursion to Rome of a few weeks were returned, recalled in a hurry, and had joined their corps. From these I collected enough, not only to assure myself of their destination, but even of more particulars than they would have chosen *before dinner* to communicate. Their object at Rome at this time was easily guessed. Considering what a number of Irish friars of every denomination abounds here, and how attached our cruel and political laws render them to the Stuart family, nothing could exceed the attention shown by the French Ministers here to these gentlemen. They were lodged in one of their houses, and received daily at their tables, and distinguished constantly from all other strangers, and their elation at the thought of a war was beyond all description. At the close of their visit they scarce made any secret of their destination, and would frequently rally me on my purchases of statues and busts, which they said must one day belong to them. If so perilous a state does not waken our Government to mitigate the penal laws against the Papists, and to win by gentleness whom they cannot subdue by severity, if the most uniform acquiescence under the most impolitic and undeserved oppression that ever disgraced any legislature does not soften our, as yet, inflexible Government, I must confess I shall suspect some treachery, and that there is a latent scheme for driving them out of the island.'[4]

A similar letter was sent the following month (3 June 1778) to Sir William Hamilton in Naples, adding the news that the Count of Albany (the name used by the 'Young Pretender') was said to be in considerably better spirits of late. 'Surely', the Bishop asked 'they cannot be hard driven enough to employ such a sot?' He passed on to Sir William his fears about the activities of the Irish friars and once again deplored the folly of the British Government's attitude towards the Catholics: 'What a madness in our Government not to legalize the daily exercise they make of their Religion, as if a man was a less faithfull subject or a less brave soldier for being fool enough to believe that to be Flesh which all the world sees to be only Bread; or, as if doing that legally which he now does illegally would render him a more tumultuous or a more dangerous Cityzen.' To these liberal but unfashionable views he appended the ominous conclusion: 'But this I fear is a Gordian knot which only the sword of a Civil War can cut.'[5]

The Bishop's hopes and fears for Ireland had a particular significance at this moment as Lord North's Government had at last begun to show some consideration for the problems of that island; a solicitude induced more by fear of what was happening in America than by any sudden conversion to the ideals and aspirations of the Irish patriots who in this year began to form volunteer companies for the protection of their country from foreign invasion.

Various concessions in favour of Irish trade were passed by the Westminster Parliament. In Dublin, Luke Gardiner's first Relief Act for Catholics was introduced into the Irish House of Commons. Hervey's absence in Italy prevented him from taking any active part in the debates but he made his views known in a long letter to Speaker Edmund Pery. His ideas went far beyond those of Gardiner, who promoted the Act, and included the suggestion that nomination to Catholic Sees in Ireland should be made by the King in the same manner as that adopted by the Prussian King in Silesia. To induce the Catholic hierarchy to accept this novel scheme (for until his death in 1766 they had been more used to being appointed by the 'Old Pretender' from his exile in Rome) Hervey suggested that 'in order to give this clergy an attachment to government as well as an attendance upon them, I would propose, in imitation of the practice at Heydelberg, Frankfort, Oppenheim, etc., that every priest should be enabled to receive for himself and his successors, an endowment in land to the amount of 25 acres, and each archbishop and bishop 40. No priest unappointed by government to be capable of such endowment or of suing for it.' He added two arguments in favour of his scheme which were typical of his general view of affairs; it would benefit tillage, and would also relieve the poor Papist who at present had to carry the burden of maintaining the Catholic priesthood. 'I am certain', he concludes, 'there is no other method of emancipating Ireland from the Roman yoke but by discriminating the harmless members of the Church of Rome from the dangerous partisans of that ambitious and wily Court. Reduce Popery, as France and Holland have done, to a sect of speculative dogmas, and you will render an Irish Papist as innocent as a Dutch or a French Papist.'[6]

To his daughter Elizabeth Foster he showed a more practical concern for the welfare of the Irish Catholics. 'Tell your husband . . .', he wrote to her from Rome in September 1778, 'that I should be much obliged to him for a list of the speakers in our house [the Irish House of Lords] on the Popish bill; that I wish also to know if the bill to tolerate their religion is to take place, without which I do not know how the multitude are benefited. . . . If such a bill should pass, I *pledge myself* to bring sixty thousand pounds sterling within eighteen months into the kingdom for the purpose of building cathedrals, churches, and chapels. The Pope will give us five thousand and one single convent in Bohemia, of Irish friars, subscribes one thousand pounds; the seminaries of *Valladolid* and *Salamanca* as much. There is an old Governor MacEgan is just returned from his government in Peru, an old bachelor with £70,000 who will give us £500. The Empress of Germany [Maria Theresa] if this war does not continue, has promised her confessor Father Kelly, an Irish Recolect, a considerable sum for the benefit of her soul in Pergatory – the other lesser subscriptions are numberless, but such a sum would be deeply felt in our exhausted country. Adieu! my dear, you see how much I have this matter at heart. . . . I have myself destined one thousand pounds for our [Catholic] chapels in the diocese of Derry, having seen the excellent effects of a reciprocal toleration through all the great towns of Germany, and the bad effects of intolerance through all the great towns of Italy.'[7]

No Act of Toleration was passed, and the Relief Act fell far short of his hopes, though it went some way towards improving the lot of Catholics, particularly with respect to the tenure of land. But it was a timid measure by Hervey's standards and showed none of his vision and liberality. It was only after his return home in November 1779 that he gave full vent to his feelings of disillusion. 'Can any country flourish', he then asked his daughter Elizabeth in a letter from Belfast, 'when two-thirds of its inhabitants are still crouching under the lash of the most severe illiberal penalties that one set of citizens ever liad upon the other?'

This letter gives us some insight into the Bishop's political activities in Rome. He explains once again the efforts he made for the Catholics in 1774 and his disappointment when many of them failed to avail themselves of the benefits of the Act passed in that year. It was only when he reached Brussels on his present visit to the Continent that he discovered the reason; that hopes of preferment in what he describes as 'their miserable hierarchy' deterred them from taking an oath which abjured the purely temporal claims of the Pope.

'On this I resolved to visit the fountain head of such a defection and to trace it to its source,' his letter continues. 'I did it so effectually, bribed so many clerks and under-clerks in the different offices that I obtained the whole course of the correspondence between Rome and her clergy in Ireland on this topick. I did more. I detected the whole plan of invasion for the last year, which could not have been attempted without the assistance of the Irish friars conversant in the English, Irish, and French languages, and I have good reason to believe that the whole proceedings in England in favour of the Catholics were grounded on the information I transmitted to Lord North and Lord Hillsborough. Had the French Ministry imagined that the Irish Parliament would have done things by halves and omitted the religious indulgence to the people whilst it granted the pecuniary one to the gentry, the invasion would still have taken place last year in Ireland, after Mr. Keppel had so scandalously left the French masters of the ocean. Don't imagine, therefore, my dear girl, that I have been inattentive to the welfare of this kingdom. Your mother can tell you how many wearisome days and studious evenings it has cost me whilst the ignorant and unobserving thought me busied in virtu and occupied by the elegant arts. . . .'

The letter then goes on to depict a scene of lively intrigue which shows how espionage could be combined with some profitable picture-dealing, and possibly also explains why the long-suffering Mrs. Hervey was excluded from the agreeable evening entertainments at the palace of the Cardinal de Bernis: 'The *committee* at Rome which governs the religious affairs of Ireland is composed of seven cardinals. . . . Every member of this committee is as venal as a Board of Aldermen, but in order to bribe them you must buy a picture off one, give a poplin to the niece or the mistress of another, a suit of cloths to the secretary of a third, and so on; so that with a good purse and a liberal hand one may know every tittle of what these Christian Pharisees have sworn not to reveal. It was by means such as these that I discovered the sentiments, the views, the interests and connexion of almost every Popish bishop in Ireland, and that at this instant I know why some have taken the oath of allegiance and why others have declined it. By these means I discovered that the King of France, through his Ambassador the Cardinal de Bernis, got the nomination of three Irish bishops in the course of one year as the most effectual means of securing the assistance of the Popish clergy and the Popish populace in the case of an invasion; and of all this I transmitted immediate information to such as could best avail themselves of it.'[8]

This letter was written after the Bishop's return home when he had had time for some reflection and self-justification, for not a few people in Ireland had considered his long absence as an indication of indifference to the plight both of his native and of his adopted country. His immediate reaction to the news from home was more dramatic and less well balanced. Writing to Sir William Hamilton from Rome in September 1778 he bluntly compared the conduct of George III to that of Charles I and declared that he trembled for the sequel of the parallel. 'When I reflect on our desperate situation,' he concluded sadly, 'I almost wish for a Vesuvius, or rather an Etna, in the midst of Great Britain. Think of what we were 16 years ago, and tell me fairly if a series of such causes could possibly have produced other effects.'[9]

The Bishop, as will be seen, had been seriously ill before he wrote this letter, and this fact may account to some extent for his sombre thoughts; but there can be no doubt that the failure of the home government to appreciate or attend to his enlightened advice (even though unsolicited) or to carry their meagre reforms beyond the merest limits of expediency, plunged his mercurial spirits into the depths of depression.

3

In May 1778 Hervey and his family took a house at Castel Gandolfo as a retreat from the summer heat of Rome, though they retained their lodgings in the city so that they would have a place to stay in the event of an occasional visit. This was in accordance with the Bishop's opulent manner of life, for he had no intention of stinting himself, even during the *villeggiatura,* and arrived at his country villa with a coach-and-four, a post-chaise, and a phaeton. Lest the evenings should prove dull he also brought his daughter Louisa's music master together with two 'well behav'd young men' who played the violin, and the promise of two others who excelled on the French horn – quite a little orchestra.

Castel Gandolfo is one of the most attractive of the *Castelli Romani*, the small towns in the Alban hills some ten or twelve miles south of Rome. Dominated by the summer palace of the Popes and clustered on a hill high above Lake Albano it was a favourite subject of the contemporary view-painters who were beginning to discover a taste for the picturesque. The Herveys' house had previously belonged to the proscribed order of Jesuits but had been remodelled and furnished for the use of summer visitors and was described by Mrs. Hervey as being 'not in a village but *en plein air* – situated on an eminence which commands a vast plain that is bounded by the Mediterranean – the *ridge* of hill on which we are plac'd is for several miles very beautiful, being a mixture of gardens, vineyards, corn, and two or three pretty lakes at an agreeable distance – fine old trees rejoice the sight and give delicious shade to our walks.'

The Bishop prepared himself for a period of repose after his months of busy intrigue in Rome. 'We are here in a delightful habitation,' he told his daughter Elizabeth. 'Wood, water, hills, plains, rivers and the sea, while beautiful buildings decorate all the villages which are chiefly on an eminence, and from our house to Albano the road leads to a birdcage walk of about a mile, shaded by the largest, the oldest and the most venerable oaks as well as chestnuts that I ever saw. Under the branches of these patrician trees one frequently discovers the principal buildings of Rome, and specially the numerous ruins of ancient ones that fill the immense plain between this hill and the city. In short a more romantic spot cannot be seen.'

Hervey spent much of his time walking in the surrounding countryside with an Irish companion called O'Reilly with whose family they shared the villa. For the most part politics were forgotten, though when the news reached them that Gardiner's Relief Act was concerned only with property and not with freedom of worship all thoughts of the day's ramble were driven from the Bishop's head and Mrs. Hervey found her husband 'at 5 o-clock sitting like a *dart* at his writing table and working his thumbs into his nightcap', while the news of Lord Chatham's death, followed shortly after by that of Voltaire (both died in May 1778) cast a gloom over this Whig household where both names were held in honour.

It was to Chatham's Ministry that Hervey owed his promotion to the Irish episcopal bench and he had always held the great statesman in high esteem. This reverence was to take an odd but characteristic form. In 1770 he commissioned a large canvas from William Hoare, R.A., of Bath. In the centre of the picture is a table with the Minister seated in an armchair on its right holding a paper in his hand and looking straight ahead apparently unaware of the presence of the Bishop of Derry, who sits at the other side of the table. The Bishop has one hand on the shoulder of his young son, John Augustus, dressed in midshipman's uniform, while the other hand indicates the statesman with a gesture of admiration and respect. It was a curious tribute, showing, perhaps, more sentiment than taste, for the resulting picture can hardly be called a work of art; indeed the almost total indifference displayed in Chatham's expression to the veneration offered him by the Hervey family gives the whole scene a rather comic air.

The loss of these two great figures filled Hervey's mind with anxious thoughts, and a first cloud passed over the happy retreat at Castel Gandolfo. He was too much of a Whig not to regret the death of Chatham, especially at this critical stage of the American war; and as that somewhat contradictory thing, a Voltairean bishop, he realized how fine a champion the enlightened causes he upheld had lost in the passing of that other great spirit. Both he and his wife were shocked when their daughter Lady Erne, then still in Paris, sent them an account of the old philosopher's last days. 'What a miserable end!' Mrs. Hervey replied. 'What a ridiculous farce about his Funeral, and what a refinement about giving his plays.'

A second cloud came to darken the household at Castel Gandolfo when serious illness struck them in July. A particularly violent epidemic of malaria affected the whole area claiming the Bishop, his wife, and their daughter Louisa, the latter nearly succumbing to the disease. 'I saw the fatal vapor one morning rising like a pest from the Pontine marshes and overspreading the hills of Veletri, Gensano, Laricia, Albano and the house where we reside', Hervey wrote to Sir William Hamilton when the worst was over. 'I immediately ordered my trunks to be pack'd up and prepared for a timely departure, but it came like a thief in the night and stopp'd me upon the threshold of my door; we have all suffer'd by it more or less; some have been with one leg in the grave and by the care of physicians drawn out again; a succession of servants, male and female, from Rome have not suffic'd to attend the sick; the physicians themselves have yielded to the contagion, and the nurses both from Rome and the neighbouring villages have attended like centinels by relays.'[10]

It was September before Mrs. Hervey could assure her daughter in Ireland that 'Your Father . . . is now, thank God, eating, sleeping and laughing himself into health', but it was another month before Louisa was even convalescent. She had nearly died, and the anxiety of it all had had its effect upon her mother who early in the summer had described herself as almost as much a skeleton as Voltaire had been. Even without illness life was trying enough for the poor woman. Her weak frame, she declared, would not allow her to get up at four in the morning, which was the Bishop's favourite hour for rising, while his insistence on retiring to bed early 'takes off the amusement which the freshness of the evening invites to after supper'.

When Hervey was better he returned to Rome on his own, leaving his wife to look after Louisa and occupy herself with her melancholy reflections, but perhaps not entirely sorry for a few weeks of peace and quiet. The Bishop must have felt a twinge of conscience for abandoning the invalids at Castel Gandolfo after his recovery for he contrived a delightful welcome for them when they joined him again in Rome. 'I brought Louisa to Town the day before yesterday', Mrs. Hervey wrote to Lady Erne on 6 November. 'She bore it very well and was in great spirits both at leaving the Place of her sufferings and returning to her Papa, whom we found surrounded with busts and pictures and almost as fresh and well looking as ever – he welcom'd us with a band of music which struck up unexpectedly in the next room whilst we were at Table; and was an idea quite in his own style and very flattering to us.'

4

The return to Rome brought welcome news from home; Lady Erne and Elizabeth Foster both announced the expected arrival of children. The prospect of becoming a grandfather delighted the Bishop. Letters were dispatched full of advice. Mrs. Hervey deplored the ineptitude of the Paris doctors who had failed to diagnose her eldest daughter's condition and nearly caused a miscarriage by ordering warm baths, while Hervey took his younger daughter to task for wishing to have her lying-in at Dublin. The air, he warned her, was insufficiently 'elastic' in that otherwise agreeable city, and the consequences might be disastrous.

For the first time since he set foot on the Continent the Bishop showed signs of wanting to be home. 'Have you seen Lord Erne?' he asked Elizabeth. 'Is he on tiptoes? Isn't Mary a sweet creature to be at last multiplying herself, and providing comforts for her old age and mine? I am in raptures with the thought of seeing you all at Downhill, and have some thoughts of building barracks for children. Go on, my dear Eliza, and never fear hurting your constitution by honest child-bearing, since for one mother that grows thin with this work there are five hundred old maids that grow more thin for want of it.'[11]

For his eldest daughter Hervey had words of counsel on the subject of the education of his future grandchildren: 'Your situation, my dear Mary, gives me the greatest satisfaction, for you have a warm capacious heart full of affection, and want more objects to fill it, especially when those which now engross it must in the course of nature leave a void in it – and what so natural as one's own children. All I entreat you is to insist on monopolising their education and having form'd yourself on those admirable models of Locke and Rousseau not to suffer feminine fears and the apprehensions bred by distemper to direct you from them. Without a strong and vigorous constitution 'tis almost impossible to have a Firm and Stable mind: the infirmities of the body will communicate themselves to the mind and weaken it in proportion as the other suffers: hardness is the first step towards making a virtuous woman and a steady man.'

Though Locke had written on *The Reasonableness of Christianity* and Rousseau professed a belief in 'natural religion' it is curious to find these two philosophers so cordially recommended by a man who was, when all was said and done, a bishop of the Established Church in whose calendar neither name was likely to be discovered. It is also significant that Hervey did not include any suggestion of religious instruction in his letter to his daughter. It could be argued, of course, that such advice was implicit in his office and therefore needed no stressing, but it could as easily be maintained that such an argument falls down in the case of the forty-eighth Bishop of Derry. Advice such as he gave to Lady Erne caused no comment when confined to his family; but Hervey was quite unrepentant in his enthusiasm for Locke, Voltaire, Rousseau, and the *philosophes* of his own generation, and expressed his admiration for them irrespective of the company or the occasion. It was this somewhat too reckless (or too honest) conduct that gained him the reputation for being that alarming species of humanity a 'free-thinker'. That this often shocked people caused him no concern at all; but it certainly made him more enemies than friends.

How strange a bishop he must have seemed to the subjects of Pope Pius VI (who had succeeded Clement XIV in 1775) as he paraded the streets of eighteenth-century Rome in his curious dress, always on the look-out for pictures, marbles, and other treasures for his house at Downhill; talking in English, French or Italian according to the company of the moment, liberal with his money as with his ideas if it was a question of sealing a bargain or snubbing an opinionated bore. But strangest of all to the Italians who hailed him indifferently as *Milordo Hervey* or *Milor il Vescovo,* here was a bishop who returned home each day to a wife and family. In the presence of such a phenomenon his liberal-egalitarian opinions would not have appeared the least of his peculiarities and probably passed unnoticed. It is one of the ironies of history that it was not the Roman Inquisition but the republican liberators of Milan who would in due course send the Bishop to cool his heels for a period in prison.

5

Hervey resumed his pleasant life in Rome for the months of November and December 1778 before leaving for Naples. He was delighted to meet a Mr. Thomas Pitt, a nephew of his hero Lord Chatham and so very like him in appearance that the Bishop (according to Mrs. Hervey) 'devours him with his eyes'. But his main occupation still consisted in buying works of art for the adornment of his new house in Ireland. 'I am purchasing treasures for the Downhill which I flatter myself will be a Tusculanium', he told Elizabeth Foster, and to John Strange he wrote that he had become a great collector of *virtu,* but unfortunately he gave no details of his actual purchases or commissions.

Fortunately one of the artists he dealt with kept a diary and has left a record of some of the purchases Hervey made from his studio. This was Thomas Jones, the Welsh landscape painter, a pupil of Richard Wilson and the Bishop's exact contemporary. Hervey had admired a view of Lake Albano but had shown some reluctance to commit himself. 'I believe his Lordship's final determination was fixed by the following circumstance', Jones noted. 'I had a handsome *Carlos Marat* frame made into which I put the picture, and one morning when his Lordship called, told him I was going to send it to England. He remonstrated some time on the Hazards, but I said I was determined to run all risques. The Bishop, upon hearing this Declaration, which was delivered in a kind of indifferent but resolute tone, immediately replied: 'That Picture Sir, shall not go to England – it is mine', and directly gave me an Order on his banker for the money.' The sum agreed upon was £40.[12]

The Bishop had probably been recommended to Jones by Sir William Hamilton who made a point of helping such British artists as made their way to Italy, and who later offered part of his *palazzo* in Naples as a studio to this same artist while he himself was away on a tour of Calabria. The episode just described took place in Rome, but when Hervey reached Naples late in December, travelling in the company of the young architect John Soane (then in Italy on a travelling scholarship from the Royal Academy), the Welsh painter had already arrived there and presented himself at the Bishop's levée, which with that early riser took place at six o'clock in the morning.

'I found him', Jones declared, 'combing and adjusting a single curl which was fixed by a string to his own short hair. "You see, Mr. Jones," said he as I was entering the room, "I am my own Valet. I am not like the generality of our Noble families – poor half-begotten creatures who have no use for their limbs, and cannot stir without a coach." After a few minutes conversation he mounted his horse and, attended only by his groom, set off according to his usual custom on a ramble till dinner.' The Bishop commissioned two other canvases from

Jones while he was in Naples. One, a storm scene, is described by the artist as 'a view of a Rock at Terracina', while the other was a view of Lake Nemi. Hervey certainly seems to have admired the work of this painter, for some years later Jones noted in his diary: 'About this time [i.e. March 1783] I received letters from the Earl of Bristol with the most friendly proposals of disposing of, in Ireland, all the Pictures I should happen to have by me, with the exception of those which he had already bespoke or, upon view, should take a fancy to.'[13] In situations of this sort the Bishop liked to refer to himself as 'the midwife of talents'.

It was, however, largely to give his daughter a chance to regain her health that had decided Hervey to winter in Naples. Mrs. Hervey and Louisa were the first to reach the city and took rooms in readiness for the Bishop's arrival. 'We have got a most delightful apartment almost in the center of this bay, which is the South, and consequently we have all the advantage that it is possible to have from a fine view, good air, and cheerful scenery. . . .' Lady Erne was informed on 30 December. 'They fish all day under our windows, which being 72 steps from the street gives us amusement without annoyance – it is also the constant promenade, in short, it is everything – and I thought it so certainly to your Father's taste that I ventur'd to take it before he came. The apartment is very extensive and convenient, but the great point is a room 50 feet long to the sea and the sun at one end. He has two rooms in front, likewise on the other, and I have the same with accommodation for all our people behind them.'

A happy circumstance for the Bishop was the presence of his old schoolfellow Sir William Hamilton at the neighbouring Palazzo Sessa. The Hamiltons were out of town but returned specially to entertain their English friends, and provided a dinner at which forty-six guests sat down at table. But it was their more intimate evenings that the Bishop most enjoyed when he could examine his friend's 'cabinet' with its growing collection of pictures, Greek vases, and the geological spoils of Vesuvius. They also shared a taste for music. The British Minister was a modest but proficient performer on the violin while his first wife was considered by no less a judge than Dr. Charles Burney to be the best harpsichord player in Italy. As the Herveys had done at Castal Gandolfo, the Hamiltons always included a few musicians among their servants so that a trio or quartette could be arranged when music was required. Certainly Mrs. Hervey preferred these simple evenings and was glad when she could be excused the grand ambassadorial dinners.

Naples as usual had a number of British visitors among whom Mrs. Hervey observed Lord Tylney 'playing at cards incessantly and devour'd by his servants', and Lady Berkeley whose terror of Vesuvius was such that she was 'in agony to get away before the earth opens and swallows up all this city which she is convinc'd will be the case'. But oddest of all in comparison to the forthright and often bawdy Bishop of Derry was the appearance in Naples of Thomas Bowdler, the later 'purifier' of Shakespeare. It is not surprising that Hervey, whom many people considered due for a little Bowdlerizing himself, and the future editor of the Family Shakespeare did not exactly appreciate each other's qualities. The young man (he was then no more than twenty-five) was at this period more interested in natural history than literature and was contemptuously dismissed by the Bishop in a letter to Strange as 'that would-be naturalist, and half natural, poor Bowdler, whose mind and ideas seem to limp more than his body'. It is amusing to imagine the encounter between the prudish Bowdler, surely one of nature's curates, and the ribald and outspoken Frederick Hervey upon whose head fate had so ironically placed a mitre.

At the end of March 1779 the Hervey family left Naples for what was to prove a very leisurely journey back to England, a journey that was to take them a full six months with many halts and detours on the way. As usual the Bishop rode on horseback, his wife and daughter (now considered well enough to travel) following by coach. Rome was reached in time for the Easter ceremonies at St. Peter's. Here Hervey's predilection for the peculiar dress of his order placed him in a position of public ridicule which must have been very unwelcome to a man of his temperament.

At the Maundy Thursday celebrations held in the Sistine Chapel Hervey arrived to watch the ceremonial washing of the feet clad once more in the dress of an English bishop. He had done this before in Rome. The difference on this occasion (to judge by the commotion that followed) was that he had chosen for his sartorial display a religious rite performed by the Pope himself, and that he seems to have adopted his full canonicals of rochet and chimere, for he would hardly have been noticed in so vast a congregation wearing the sober black of apron and gaiters.

It was a tactless act to say the least, but knowing the Bishop's character there was no doubt a note of bravado in it as well. The result, however, was a public humiliation. Sir Edward Newenham, an Irish politician, was present and recorded in his diary: 'The Bishop of Derry most absurdly appeared in his English bishop's dress. He was laughed at by everyone. For this piece of absurdity he was obliged to go to the lowest part of the chapel among the common people while my sons and I were in the same upper division with the Cardinals. After this behaviour the eccentric bishop was held in the greatest contempt. Scarcely a nobleman would visit him.'[14]

Snubs, indeed, seemed to be the order of the day at this period, though the one that followed was delivered indirectly to the British Minister in Florence. The Herveys proceeded there in April and their arrival at the Tuscan capital was duly reported in a letter from Sir Horace Mann to his friend Horace Walpole at Strawberry Hill, but only to receive the rather crushing reply: 'I am not at all acquainted with your Lord Bishop and my Lady, his wife. His mother, who was much my friend, I believe, did not highly reverence his sincerity; I never in my life met him at her house.'[15] Difference in generation was not usually a handicap to friendship with Walpole and it is rather surprising that he did not know the Bishop with whom, in fact, he had so many tastes in common as well as a mutual friend of Hervey's own generation in Sir William Hamilton. Later on, when the Bishop became more involved in Irish politics, Walpole was to refer to him with the greatest animosity; but the rather tart note of the reply to Mann's letter suggests that even at this time he had no great desire to repair this particular omission in his circle of friends.

The Bishop, meanwhile, was heading for France by way of Turin and Lausanne, being cheered *en route* by news of the birth of a daughter to Lady Erne. From Turin, on 18 May, Mrs. Hervey wrote to the young mother: 'Your father is this moment arriv'd as well and as cheerful as Mountains can make him, and full of the extraordinary things and Persons he found among them. He sends you his blessing and best affections, and longs very much to see you in your new occupation and character, which he very *highly approves*.' The stay in Italy was not prolonged after Turin, and the Bishop spurred on to France. Having whetted his appetite for ecclesiastical intrigue in Rome he was now to try his hand at secular politics in Paris.

6

When Hervey arrived in Paris in August 1779 a state of war had existed between his native country and France since February of the previous year when the French Government had entered into an offensive and defensive treaty with the American Colonies. This fact in no way affected the cordiality of his reception at the French capital though his conduct there, never tactful at the best of times, would cause him to leave the city in a hurry after a stay of little more than a month.

It was not a propitious moment in Anglo-French relations. Nothing was more welcome in Paris than news of an English reverse in North America and the fact that in this very month of August the French fleet was in temporary control of the English Channel gave a grim reality to the possibility of an invasion of England or Ireland on the very lines Hervey had feared so much when he was in Rome. It was for this reason that he sought the company of Benjamin Franklin, who was then living at Passy, in the hope that between them they might find some formula of reconciliation between the British Government and her estranged colonies. His mission was quite unofficial and undertaken entirely on his own initiative. It is not impossible that he hoped, should his efforts prove successful, that he might be able by this means to regain the trust of George III whose confidence in the Bishop of Derry had by no means been improved by this further prolonged absence from his ecclesiastical duties in Ireland.

Franklin had been the best part of three years in the French capital where he enjoyed great social acclaim. Caressed and petted by the more exclusive Parisian hostesses, revered in literary and scientific circles, he was not without success at court even though he had shocked and amazed the more conservative courtiers by appearing at Versailles without wig or sword. His prestige was immense and his diplomatic achievements had been considerable, but at the time when the Bishop arrived in Paris his position was made somewhat insecure by the knowledge of plots against him in the Congress at Philadelphia. New contacts might well come in useful, and this may indeed have been one of the reasons why he welcomed Hervey's visits, for there is no reason to suppose that he had much respect for the Bishop or expected any great results from their meetings.[16]

The results of Hervey's conversations with Franklin and with Turgot, the former Comptroller General of Finance, were set out in a letter to Lord George Germain, Secretary of State for American Affairs, in a letter dated from Passy on 4 August. 'I have seen Franklin four times', the Bishop wrote. 'He is thoroughly dissatisfied with the Congress, and more so with Versailles, and told me he would go to Italy, but I believe wishes for a more honourable retreat and would gladly contribute to a reunion of the Empire. I shall remain a month here if you think it worth while to take any notice of this information. Mons. Turgot himself despairs; surely the iron should be well struck while it is so hot, and it is better to give too much (with regard to America) than risque all by offering too little. I fear most for Ireland; there is a kind of Quixotism about making that country independent, and *Spain* has no Ireland to fear, for Application was made sometime ago to the Irish Seminary here for two Missionaries who could speak Irish, French and English but the Superior could not find two so qualified. The bearer can tell you more. I forgot to mention that Turgot himself told me one night at Madam Blondel's that the Congress had us'd Franklin shamefully, and did not deserve him.'

A little over a month later (on 10 September) Hervey was writing to the Secretary of State from Ostende a letter largely concerned with French military designs on Ireland. In the intervening period he had left Paris, apparently rather suddenly. According to Horace Walpole this was because he had become 'so abusive of Dr. Franklin and the American colonists that he was ordered to depart from Paris under pain of the Bastille'. This explanation seems unlikely, especially when coming from so unfriendly a source. There is no indication in either of the letters that he subsequently wrote to Lord George Germain that he had any ill-feelings towards Franklin, indeed he refers quite sympathetically to the latter's difficulties with the American Congress. It is much more likely that his all too evident interest in French military plans was the cause of his hurried departure, for these form the chief content of his letters from Ostende. The Bishop was never one to keep his opinions to himself or to express them in moderate language. If he sought out information on France's invasion plans as assiduously in Paris as he had done in Rome it is not surprising that the French Government encouraged his speedy departure and possibly added threats to their encouragements.

The letter from Ostende is important not only for its military information, which was surely of value to the British Government, but also because it shows (even at this moment of crisis) the consistent and uncompromising nature of Hervey's liberal ideas in relation to the suppressed majority of the Irish people. Unfortunately the letter's recipient was no less uncompromising, but in the opposite direction.

'I cannot omit so safe an opportunity as the present', the letter begins, 'of renewing my assurance to yr. Lordship that the great armament is levelled against Ireland, tho' a ridiculous feint will be made on the Isle of Wight. The coast of Galway is the place of landing as the bearer can inform you who knows much of the detail. The Manifesto intended to be dispers'd exhibits *Independence, Liberty of Religion* to all sects, and *free trade*. One man who gave the plan is son to a late Minister, well acquainted with England and therefore dissuaded them from their first intentions. They are encouraged likewise to fix on Ireland by letters and emissaries from both ends of the kingdom.

'Your Lordship will please to remember that nothing has yet been done for the Romish Clergy, and for the people of that persuasion who hold everything cheap in comparison of their religion; that the Romish gentlemen are few and of course have little interest either over the Clergy or the peasantry; that to my knowledge they think the gentlemen sacrificed the liberty of religion to the security of their property, which idea has considerably lessen'd the little influence they had. If something therefore be not speedily effected to pacify both the Papists and the Presbyterians, we risque a general insurrection even upon the appearance of the French.

'With all the regard I have for the Presbyterians, many of whom I know to be excellent men, yet I deem them much more dangerous at this crisis than the Papists. Their principles are truly republican and the proffer of independency, which will be instantly exhibited by the French, cannot fail of success among them. . . . For God's sake then, my Lord, let us not be sacrificed either to the Indolence or Incredulity and much less to the fear of disgusting a venal faction in Ireland. The rights of humanity demand a general and unlimited toleration at all times. Policy peculiarly demands it at present. A reasonable indulgence to the Presbyterian and Papist may save the kingdom. The Presbyterians cannot believe the King loves them – let his Attorney General or rather his eloquent Prime Sergeant, move a repeal of the Test Act. It can disgust only a few ignorant High Churchmen among ourselves, and will reclaim some thousands of ill-dispos'd subjects among those sectaries. Place us all, my Lord, on the same footing, and we shall all be equally good subjects. . . . One happy masterly stroke may save Ireland for ages; its ruin shall not lie at my door.'

In a further undated letter written from Dover, concerned chiefly with an account of the French capture of Granada in the West Indies and of the factions in America scheming to undermine the influence of Franklin, the Bishop ends with a final plea for the country of his adoption: 'if it be possible to raise Roman Catholic regiments in Ireland there may be a supply of such Officers as would be no indifferent acquisition towards the speedy reduction of America. I throw out this for your Lordship's attention, before I have the honor of seeing you, and I hope you will forgive the importunity of one who feels deeply for the misfortunes of his country and the miscarriages of some of the noblest plans that ever were concerted, and which seemed to have every title to success except the indolence of those appointed to execute them.'

This letter, written from English soil, seems to lack the note of confidence and hope which had characterized the many other letters on the subject of Ireland which the Bishop had written in the course of his travels. It was as though the return to these familiar shores had brought home to him the essential indifference of the British Government to the fundamental problems of the Irish nation. There was no sign of any favourable response to his schemes for reform. The general feeling of those in authority when faced with his proposals for improving the lot of Catholics or Presbyterians was aptly summed up in the opinion of the King himself. No man in his senses, declared George III, could approve such dangerous democratical remedies.[17] In future the Bishop would find other ways of attempting to put his ideas into practice.

7

The Bishop spent the months of September and October 1779 in London, where he talked a good deal in his usual unguarded way about his conversations with Benjamin Franklin. This was to have an amusing sequel, as Lord Shelburne (a friend to both Hervey and Franklin) later related to Jeremy Bentham. 'Coming from Paris directly to London', Bentham recorded, 'he [the Bishop] carried a verbal message, as he pretended from Franklin to – whom would you think of all men in the world? – Lord Spencer; telling him that if he would come to Paris immediately they two would be able to settle a Peace. Lord Spencer was very much distressed; would scarce credit the information; but willing to do what he thought right, thought he would not justify himself by taking no notice of it. He accordingly set out, and actually got nearly as far as Calais, but the wind proving contrary, or some other obstruction arising, he fancied it impossible to get to Paris in time enough, so he went back again.'[18]

Whether this was one of the Bishop's elaborate and often heartless practical jokes or merely the result of his rather wild talk, it does not seem to have done any permanent damage to his relations with Lord and Lady Spencer. The latter he called 'my model of women' and spent some time with her at Althrop on his way back to Ireland where, as he confessed to his daughter Mary, 'we discussed almost every topick of the human mind, and I scarcely know one on which we differ'd and on which we did not almost anticipate each other's ideas.' The Bishop does not say whether Lady Spencer's husband was present at these animated discussions. Perhaps he was still contending with contrary winds in the English Channel; but Lady Spencer was a woman of exemplary character, as Fanny Burney later testified, and the Bishop assured his daughter: 'if ever I should pass a winter in Town I will make you know her thoroughly and then you will admire her as much as I do.'

The possibility of a union between England and Ireland on similar terms to those between England and Scotland was being discussed in political circles while Hervey was in London. Though the union in fact lay just over twenty years ahead the Bishop seems to have thought it much more imminent. 'No one in London doubts of a Union,' he wrote to his daughter Elizabeth on 6 November, 'nor do I believe there will be much difficulty about the terms. The Peerage, to be incorporated with the British House, is to be hereditary, and the remaining Irish peers are to be admissible as at present into the lower House. The proportion of each will be a little more difficult to ascertain, but all agree that we Bishops shall remain in our dioceses. God grant this may be true. Another scheme has been prepared of leaving the Parliament in Ireland for the internal administration of the kingdom, and assessing it once for all in proportion with England, but I cannot imagine the Irish will endure this: it would reduce them to the insignificance of a mere corporation of Aldermen and Common Council, and would multiply the number of non-residents beyond endurance, for who would condescend to become a member of such a legislature?'

The Bishop had discussed the scheme with James Boswell while in London, and found him strongly opposed to the whole project. On returning to Ireland Hervey assured Boswell that the inhabitants of Dublin were violently against a union with England but that he himself considered that the rest of the country was likely to benefit from it. Boswell had claimed that Edinburgh had suffered as a result of the Union of 1707; Hervey now asked him if he would ascertain what the present number of houses was in Edinburgh and how it compared with the number at the time of the Union. Boswell, however was impatient of mere statistics: 'Let us, my Lord,' he replied, 'be satisfied to live on good and equal terms as we might have done with our Sovereign's people of America had those been allow'd to enjoy *their* Parliament or Assemblies as Ireland enjoys *hers,* and instead of calling Ireland a deluded people and attempting to grasp them in our paws, let us admire their spirit. A Scotchman might preach a Union to them as the fox who has lost his tail. But your Lordship is an Englishman and brother to the Earl of Bristol.'[19]

Hervey was certainly at that moment both; but though he would of necessity remain an Englishman, he was very soon to revise his ideas on the constitutional question and become closely associated with the patriotic party, now organizing itself in the Volunteer movement which had started while he was abroad. It was to be an association which the Bishop would conduct in his own flamboyant and intemperate style. As to being brother to the Earl of Bristol, that he would remain for another week. Boswell's letter was dated 15 December 1779. On 22 December Hervey's brother Augustus died at Bristol House in St. James' Square, London, and Frederick succeeded him in the family honours as fourth Earl. 'Lord Bristol has outran me,' declared Horace Walpole on hearing the news, 'and leaves an Earl-Bishop and a Countess-Duchess.'

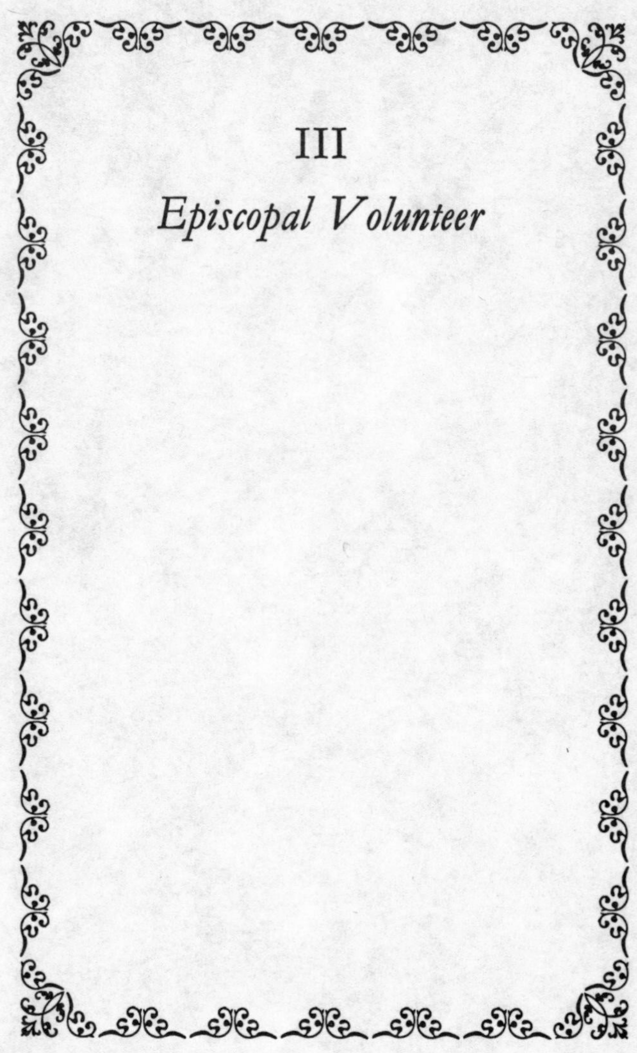

III
Episcopal Volunteer

I

Probably the most important consideration to Frederick Hervey as he succeeded to the Earldom of Bristol was the fact that his income was now augmented to the extent of about £20,000 a year. This was the estimated annual revenue from the entailed property in which he now enjoyed a life interest. There had been no love lost between the two brothers, and the departed Earl had left his successor not a penny more than he could help, providing for a bereaved mistress and a natural son out of the unsettled estate, leaving all his father's manuscript writings to the latter with the injunction never to publish them during the present King's (George III's) lifetime, 'nor ever at any time to lend them to my brother Frederick, the present Bishop of Derry'.

When it is recalled that the emoluments of the See of Derry rose to 'a princely revenue not far short of £20,000 a year'[1] under Hervey's skilful management it will be seen that for most of the latter part of his life he had at his command a yearly income in the neighbourhood of £40,000. For a man who had started life as a younger son with an annuity of '£200 a year clear', the Earl-Bishop of Derry had not done so badly.

He appears never at any moment to have thought of resigning his bishopric. The only change in his style after becoming Earl of Bristol was that he adopted the signature 'Bristol' in place of his episcopal signature 'F. Derry' (though when travelling abroad he would sometimes sign himself with the full flourish '*Le Comte de Bristol, Evêque de Derry*') while in society generally he was more usually referred to as Lord Bristol than Bishop of Derry. 'How do you like an Earl-Bishop?' Horace Walpole wrote to the Rev. William Cole a few days after Hervey's succession. 'Had we not one before in ancient days? I have not a book in town; but was not there Anthony Beck, or a Hubert de Burgh, that was Bishop of Durham and Earl of Kent, or have I confounded them?'[2] In fact the last Earl-Bishop seems to have been William the Conqueror's half-brother Odo who was Bishop of Bayeux and Earl of Kent.

The Bishop spent the greater part of the year 1780 in his diocese, which was the least he could do after nearly two and a half years of neglect. Work was still in progress on the enlargement and embellishment of Downhill and he had to supervise the placing of the collection of pictures and works of art he had made in Rome and Naples. To the colony of British artists in Italy the news of his recent increase in fortune was hailed with delight and the liveliest anticipation of further patronage and commissions. Henry Tresham, later a Royal Academician, according to Thomas Jones's diary 'gave a great entertainment to a large company of artists on the occasion of the Bishop succeeding to the title and estates of his brother the late Earl of Bristol'. As far as they were concerned the sooner the Earl-Bishop was on his travels again the better contented they would be.

For the next five years, however, the Bishop was to find enough to occupy his energy and ingenuity nearer home. During his absence abroad, as has been briefly noted, Ireland had been arming herself against the threat of foreign invasion. The Volunteer Corps, which was formed for this purpose, owed its origin indirectly to that colourful figure, the American privateer Paul Jones. In April 1778 (while the Bishop of Derry was enjoying the enchantments of a Roman spring) Jones had sailed into Belfast Lough and captured a naval ship with a minimum of military opposition. Alarmed and provoked to action by this hostile act the citizens of Belfast had formed their own defence force, and so the Volunteer movement had begun.

In the two following years the Volunteers had grown into a considerable force, and in the situation of Ireland at the time it was no surprise that they had taken on a strong political complexion. It was to the Volunteers, with their resplendent uniforms and all the glamour of military rank, that those Irish patriots rallied whose ultimate objective was the legislative independence of their country. They represented, however, only the 'Protestant nation'. The adherents of the Established Church and the Presbyterians of the north (whose hatred of the French outweighed their admiration for the American republicans) were able to unite in the Volunteer ranks; but the movement held aloof from the Catholic majority.

The Government, as represented by Dublin Castle, viewed the

movement with distrust and clearly feared its growing strength, but while the danger of an invasion persisted and while the American war absorbed all available regular troops, they had no alternative but to accept the Volunteers with what good grace they could muster.

It was to an Ireland in which the Volunteers were now widespread and conscious of their strength that Hervey returned with the added prestige of his British peerage joined to his rank as an Irish bishop. He was completely in sympathy with their political outlook which corresponded to his own often expressed sentiments of patriotism for his adopted country; but at this period he did not associate himself with them so completely as was later to be the case, when he would add the military rank of colonel to his temporal rank of earl and his spiritual rank of bishop. It was, however, very much the presence of the Volunteer corps that helped to get some much needed reforms through the Irish parliament; reforms for which Lord Bristol was prepared to take a good deal of credit.

His travels on the Continent had prevented Bristol (as we must now call him) from taking part in the debates in the Irish Parliament when Gardiner's Relief Act had been passed; an Act which, as he declared at the time, fell short of his expectations. He was now able to lend his support in person to the debates that resulted in the repeal of the Test Act in March 1780. The Act had originally been passed in 1704 as a measure directed against Roman Catholics, but when the Westminster Government gave it their sanction they added a clause which required all office holders to qualify by taking the sacrament in the Established Church, thus excluding Protestant nonconformists from office as well as Catholics. It was this discrimination against the Protestant sects that the Irish Parliament, with strong pressure from the Volunteers, now set aside.

Bristol, as usual, would have wished the toleration to go further. Just over a year later (August 1781) he was staying with Lord Shelburne at Bowood where he met Jeremy Bentham who found the Earl-Bishop 'a singular sort of personage who, not in Falstaff's sense, but in another sense, may be termed a *double man*'. According to Bentham 'Lord B. assumed to me . . . a principal share in merit of carrying the toleration act through the Irish House of Lords. He was, in his own mind at least, for going further, and admitting them to all offices, that of Member of Parliament not excepted.'[3] On this point of reform, however, his ideas outstripped those of his fellow Anglicans as his ideas of a Catholic franchise were later on to outstrip those of his fellow Volunteers.

At this period he was still set on a course of moderation. 'Is it possible', he wrote to his daughter Elizabeth in April 1780, 'that the Chief Governor or any of his friends can think me capable of distressing an administration both in England and Ireland to which I wish so well, and for the sake of which I have separated from some of the oldest and most intimate connexions I have in the world? Believe me, I think this cause too good either to desert it or embarrass them. When I judged them to be better informed than myself, as in all foreign politicks, I should without either scruple or reserve deliver my political conscience into their hands; but with regard to their interests in Ireland and the intrinsick unalienable rights of Ireland itself (which are the rights of mankind) in which I deem myself much better informed than they, having not only taken more pains on the subject but being also an ocular observer on the spot, if, either through inattention or presumptions, they will not take the advice I have given them, but persist in the same infatuated system of despotism towards Ireland which has almost lost America – what is then the part of an honest man or a true friend?' He was sure, he told her, that civil war would break out 'which bids fair for being one of the most sanguinary and most general that this country has known' if the Government in England continued in its policy towards Ireland, but for the present he still saw his role as one who should warn the government of its dangers and oppose it only when he could take no other course, rather than as one who should oppose it *à l'outrance*.

The Bishop made no further escapades into Irish politics during this year. The affairs of his diocese and his personal concerns kept him either in Derry or at Downhill for most of the time. In March Lepel, Lady Mulgrave, died, and the loss of this favourite sister left him 'totally unfit for anything but the solitude in which I live and move and have my being', and by August he had retired to Downhill in ill-health. The illness does not seem to have been serious: a sort of nervous exhaustion that attacked him from time to time.

During all this time his wife had been at Ickworth, the scene of her early married life, and from there she wrote to him on 13 August: 'We drank your health yesterday, but I am much concerned to find on pressing Elizabeth on that subject that it is not altogether so good as, in your ardour for the mountains, you represent it to me: and though Mary says that you have no other complaint than a sore finger, yet she seems to think your spirits low, and I much fear that you have taken too much fatigue for your strength. . . .' In spite of this show of wifely affection he did not seem to be in any hurry to rejoin her. There were, none the less, pressing reasons for his return to England. His daughter Elizabeth's marriage to Foster, 'little f', appeared to be on the verge of collapse, and he had not yet visited the estates in Suffolk which had become his on his succession to the peerage. Even so he did not return to Ickworth until just before Christmas.

2

Bristol spent nearly two years in England, during which period he made his home at Ickworth Lodge where his wife had been living since their return from the Continent. The time which elapsed between his arrival there in December 1780 and his departure for Ireland again in November 1782 was to see the break-up not only of his daughter Lady Elizabeth Foster's marriage, but also of his own.

Elizabeth Foster's marriage, which had started with such promise, had not long survived its first period of bliss. A total incompatibility of temperament seems to have caused its early disruption. From the safe distance of Downhill the Bishop had attempted (with a minimum of discomfort to himself) to restore some harmony to the estranged couple. He arranged for them to meet, not under his own roof, but at Ickworth. Perhaps he thought Lady Bristol a more likely person to preside over a reconciliation than himself, and in this no doubt he was right, but even so the meeting failed in its purpose.

Foster was at Ickworth by the end of August. Early in September Lady Bristol reported on the failure of her hopes in a letter to her daughter Mary. 'With regard to the reconciliation,' she wrote,

'I do not think there is a ray of comfort or hope in it. It was totally against my opinion as to *happiness*, but yr Father's orders and her *situation* call'd for it – it is apparently well establish'd but it cannot produce any good effect – dejection and despair are wrote on her countenance, and tho' I have no doubt that time might wear out her *attachment*, I believe nothing *can remove her* disgust. . . . I have no hope of getting rid of him, and yr Father seems to wish his countenance here – for his part I am convinced that he is perfectly well pleased – affection, vanity and avarice being all gratified.' The reference to Elizabeth's 'situation' arose from the fact that she was expecting her second child.

The baby, a son, was born at Ickworth on 4 December, not long before the arrival of his grandfather from Ireland. Four months previously he had been presented with another grandchild when his eldest son's wife, Lady Hervey, had given birth to a daughter. But these births do not seem to have produced the loud acclamations that heralded the arrival of his first grandchild; indeed, the Bishop seems to have been thoroughly out of humour with all his family.

In April 1781 Lady Elizabeth left for London. The marriage with Foster was at an end; nothing remained but to agree to the terms of the separation. Bristol, though he had been back in England for some time, appeared to show very little concern for his daughter's troubles, going off on a tour of Norfolk and leaving everything for his wife to settle in his absence.

The Bishop's selfishness and lack of consideration for others had not diminished with the passage of time. His affection for his family, though superficially cordial enough, tended quickly to wane as his own schemes and projects, in which they found no place, grew and blossomed. His interest in his family only revived when he found that they could be of some practical use to him. He was as often as not quite unaware of the unhappiness that surrounded him.

It is no surprise, then, to learn that the family circle at Ickworth, apart from the Earl-Bishop himself, was not a particularly merry one at this period. In November 1781 one of his nieces, a Mrs. Dillon, daughter of his sister Lepel, paid a visit to her uncle, and from the letter she wrote to her husband we get a rather grim view of the Hervey family gathered at their family seat.

'I came down here on Thursday,' she wrote, 'and was received with the greatest kindness. Lady Bristol is a charming woman – I am sure you would like her. She has great good humor and a great deal of dignity and good breeding. . . . Lady Erne you know, but she has grown *languissante*, and really looks stepping into her grave, poor creature. Lady Elizabeth Foster has the most pleasing manner in the world. She is just at this moment in the most terrible situation. Her odious husband will settle so little on her that she must be dependent on her father, which is always an unpleasant thing. Her children, who are now here, are to be taken from her. All this makes her miserable. . . .

'The only happy looking creatures are the children, of which there are a heap, and my noble uncle who cares for nothing but himself, and therefore being gratified in every wish he has, could not be otherwise, unfeeling others' woes. He has not taken his seat [in the House of Lords], nor will he let Lady Bristol go to Court or to town since my late uncle's death. Henry told me he believed he was disappointed in something he asked for, *et qu'il boude*. He is vastly fond of me at this moment, but the winds are not more variable than his character. Notwithstanding all I have said on our melancholy, this is a charming pleasant place. He lives magnificently, has an excellent cook, is himself in high spirits, and we pretend to be so.'[4]

Yet when it came to his own guests and companions a different atmosphere prevailed. He could be a genial enough host when he wished it. It was on this visit to Suffolk that he became acquainted with Arthur Young who was soon a constant and welcome visitor. To Young he seemed the most extraordinary man he had ever met with. 'This year', he recorded in his *Autobiography,* 'the Episcopal Earl of Bristol lived at Ickworth both summer and winter, and having very early called upon me after coming to the title and estates, a great intimacy took place between us; and Lord B. desired me to dine with him every Thursday, which I did through the whole year. Mr. Symonds, Professor of Modern History at Cambridge, Sir John Cullum, author of the 'History of Hawstead', a very learned antiquary, and the Rev. George Ashby, Rector of Barrow, another antiquary and a man of universal knowledge . . . being constantly of the party. It was a trait in this nobleman's character, which deserved something more than admiration, to select men distinguished for knowledge and ability as his companions.'[5]

The picture which Young draws certainly shows a more pleasant scene than that depicted by Mrs. Dillon. The Bishop was obviously more agreeable in the company of his friends than in the bosom of his family. There is no mention of Lady Bristol or of his daughters at these Thursday gatherings, perhaps because Bristol, who, as Young admits, often 'lived in a manner that was not very episcopal' and according to another testimony could 'drink a bottle of Madiera and swear like a gentleman',[6] liked the conversation to be free as well as scholarly. Surrounded by scholars, antiquaries and artists, he created a world in which the claims of a wife and family had very little place. That he liked them well enough when he remembered them was still true (at least in so far as his daughters were concerned), but he tended to remember them less and less often. Even in their company, as Mrs. Dillon pointed out, he was generally oblivious of their true feelings.

At the beginning of February 1782 the Bishop brought Lancelot Brown, better known as 'Capability' Brown, to Ickworth presumably with an eye to improving the general layout of the grounds. Brown is said to have brought the plans for a new house with him, though he was more of a landscape gardener than an architect. Whether they were his own plans or someone else's is not made clear, for neither the plan of the house nor Brown's scheme of 'improvement' has survived. Perhaps he was simply called in—to select a suitable site for the new house which Bristol must already have had in contemplation, the great mansion that he was later to build but never to see.

At the end of the month he was off to London to be admitted a Fellow of the Royal Society, an honour due more to his position as a peer of the realm and a bishop than to any particular preeminence in scientific knowledge; for though he was a keen amateur he could not, like his friend Sir William Hamilton, claim to be an equal in any field with the professionals. It was none the less a coveted distinction.

While in London he made a brief but unsuccessful entry into the world of literary patronage. It was perhaps unfortunate that he should have chosen Horace Walpole (who now at last met him) as the person to whom he would display his great dramatic discovery, for few people could be more devastatingly the deflator than Walpole when the mood so took him.

'I wish it was possible to give you a full account of a tragedy that has just been lent to me; an adequate one is totally impossible', Walpole wrote to William Mason. 'The Bishop-Count of Bristol, whom I met t'other night at Mrs. Delany's, desired to send me a play, that he confessed he thought equal to the noblest flights of Shakespeare. Such an honour was not to be refused. Arrived the thickest of quartos, full as the egg of an ostrich; with great difficulty I got through it in two days. It is on the story of Lord Russell. John Lilburne himself could not have more whig-zeal. The style, extremely deficient in grammar, is flogged up to more extravagant rants than Statius's or Claudian's, with a due proportion of tumbles into the kennel. The Devils and damnation supply every curse with brimstone, and Hell's sublime is coupled with Newgate, St. James's, and Stock's market; every scene is detached, and each as long as an act; and every one might be omitted without interrupting the action – for plot or conduct there is none.' Walpole extracts one line for the admiration of his friend, a 'nine-hours' sermon' described as delivered

Through the funnel
Of noses lengthened down into proboscis.

'This is the only flower', he declared, 'that I could retain of so dainty a garland.' After this the Bishop confined himself to art criticism, where he was more at home. If his enthusiasm here was misplaced, as seems clearly to have been the case, it was perhaps due to the 'whig-zeal' which he undoubtedly shared with the author and, for the present at least, with Horace Walpole.

While Lord Bristol was enjoying himself in London and Suffolk Elizabeth Foster had retired to Bath with her sister Mary, who was also temporarily at loggerheads with her husband. We get a glimpse of the younger sister's plight in another outburst from her cousin Mrs. Dillon. 'Never was a story more proper for a novel than poor Lady Elizabeth Foster's', she told her husband in an angry letter. 'She is parted from her husband, but would you conceive any father with the income he has should talk of her living alone on such a scanty pittance as £300 a year! And this is the man who is ever talking of his love of hospitality and his desire to have his children about him! Might one not imagine that he would be oppos'd to a pretty young woman of her age living alone? It is incredible the cruelties that monster Foster made her undergo with him; her father knows it, owned him a villain, and yet, for fear she should fall on his hands again, tried first to persuade her to return to him.'

The Bishop was in London at the time, occupying Bristol House in St. James's Square, from where he managed to send his unfortunate daughter the present of £100. More substantial help was to come from another quarter. The Duchess of Devonshire (the beautiful Georgiana Spencer) wrote to Lady Bristol suggesting that Elizabeth should take charge of the Duke's natural daughter and live with her abroad on an allowance from the Duke of £300 a year. This proposal, which solved Elizabeth's immediate problems and no doubt appealed to the maternal instincts of a woman who had just been forced to part from her two sons, was gratefully accepted, but it was an arrangement which reflected no credit on her father and resulted a year later in another broadside from Horace Walpole. 'The mission of [Lord Bristol's] daughter, and her circumstances, are just as you have heard them', he told Sir Horace Mann. 'You may add, that though the daughter of an Earl in lawn sleeves, who has an income of four or five and twenty thousand a-year, he suffers her from indigence to accept £300 a-year as governess to a natural child.'[8]

To describe her as 'governess' was to make her position look as miserable as possible, which was, of course, just what Walpole intended. In fact Lady Elizabeth was not to be miserable at all in her new role, though neither Walpole nor she herself when she first undertook the charge could have guessed that it was to be the first step in the evolution of the extraordinary *ménage à trois* that was to develop between Lady Elizabeth and the Duke and Duchess of Devonshire. Nor could Walpole foretell that the young woman whose sad destiny he was describing would one day be Duchess of Devonshire herself.

It is in this same letter to Mann that Horace Walpole comes out with the surprising information that Lord Shelburne intended to send the Earl-Bishop to Versailles as a plenipotentiary in the peace negotiations with France, but that Lord Bristol refused because the bad treatment he had received in Paris (that he was ordered to leave on pain of the Bastille) still rankled in his heart. For this reason or because, as Walpole preferred to think, 'to be a peace-maker was too much in the character of a

Bishop for such a *Bishop* to accept,' the offer was declined. If Walpole's earlier account of the Bishop's adventures in Paris was true then he would indeed be the last person one would expect to find opening the negotiations with Franklin and the Count de Vergennes. In fact Thomas Grenville was sent to Paris and we have only Horace Walpole's word that the post was ever offered to Lord Bristol.

In November 1782 the Bishop returned once more to his Irish diocese. His period in England had not been fortunate and little had happened there to add much lustre to his reputation, either public or private. During the last months he had a final rift with his wife. The immediate cause of this is obscure but there are many indications that his growing impatience with interference from others as well as his selfish indifference to their feelings had tended increasingly to make him an impossible man to live with, certainly on any level of equality. The breach came at Ickworth. On the evidence of a servant[9] we are told that 'the Bishop and his wife went out for a drive together, and in the course of the drive something was said, something passed between them, and they came home and never spoke to each other again.' For anyone but the Earl-Bishop such a situation would appear ridiculous; but with his vehement temperament and sharp, unguarded, wounding tongue, some such incident is not impossible.

All we learn from Lady Bristol is of a dispute over the letting of the house in St. James's Square. 'I am sorry that my situation has sat so heavy on your mind,' she wrote to Elizabeth after the Bishop had left her, 'for I can give you no comfort on that subject except by assuring you that my mind is quite above and out of the reach of the oppression I receive and the insults which accompany it, and that I have pride enough to bear being told that my advice is presumptuous; and that I am being so made up of vanity and ostentation as not to be capable of co-operating in so laudable a plan without feeling the least humbled by it; and even my resentment is softened down into compassion for the frailties of human nature, and for the wreck which warring passions bring upon it: my own happiness has long been an empty sound, and I am now only intent on drawing all the good possible out of this evil in favour of Louisa.'[10]

Later, in writing to tell Lady Elizabeth that her father intended to increase her income by £50 a year 'and perhaps £100 if you conduct yourself prudently', Lady Bristol adds the warning: 'I beg you will be very cautious in speaking of him to others; how you throw any blame on him on my account. I leave him to Heaven, and to those thorns that in his bosom lodge to prick and sting him.'

After he left Ickworth in November 1782 the Bishop never met or spoke to his wife again. If the thorns in his bosom pricked or stung him he gave not the slightest indication of discomfort. His character remained as ebullient as ever; indeed, it now took on a military dash that had not been in evidence before. After thirty years of marriage he seems to have parted from his wife without a pang.

3

When Bristol returned to Ireland he launched almost at once into a flirtation, more innocent in fact than in appearance, which was soon to cause a considerable scandal. The object of the Bishop's gallant attention was a close relative, a Mrs. Mussenden, who had been born Frideswide Bruce, a daughter of his cousin Mrs. James Bruce, who was herself a daughter of Lord Bristol's clergyman uncle Henry Hervey-Aston. She was about twenty years old and acknowledged one of the prettiest young women in Ireland. Indeed, she was so beautiful that the Bishop's many detractors found it hard to believe that she was also virtuous.

A letter to Lady Erne, written from the house of this *chère cousine* (at whose elbow, he declared, he was writing) shows him in a very different spirit from that of the wife he had so recently abandoned in England. 'From morning to night,' he told his daughter, 'and much beyond the *even* I have not known for months together, and especially within these last six weeks, what a gloomy cloudy moment meant. "Eternal springs and cloudless skies" have been the unremitting appanage of this *chère cousine's* innocent spirits, gay society and indefatigable attentions to me, indeed nothing can pass more deliciously than our time ever since we lived so much together, tho' we are never separated till eleven at night, yet the slumbers pure and spirits light send me bounding out of my bed about seven in the morn, after having pass'd a full hour in voluptuous meditation of some extensive prospects big with comfort either to my friends or dependants whom I have the happiness to find my friends.'

These lines, and much more in the same lyrical strain, were written by Mrs. Mussenden's fifty-two-year-old swain from her house at Larchfield near Hillsborough where the Bishop was staying as a guest. The offspring of this innocent amour was an architectural folly, the Mussenden Temple, which Lord Bristol built at Downhill and dedicated to his cousin. It is perhaps the happiest of the Earl-Bishop's architectural conceits. The temple is circular with a domed roof supported by Corinthian columns and with an urn crowning the top. The main apartment housed the Bishop's library. Below was a vault which he later allowed the Roman Catholics of the neighbourhood to use as a place of worship. It was built between 1783 and 1785 under Shanahan's supervision, but in the year of its completion Mrs. Mussenden died while only twenty-two, yet not before a storm of scandal had broken over her association with the Bishop.

In December 1783, at a time when the Bishop had many political enemies, an anonymous letter in the *Freeman's Journal* accused him by implication (he was not actually named) of being Mrs. Mussenden's lover and seducer. If the charge was a false one there can be little doubt that the Bishop's general behaviour and unguarded conversation, which always dealt in the wildest hyperbole, was of a sort ideally calculated to produce smoke where in fact there was no fire; and though his conduct in this case was without blame his total lack of discretion and of any sense of decorum was not.

A reply in the *Volunteer Evening Post* vindicated his character. 'With regard to your imputation on him,' it pointed out to the author of the libel, 'it seems to lie in a very small compass; either the lady, whom you suppose him to be base enough to seduce, corresponded with his love or she did not. If she did, how came you to know what nobody heard or believes of a most virtuous, chaste, and innocent lady? If she did not – then, she herself may hold this relation and seducer in the utmost abhorrence. Now, it is well known here, and in this neighbourhood, that she holds him in the utmost esteem, reverence, and affection . . . that her husband allows her still to receive such presents from her noble relation (which bye the bye is no less than a first cousin once removed) as suits the generosity of his mind and the tenderness of his affection. . . .'

If any further argument were needed to prove the propriety of this fatherly infatuation (he described himself in relation to her as being '*comme un bon Papa*') between Bristol and his *chère cousine* it would consist in the cordial affection which continued to subsist between her so-called seducer and the rest of her family. Her brother, the Revd. Henry Hervey Bruce, became the Bishop's right-hand man and acted virtually as vicar general of the diocese during his long absences and was destined ultimately to inherit Downhill and the Irish estates under the Bishop's will. The whole episode would have passed off as yet another of those ludicrous situations into which Lord Bristol's impetuous temperament so often led him had not the young lady herself died so suddenly and at so tragically young an age so soon afterwards. The Temple which was raised to celebrate this harmless *amitié amoureuse* (a type of friendship in which the Bishop perhaps too thoughtlessly indulged) was now fated to become her memorial.

4

It was not to be the Earl-Bishop's private life that brought him the most notoriety in 1783, for it was in this year that he threw in his lot publicly with the Volunteer movement and became, if only for a brief space of time, a formidable and (from the British Government's point of view) an alarming force in Irish affairs. His love of display, his thirst for applause, his passion for intrigue as well as his very genuine concern for Irish independence and freedom were all to find an outlet in the political convulsions of that momentous year.

Bristol had been in communication with the Londonderry Volunteer Corps while he was still in England. At the time when Henry Grattan established the legislative independence of the Irish Parliament the Bishop had written declaring his sympathy with the Volunteers and had provided funds for arms and equipment. He realized that their presence as a pressure group had greatly assisted Grattan in this task, as had been the case with the repeal of the Test Act in 1780, and he saw his one chance to implicate his own schemes for Catholic emancipation with help from the same source. The Volunteers had now become frankly political in their demands though still military in their organization, and the Bishop decided to make a bid for their leadership. As a first step in this direction he was able to get himself appointed Colonel of the Londonderry Corps soon after his return to his diocese. It was his mixed episcopal and military rank that gave rise to the unconfirmed legend that he had presented some cannon to the Volunteers with the text engraved on their barrels, 'O Lord open thou our lips and our mouths shall show forth thy praise'.

At the head of the Volunteers was the commander-in-chief James Caulfield, Earl of Charlemont. He was a cultivated and urbane man of the world who when in London moved in the literary circles of Samuel Johnson. Two years older than the Earl-Bishop he was a connoisseur of art, a member of the Society of Dilettanti as well as a fellow of the Royal Society and the Society of Antiquaries. He collected pictures, encouraged archaeological research and had travelled abroad. With such a multitude of common interests it would seem a foregone conclusion that he and Lord Bristol would get on well together, but in fact their mistrust was mutual, instantaneous, and profound. Charlemont had none of Bristol's bluster or verve; he was cautious, painstaking, and a trifle dull. He did not scintillate. Of his foreign travels Dr. Johnson remarked: 'I never but once heard him talk of what he had seen, and that was of a large serpent in one of the Pyramids of Egypt.' His character was one of reserve; there was nothing of the demagogue or revolutionary about him. He considered Lord Bristol to be both dangerous and shallow, 'more brilliant than solid'.

The Bishop's first opportunity for intervention in the affairs of the Volunteers came in September 1783 when a Convention of the Ulster Volunteers was held as a follow-up to a Convention that had taken place at Dungannon in February of the previous year, and as a preparation for a later more general gathering to be held in Dublin. The Ulster Volunteers also chose Dungannon as their place of meeting. It was a moment of crisis for the whole Volunteer movement. The programme of reform which they supported and hoped to see enacted had as yet made little progress in Parliament while the conclusion of peace on the Continent had rendered their existance as a military force no longer justified or necessary. It was therefore a time for action if any of their objectives were to be achieved.

It was a fortunate occasion for Lord Bristol to display his demagogic prowess, for his two chief rivals in fame were absent; Lord Charlemont for reasons not stated and Henry Flood, the great orator and patriot, because of a sudden attack of gout.

The Bishop lent his vociferous support to a call for the reform of the Irish House of Commons, in particular for a resolution demanding that 'the elective Franchise ought of right to extend to all those, and those only, who are likely to exercise it for the public good.' In spite of a significant saving clause this resolution, at least to Lord Bristol and to those who shared his view, implied an extension of the franchise to Roman Catholics; a notion, as was later to be proved, which was not shared by the majority of the Volunteers. For the present, however, the full extent of his reforming schemes was not widely understood or appreciated, and the Convention returned an unanimous vote of thanks to the Bishop of Derry for attending their gathering and for proving himself 'the steady friend of the liberties of Ireland upon all occasions'. With the plaudits of the assembly still ringing in his ears the Bishop was himself struck down by gout and compelled to retire from the proceedings, but not before he had established himself as a power to be reckoned with. For Lord Charlemont and his fellow moderates there was much in the proceedings of the second Dungannon Convention to cause them alarm.

This Convention was, as it were, a sort of dress rehearsal for the Grand General Convention of the Volunteers of all Ireland which was due to be held in Dublin in November. The behaviour of the Earl-Bishop at this preliminary gathering gave the commander-in-chief considerable food for thought. Though sincere and single-minded in his patriotism Lord Charlemont had no desire to carry the campaign too far. He gave his full support to Grattan in his fight for legislative independence, a battle that was now fought and won. His support for Henry Flood's Act of Renunciation by Great Britain was more grudging; he saw that it could add little to what was already gained and probably realized that it sprang more from the personal rivalry between Flood and Grattan than from motives of pure patriotic zeal.

On the question of votes for Roman Catholics Lord Charlemont's mind admitted of no question of doubt. Himself a staunch Protestant he considered the Bishop of Derry's proposal to give the Catholics a voice in parliamentary elections as nothing less than an attack upon Protestant liberty: such an idea was to be dismissed as an 'unaccountable frenzy'. In this he shared the opinion of Flood, who declared in the House of Commons: 'I admit the merit of Roman Catholics, and that merit makes me consent to enlarge their privileges; but I will not consent to their having any influence in choosing members of this house.'[11]

It was most important to Charlemont that these views should triumph at the forthcoming Convention in Dublin. So long as the Roman Catholic cause had no leader he had no serious fears, but with the prospect of the Earl-Bishop rallying the extremists or (frightening thought!) actually being elected to the presidential chair, there was no end, from Charlemont's point of view, to the damage that might result. The thought of a civil war haunted his mind and he was ready to do anything to prevent it, for he considered it a far worse evil than any of the evils it might hope to overthrow. He had no great relish for the Convention at all as he privately believed that reform had gone far enough. However, as the Convention must inevitably take place he determined 'that to render the assembly as respectable as possible was the next best mode to the entire prevention of it'.

In preparing for the Convention, therefore, Lord Charlemont took care to see that his own moderate views should be echoed in the minds of as many delegates as possible, and that the designs of the Earl-Bishop should be frustrated at all costs. 'The same reason', he later admitted, 'which has induced me to accept the nomination from Armagh, and to persuade many moderate friends of mine, much against their wishes, to suffer themselves to be delegated, namely that there should be in the assembly a strength of prudent men sufficient, by preventing or withstanding violence, to secure moderate measures, induced me to accept the troublesome and dangerous office of President, which was unanimously voted to me. Another reason also concurred to prevent my refusal. The Bishop of Derry had, I know, done all in his power to be elected to that office, and I feared that, if I should refuse, the choice might fall upon him, which would indeed have been fatal to the public repose.'[12]

Meanwhile the Bishop himself had been preparing for his

entry into Dublin in a fine state of euphoria; but in planning to arrive in the capital *en prince*, complete with military escort, he quite overlooked, or at least seriously underestimated, the strength of his opponents.

Charlemont may not have been a man to dazzle the multitude but his unshakeable Protestantism appealed strongly to the mass of the Volunteers who wished to be reassured rather than astonished, while behind Charlemont stood the tremendous figures of Grattan and Flood. To the former the Irish Parliament owed its freedom from the overriding power of the British Privy Council, while the latter stood out as the champion of patriotism and reform. Both were powerful orators, both enjoyed enthusiastic popular support, and both (unlike the Earl-Bishop of Derry) were Irishmen born and bred. Grattan, though a Volunteer, was a parliamentarian first, and did not attend this Congress, for Parliament would be in session at the time, and his view now was that having given a free parliament to the people it was the duty of the Volunteers to leave the people to Parliament. Flood, however, not only planned to be present but had every intention of dominating the proceedings. It was Flood, and not Charlemont, who would steal the limelight which the Bishop had hoped would shine upon himself alone, and it would be the Bishop who would inadvertently place his rival in the position to enjoy it.

5

The delegates began to gather in Dublin at the beginning of November in readiness for the opening of the Congress on the tenth of the month. The journey from Derry to Dublin was a triumph for Lord Bristol. He travelled with a cavalcade of supporters and was received everywhere with military honours.

On reaching the capital he made his way to the meeting of the Congress in a manner calculated by its splendour and audacity to astound the population and confound his opponents. He sat in an open landau drawn by six horses, their harness decorated with purple ribands. Several other carriages containing his supporters followed behind him. The coachmen, footmen, and postilions were fitted out in sumptuous liveries and an escort of light cavalry formed a guard of honour. The Bishop himself was clad in purple, his knee and shoe buckles blazing with diamonds. His gloves were white with gold fringes at the wrists and had large gold tassels hanging from them. Upon his head, somewhat incongruously, he wore the hat of a colonel of the Volunteers as an indication of his military rank. The escort of soldiers was commanded by his nephew, George Robert Fitzgerald, a young man who had already been in prison and was later to be hanged.

As this extraordinary procession made its way through the streets of Dublin it was greeted by cries of 'Long live the Bishop,' a salutation which was acknowledged with a gracious flutter of the white-gloved hand. Indeed, as one observer later recorded, the Bishop 'never ceased making dignified obeisances to the multitude'.[13] On reaching College Green Lord Bristol halted the procession before the Houses of Parliament and ordered his trumpeters to blow a fanfare. The Lords and Commons, who were in session at the time, were not a little amazed at this brazen interruption of their deliberations and some ran to the door to see what it was all about. The Bishop claimed that it was no more than a salute, but it could also be taken as an act of gross impertinence to a body of which he was himself a member.

The procession next made its way to Lord Charlemont's house. The ostensible purpose of this visit was for Lord Bristol to pay his respects to the commander-in-chief; but, though officially a call of courtesy, there can be no doubt that the Bishop also intended to impress his rival with a demonstration of his own popularity and power. Charlemont, however, was not only ready for the visit but had prepared a counter-attack. 'As I was well acquainted with his dispositions and already dreaded his designs,' he afterwards recalled 'it was necessary that I should be circumspect in the manner of his reception. It was fitting that the Derry troup should be received in a military manner, and accordingly a guard of infantry and a squadron of horse were drawn up at my door who saluted them at their arrival. But lest the Bishop should suppose that any particular honour were paid by the Volunteers to his person, I took care, by my orders, that his coach should be prevented from coming close to the door, that so, under appearance of respect I might receive him at some distance from this house, and that returning with him from his coach, the subsequent salute should appear to me as general, and not to him.'

The plan worked admirably and the significance of it was not lost on the Bishop, who did not much relish the situation in which he found himself after his triumphal progress through the streets. 'This manoeuvre', Lord Charlemont declared complacently 'he clearly understood, and appeared with some difficulty to refrain from showing some symptoms of displeasure.'

It was necessary for Bristol to attempt to retrieve something of his self-imposed ascendancy after this irritating set-back. His continued progress to the Convention, therefore (which owing to the great number of delegates present had removed from its first meeting-place at the Exchange to the more commodious Rotunda), was accompanied by a similar display and his arrival was greeted with further gratifying shouts and cheers from the crowd. He entered the assembly in style, seeming, according to one young witness,[14] in point of dignity and importance to surpass the whole of his brother delegates. 'He entered the chamber in the greatest form, presented his credentials, took his seat, conversed a few moments with all the ceremony of a temporal prince, and then with the excess of that dignified courtesy of which he was the perfect master, he retired as he had entered, and drove away in the same majestic style, and amidst reiterated applause, to his house, where the Volunteers had previously mounted a guard of honour.' In spite of this display, however, it was Lord Charlemont and not the Bishop who was elected President of the Convention. 'This was the very step the Government desired,' the same witness tells us. 'Lord Charlemont might be managed, but the Bishop of Derry would have been intractable.'

Charlemont's election to the chair was due to his own careful packing of the assembly and also to the presence of a number of delegates whose sympathies lay with the viceregal Government or who were in its pay as placemen or unofficial agents. Indeed, the newly elected president himself was all the time on a friendly footing with the Court at Dublin Castle and was on the best of terms with the Lord Lieutenant, the Earl of Northington. When he contemplated the Government of Ireland as represented by the Castle and compared it to the wild schemes of the Bishop of Derry, whose pro-Catholic sympathies threatened to challenge the whole existence of the Protestant ascendancy (which to Lord Charlemont was synonymous with freedom itself) he did not doubt where his duty lay. If the Bishop were to bring forward his proposals in favour of the Catholic population then Charlemont would see it as his mission to oppose them as strenuously as he could.

It was in this atmosphere that the Grand General Convention met and got down to business. Reform was the only topic, but how much reform was the issue at stake. That there was need for parliamentary reform no one doubted, not even Parliament itself. As the historian William Lecky later wrote: 'The abuses of the unreformed British Parliament, great as they were, were almost insignificant compared with those of the Parliament in Dublin. It was computed that out of 300 members, 200 sat for pocket boroughs, that 124 members were nominated by 53 peers and 91 others by 52 commoners.' In the Upper House things were no better. 'Nothing in the Irish history of the latter half of the [eighteenth] century', Lecky recorded, 'is more conspicuous than the lavishness with which peerages were then granted as a means of parliamentary management. It was stated that between 1762 and 1783 inclusive, thirty-three barons, sixteen viscounts, and twenty-four earls had been added to the Irish peerage.'[15]

A committee of the Convention was formed to receive and consider the various plans for reform, but as almost every delegate appeared to have brought his own plan with him the committee was soon inundated with scores of panaceas, some of them, in Charlemont's words, 'of the wildest and most ridiculous nature'. Not a few of these crazy proposals were inspired by agents of Lord Northington who confessed to Charles James Fox (this was during the brief Fox–North coalition which lasted only until December) that he hoped by this means to divide and confuse the assembly and bring its deliberations into public contempt.

The confusion raged for some days. It began to look as though nothing would be achieved, which was precisely what the Lord Lieutenant hoped for and would not unduly have distressed the President. But the Bishop of Derry was not prepared to give in. He saw that the committee would make no headway unless there was at least one strong-minded and determined character among its members who would dominate the proceedings and get the Convention out of its impasse. He therefore proposed that Henry Flood be co-opted on to the committee as assessor.

By this act, which saved the face of the Convention, the Bishop's own hope of gaining some relief for the Catholics was irrevocably lost. On the general question of parliamentary reform he had no differences with Flood; both were equally committed to a thoroughgoing attack upon corruption, and Bristol must have hoped, in securing for Flood this commanding position in the Convention, to reach a compromise with him on the question of Catholic suffrage. But if he thought this he had seriously underestimated the extent of Flood's Protestantism, which was no less strong than Lord Charlemont's and no less openly expressed. The Bishop, in fact, had made a serious blunder. It was his second major defeat in the assembly. He had failed to secure the presidency, and now he saw all his attempts to gain concessions for the Catholics frustrated by the insurmountable prejudices of the very man whom he had nominated to a position of decisive authority.

These set-backs did not improve the Bishop's temper. If he was (as had been observed) the perfect master of dignified courtesy he was also something of an artist at the wounding gibe and stinging retort. It had not escaped his notice that the President's devotion to reform had been much more fervent at the time of the first Duncannon Convention than it was now, and meeting him during a moment's recess in the proceedings of the present Convention he was not above taunting him with this change of heart. This conduct, declared Lord Bristol, was not generally approved of and Lord Charlemont was considered as rather lukewarm in favour of reform.

Charlemont listened to the Bishop with a frigid dignity. 'The difference which I make between the present and the former objects of our exertions is this,' he replied. 'Whilst Ireland was in effect subject to a foreign legislature there were no lengths I would not have gone to to rescue her from a state which I considered as positive slavery. To that point I had pledged my life and future, and towards the attainment of it I would willingly and cheerfully have hazarded not only them but what was, and still is more dear to me, and far more important, the peace of my country. Our present object I esteem great, and of high importance, and to obtain it will do everything not inconsistent with the public peace. But I will go no further. Make what use of this you please.'[16] At that moment the Convention was called to business and their further exchange was cut short.

It is difficult to see the point of Bristol's peevish attack except as a manifestation of his own exasperation. He had himself been enjoying the varying pleasures of Suffolk and London at the time of the Convention in question, which he had not bothered to attend, and so was hardly in a position to criticize someone who had been there. The outburst was another regrettable example of his lack of self-control and it did nothing to help the cause he still championed in the assembly. He was later to startle Lord Charlemont even more at a time when tension both inside and outside the Convention was running high. The timid President was full of apprehension, but Lord Bristol came in rubbing his hands together and declared: 'Things are going well, my Lord; we shall have blood, my Lord, we shall have blood!'

Meanwhile, he continued to press for some measure of Catholic enfranchisement as long as he could get any support at all from his fellow delegates. But towards the close of the deliberations his efforts received a fatal blow from what was proved, in the end, to be no more than a scandalous trick.

A certain Sir Boyle Roche, a delegate to the Convention and a member of the Irish Commons, intervened in the debate to say he had been authorized by Lord Kenmare, a leading Catholic peer, to declare upon his authority that the Catholic population had no desire to take part in any elections and only asked to be left alone to enjoy in peace the favours already bestowed upon them. It was only later, but too late for Lord Bristol's supporters to recover themselves, that it transpired that Lord Kenmare's message had had no existence outside the imagination of the mendacious Roche, who admitted that he had invented the whole story simply to foil the dangerous schemes of the Bishop of Derry.

It was, however, not so much the efforts of people like the deplorable Roche or the Castle agents who prevented a motion in favour of the Catholic vote from being introduced into the final programme of reform adopted by the Convention. The Bishop, it may be said, was defeated by his own hand, for it was Flood, the champion whom he had himself proposed, who carried the day with his oratory, his skill at managing debate, and his implacable hostility to the idea of any parliamentary representation for the Catholics. His final plan, accepted by the Convention, called for an extension of the franchise, attacked closed boroughs, condemned the bribery of members, and exposed many abuses, but in every detail it preserved the character of the Irish Parliament as an exclusively Protestant assembly. All the efforts of the Earl-Bishop had come to nothing.

In the final dramatic stages of the Convention, when Flood proposed to carry their motion of reform and place it before the House of Commons, the Bishop prudently, but somewhat out of character, recommended a note of caution. Let the Convention, he declared, put forward a general purpose of reform, but leave Parliament to decide upon the details. He also suggested that the Convention should no longer remain in session now that its work was done: 'it would be for the public good they should make an end of their session tomorrow [28 November], in order that the Bill might be brought into the House of Commons tomorrow evening.'

All this was sound advice, and had it been followed Parliament might not have felt itself threatened by coercion on the following day when, at Flood's insistence, and with the Convention still in session, the reform proposals were brought to the House of Commons by those members of the Convention who were also Members of Parliament. They arrived in their Volunteer uniforms and presented a very military aspect. This gave the enemies of reform their chance. 'We sit not here', said the Attorney General, 'to register the edicts of another assembly or to receive propositions at the point of a bayonet.' All Flood's oratory could not extricate himself from a false position; Grattan, though sympathetic to the measure, could not condone the manner in which the proposals were presented; and when, after a stormy debate, the House divided, Flood's Bill was rejected by 157 votes to 77. There was to be a good deal more shouting, but in fact the cause of reform was lost.

The consequences of that day were to have sad and far-reaching effects upon the course of Irish history. That the great majority of the citizens of a country should remain unrepresented was usual in the eighteenth century and fairly generally approved during the greater part of it; even among the Protestants in Ireland the franchise was strictly limited. The tragedy behind the failure of Lord Bristol's efforts on behalf of the Catholics was that it exposed the true nature of the fear in which they were held by their Protestant fellow citizens, and must have removed all hope from those perfectly loyal Catholics who wished to have a voice in the government of their country.

This fear was expressed simply enough by Lord Charlemont. 'For my own part,' he wrote upon the issues raised by the Bishop, 'my opinion upon this important subject had long been decided, and I was clear that every immunity, every privilege of citizenship should be given to Catholics *excepting only arms and legislature:* either of which being granted to them would I conceive shortly render Ireland a Catholic country, totally break its connection with England, and force it into alliance, or rather under the dangerous protection of France or Spain.' It was clear to Charlemont and his supporters that the ascendancy of the 'Protestant nation' must depend upon the continuing link with England, and though they demanded freedom in all else the supremacy of the Crown must remain inviolate. Anything that weakened the power of the Crown would weaken the power of the Protestant ascendancy and this they could not permit on any terms. It is not without significance that the last act of the Convention was to draw up an address of loyalty to George III which Flood was deputed to carry to England and present to His Majesty. Very much to Lord Charlemont's annoyance the Earl-Bishop took no part in these final proceedings, and indeed the danger of Ireland falling under the dominance of a hostile foreign power was the one point in the argument of Charlemont and his followers to which the Bishop had no answer to offer.

The Irish Parliament remained unreformed, and as a result of the rejection of Flood's Bill, so maladroitly presented, came to appear unreformable. This was greatly to weaken its prestige, and the more ambitious parliamentarians began to cast glances in the direction of Westminster. The way, in short, was now open which would lead to its final dissolution in 1800 when as a result of Pitt's Act of Union the ancient Lords and Commons of Ireland would cease to exist.

In spite of the comedy that never failed to accompany the Bishop's public acts one can only regret that on this occasion his exertions did not have a more positive result. He returned to Downhill having achieved little or nothing in spite of all his flamboyance and zeal. And yet if Charlemont had had a little more of the Bishop's liberalism and enthusiasm and the Earl-Bishop himself a little of Charlemont's prudence and moderation, there is no guessing what they might not have accomplished for the Irish nation.

The view taken by the Government of their relative merit did not admit of much doubt. Lord Charlemont was honoured in this year by being appointed one of the first Knights of the Order of St. Patrick. Lord Bristol's activities, after the close of the Convention, came for some time under the observation of a Government spy.

6

The Earl-Bishop's behaviour at the Dublin Volunteer Convention, but especially his demand for a Catholic franchise, made him the target for some very scathing abuse from members of his own social class, and caused him to be regarded with the greatest distrust and suspicion by the Governments of both Ireland and Great Britain.

In order to understand the cause of this it is necessary to realize how generally accepted were the views of people like Lord Charlemont upon this particular issue. Horace Walpole, a liberal and humane man and a lifelong Whig, held a similar point of view. 'No change of times or persons,' he wrote, 'no heterogeneous commixture of the partisans that lead factions, can authorise or justify an adoption of Catholics into civil government. This has ever been – ever will be my ruling principle. Papists and liberty are contradictions, and so, I fear, it will too soon appear.'[17]

When Walpole heard that the Convention was adjourned but was sending a loyal address to the King he burst out into a violent tirade against the Bishop. The address, he told Sir Horace Mann, was to be brought over by Henry Flood 'who has been a principal engine of confusion, but who probably did not wish or mean to go as far as that mitred Proteus, the Count-Bishop, who, I dare say, would be glad of a red hat, and whose crimes you are infinitely too charitable in not seeing in the blackest light; nor can they be palliated, but by his profligate folly. In truth, his extravagant indecency has been as servicable to the Government as overwhelming to himself. His immorality, martial pretences, and profaneness, covered him with odium and derision. Blasphemy was the puddle in which he washed away his episcopal

Protestantism, though, perhaps, he flatters himself that as Episcopacy is deemed an indelible character, he shall be *admitted ad Eundem* (as they say at Cambridge and Oxford) into the Church of Rome.'[18]

To the ordinary people of Ireland, however, the Bishop became a hero, a champion of liberty and reform, and messages and addresses poured in upon him from all sides. In his replies, as was always his way, Lord Bristol often made use of very extravagant language, uttering expressions which appeared to his enemies as little less than exhortations to open revolt.

Thus to the Drogheda association of Volunteers he denounced the representatives of the 'mean, decayed and depopulated boroughs' who had united to throw the Reform Bill out of Parliament, and went on to point out 'that they who denied to the people their indubitable rights have yet afforded them wholesome instruction, and having overpowered by numbers the voice of reason, have now taught that people to add to their remonstrance the irresistible force of numbers'. Referring to the unreformed House of Commons he told the Londonderry Volunteers: 'I advise you therefore no longer to endure so insolent a monitor but conscious of your own rights, and indignant at their encroachments, *speak* to these *mock* representatives of *fictitious unsubstantial* constituents a language suitable to yourselves, and which freemen of every nation, and Irish freemen above all others, know how to *enforce*.'

There were many other examples of these inflammatory addresses, not the least shocking to the 'Establishment' being the occasion at Downhill in January 1784 when a unit of Volunteers calling itself the Bill of Rights Battalion formed up under arms to present its compliments to the Bishop. Eighty rank-and-file with their Lieutenant-Colonel at their head heard a spirited harangue in which they were urged to remember the plight of their Catholic fellow countrymen 'who have long crouched under the iron rod of their oppressors . . . men in whose hearts beats at this instance as high a pulse for liberty, and through whose veins pours a tide of as pure blood, and as noble too, as any that animates the proudest citizen in Ireland. . . .' It was all heady stuff; the Bishop greatly enjoyed himself, and was able to work off a good deal of the frustration he had felt after the failure of his hopes at the Volunteer Convention.

But to the authorities at Dublin Castle these antics of the Bishop of Derry were anything but a joke. 'Lord Bristol is going on like a madman . . .', Lord Hillsborough, the Secretary of State, reported at the end of January, 'the people are as mad as the Bishop, and God knows to what length they may go. The forbearance with regard to his Lordship makes them imagine that Government is intimidated.'

The Government were certainly very disturbed by Bristol's behaviour and had taken legal advice soon after the Convention adjourned. Writing to the Duke of Portland on 14 December 1783, the Lord Lieutenant's secretary concluded his letter with a few words about the Bishop of Derry: 'Your Grace has probably seen the two very extraordinary answers which were made by him to the Corps of Drogheda and Derry in consequence of their addresses to him; they are become the subject of general conversation and animadversion, and are generally considered as of such mischievous tendency that Government must take some notice of them. I have consulted the law officers about them, who think that they contain sufficient ground for impeachment, if there was legal evidence of his having published them. They have however directed the Crown Solicitor to collect all the evidence he can reach concerning them, and instruct proper people whom he can trust to watch his conduct at Derry, and I think it but proper that Government should appear to have taken the earliest notice of these letters, if it should hereafter be necessary to take further notice of them, and yet not to act openly against the Bishop until there appeared a prospect of success in any proceedings against him.'

Action on the Government's part was complicated by the fall of Portland's administration and the recall of Lord Northington. Nothing, in fact, was done, though the retiring Lord Lieutenant later admitted that at one time he had had a warrant for the Earl-Bishop's arrest in his pocket. On 19 December a new Ministry had been formed under William Pitt, and the Duke of Rutland was sent as viceroy to Ireland.

The Castle continued to keep a sharp eye on the Bishop. Letters passed between Dublin and Westminster on the question of his arrest; the King himself was consulted and expressed his horror of 'this wicked Prelate', but the general opinion was that caution was the best policy. Pitt was perhaps reluctant to take proceedings against the man who had always championed his father and anyway knew the danger of creating martyrs. Also, as he prudently pointed out, should the attempt to punish prove unsuccessful, 'it cannot fail to weaken the credit of government and give fresh strength and credit to its opponents'.

So the Bishop was left in peace. The Volunteer movement gradually petered out, greatly assisted in its death throes by the pacifying hand of Lord Charlemont who managed, among other things, to exclude the enrolment of Catholics in its ranks. When the agitator James Napper Tandy announced a more radical programme of reform in September 1784 the Earl-Bishop refused to be associated with it, much to the annoyance of the organizers. Perhaps his enthusiasm waned when he heard that Flood would be attending their meeting in Belfast. But he continued to see himself as the friend of liberty. 'The rights of humanity, dear Arthur,' he wrote to Arthur Young in March 1785, 'the rights of humanity form a great article in my creed, and that religion, or sect of religion, which can teach otherwise may come from below, but surely did not descend from above.'[19]

The role of noble friend of liberty certainly suited him better than that of political firebrand. Reflecting upon the Bishop's part in the events of 1783 Lecky wrote: 'Vain, impetuous, and delighting in display; with an insatiable appetite for popularity, and utterly reckless about the consequences of his acts, he exhibited all the characteristics of the most irresponsible adventurer. Under other circumstances he might have been capable of the policy of an Alberoni. In Ireland, for a short time, he rode upon the crest of the wave; and if he had obtained the control he had aspired to over the volunteer movement, he would probably have headed a civil war. But though a man of indisputable courage, and of considerable popular talents, he had neither the caution of a great rebel nor the settled principles of a great statesman.'[20]

When it became clear that the Volunteer movement had lost its impetus, when he saw that he would never now take the place in Irish life that was already held by Flood and Grattan, or even by his old rival Lord Charlemont, the Bishop's interest in the whole Irish political scene began to decline. He lacked the real interest and determination to consolidate a position for himself after the shouting and the parades were over and the Dublin Convention could be seen for the failure it was. His mind, quick, alert, but never over profound, began to look for new excitements. His wealth gave him a freedom of a very different sort from that which he had clamoured for on behalf of the Irish Roman Catholics. His restlessness began to reassert itself. Soon he would be on his travels again.

IV
A Vagabond Star

I

Gradually the Earl-Bishop extricated himself from the tumult of Irish politics, or at least from actual participation in the hurly-burly, for his interest in political questions never waned. In January 1785 we find him writing to Arthur Young in the character of Cincinnatus, discoursing on the topic of agriculture and only introducing politics by the way.

'From sunrise to long after sunset I am not a moment idle in mind or person,' he wrote, 'and I can venture to assure you that agriculture, being the basis of all public and private virtue as it banishes laziness, fortifies the body, leads to fair and honest procreation, provides sustenance, and multiplies the tenderest and most enduring ties in nature, has no little share of my time and attention. Let 150 men daily employed verify my assertion; let the rocks which disappear and the grass which succeeds to them corroborate that evidence. But then what have I to do with the English plough? Neither our soil, nor our climate, nor our labourers are the same; we are poor, you are rich; when industry has approximated a little of our wealth to yours, perhaps we may be tempted to adopt your luxury in agriculture, unless before that you shall have discovered your errors, and so save us the trouble of retracting what we have not had time to adopt. As to my Presbyterians . . . all the harm which I find in them is that they love the rights of mankind, and if in pursuing them for themselves they refuse to participate with their fellow citizens, I would join in your execrations, and set them a better example than hitherto they have received from our church . . .'.[1]

This pastoral scene is in vivid contrast to Lord Bristol's militant activities and provocative policies of only a few months before when Horace Walpole, deploring his 'preposterous idea' of allowing Catholics to vote at elections, had declared it as his opinion that the Bishop would have called Mussulmans to the poll had there been any within the diocese of Derry.

Now all was peace and contentment. Dublin seemed to be forgotten. Downhill was the centre of attention: its grounds must be improved, its rooms extended, the picture gallery completed. The family begin to interest him again. His eldest son is sent packing from Downhill as a punishment for extravagance (so much to be condemned in others); Mary, now also parted from her husband, is sent consolation and more welcome financial help – for Lord Erne is proving as mean as Foster – at her retreat in France. Frederick, in England, attends the Handel commemoration in Westminster Abbey and hears an orchestra of 607 instruments. 'What a Crash!' his father comments to the unfortunate Mary on this 'most sumptious musick jubilee ever exhibited.' The Bishop seemed quite glad not to have been present. Only a short time before he had assured his eldest daughter that he had no thoughts of quitting Ireland. He was too happy there to be equally so anywhere else.

So he thought and wrote in February. By May, however, a severe illness had struck him and as always when prostrated by ill-health his thoughts turned to foreign travel, to the temperate climate of the south, and to those delectable Spas which were so well calculated to invigorate and divert a convalescent but gregarious invalid. To Mary he now wrote from his sick-room at Downhill: 'I have this moment been rubb'd all over with Laudanum especially on the Pitt of the stomach and drench'd with Aether by my poor Physician. I conclude, tho' he does not confess it to me, he took the disorder for the gout in the stomach and wishes to avert a return. I reckon I must pass the winter in a warm climate . . .'.

A series of relapses prevented his departure until July when he went to Bath, still far from well but 'crawling to the pump' where the famous waters restored him to something like his usual form. He spent the summer there before continuing his journey to the Continent. By the early autumn he was sufficiently well to appear in Oxford in a light lilac coat with his Volunteer hat 'fiercely cocked, laced, and with a cockade', a sight which caused one innocent countryman to remark that surely 'that there man cannot be a parson in them there clothes.'[2] On 3 October he landed at Calais.

While the Bishop was in England he made no effort to visit his wife nor did he make any attempt to heal the breach which existed between them. Lady Bristol and her youngest daughter remained at Ickworth from where, at the time of the Bishop's political exploits in Dublin, Lady Bristol had written to her daughter Elizabeth: 'I have accounts from time to time of his great spirits and happiness in everything that is going on in Ireland, and he seems quite unconcerned at having placed me here without a plan, view, object, or improvement of any sort to occupy a mind so much harassed; but I thank God that I have objects that are out of his reach and from which my mind receives such comfort that I hope you will not be uneasy for me. I have converted this disappointment, I trust, entirely to the advantage of Louisa. I have called forth all the best feelings of her excellent heart, and to turn her from a *selfish* and *pining* discontent endeavoured to *make herself my object* whilst she is mine . . .'[3]

Here the sixteen-year-old Louisa lived a restricted life in the company of her mother and a French governess. Her pleasures were restrained and even such novels as she was allowed to read were carefully censored by the vigilant Countess who tore out any page that might offend. When reading Samuel Richardson's *Clarissa* her mother considered her 'a little too *épris* with Lovelace' and not a few pages were sacrificed on the altar of modesty.

'I let her read it some part of the morning,' Lady Bristol told Lady Erne. 'After dinner (our little dinner in the library) we come into my dressing room, where we play at piquet till tea-time. She plays on the pianoforte whilst I drink tea – which saves her a temptation and gives me a pleasure, and about half an hour after seven she takes her work and I read to her till she is summon'd by Madlle – one book of Iliad – a little talk on the notes on it after it is over generally fills up this space. She then retires, and I read or play with great amusement and without any heaviness till after eleven.'

Though amusing enough for Lady Bristol (who was putting the best face she could on the unwelcome role of *abbandonata*) it was a dreary regime for poor Louisa. She might survive the temptation of tea drinking but a young girl needs a little more excitement than is provided by a game of piquet or by trying to guess the contents of pages torn from a romantic novel. She must also have compared her dull existence with her sisters' dramatic but, in comparison with her own, none the less fascinating lives, and her father's dazzling career in which she had no share. It is no surprise to learn that she soon succumbed to a form of nervous breakdown, 'her whole frame . . . shatter'd by an irritation of the nerves'.

This nervous collapse decided Lady Bristol to take her daughter to London in defiance of her husband's orders. They stayed for some time at Bristol House in St. James's Square where the best medical advice was available. The doctor prescribed 'moderate exercise, moderate and cheerful amusements'. Lady Louisa responded in due course to this sensible treatment and survived not only to return to the gloomy emptiness of life at Ickworth, but ultimately to become the wife of Lord Liverpool, one of England's dullest Prime Ministers.[4]

The Bishop, meanwhile, was posting across France to join his daughter Mary at Lyons. His younger son Frederick, now sixteen years old, was with him as well as a group of followers or retainers whom Bristol described dismissively as 'the clods I bring with me'. After Lady Erne joined the party they continued on to Rome where *Il Vescovo Inglese* was to be seen once more in the company of Cardinal de Bernis. The Bishop had ridden on horseback for most of the journey despite his recent illness. The only concession he made to convalescence and advancing years (for he was now in his mid fifties) was to travel on the coast route by way of Nice and the Riviera, thus avoiding the Alpine passes.

The return of Lord Bristol to Rome was welcome to the artists if to no one else and he continued to indulge in his favourite role of patron of the arts, though we have no record of any major purchases or commissions during this visit to Italy, which was indeed to be comparatively brief and dogged by ill-health.

Much to his irritation his eldest son, with whom he was at the moment upon the worst of terms, came up from Naples (where he was enjoying an amorous intrigue with the wife of a Neapolitan prince) expecting his father to help him 'quit his creditors'. The Bishop was in no mood to assist him and left Rome in order to avoid meeting with him. This, and the lack of any spectacular purchase in the field of art, resulted in old Sir Horace Mann's carping report that the Bishop 'moves from place to place, to avoid his eldest son, whom he leaves in absolute distress at a time when he himself squanders vast sums in what he calls the Beaux Arts, though he only purchases the dregs of them'.[5]

This remark was made a little later when the Earl-Bishop was 'hovering about Tuscany'. In the meantime he had himself been to Naples, where he was again ill, during the summer of 1786.

Rather surprisingly Lord Northington, the former Lord Lieutenant of Ireland, was in Naples at the time and was the witness of a curious little scene.

The Bishop, whose illness had been serious, had just received the sacrament when an Italian girl whom Northington described as 'a young and interesting female' tried to push her way into the room where Lord Bristol lay. It was explained that the rites of the Church were being administered to the sick man but the girl, who seemed to think that the Bishop was being given some medicine, blandly answered: '*Quando avrà passato, io entrerò.*' It was then that the somewhat scandalized ex-viceroy told the other people present that he had once had a warrant in his pocket for the arrest of the present invalid for seditious conduct.

It is curious to speculate whether it was on the occasion of this visit to Naples that Lord Bristol first met the beautiful Emma Hart, later to be the second and notorious Lady Hamilton. She arrived there in the April of that year to live under the protection of his old schoolfellow Sir William. They were to be on the best of terms during his subsequent visits as Lady Holland was to testify. Lord Bristol, whom she declared to be 'full of wit and pleasantry' (though she was also to call him 'a clever, bad man') was 'a great admirer of Lady Hamilton and conjured Sir W. to allow him to call her *Emma*. That he should admire her beauty and her wonderful attitudes is not singular, but that he should like her society certainly is, as it is impossible to go beyond her in vulgarity and coarseness.'[6] Perhaps the little episode that Lord Northington had witnessed would serve to show, if nothing else, that neither coarseness nor vulgarity necessarily came under the condemnation of the Earl-Bishop.

When he was sufficiently recovered the Bishop made his way to Florence where another shock was in store for him. It was in the Tuscan capital that he learnt the news that his nephew Fitzgerald had been executed for murder.

The young man who had commanded the Earl-Bishop's military escort in so dashing a manner had shot a man while attempting to ambush someone with whom he had a private feud. It was a squalid affair and resulted in his arrest, trial, and condemnation to the gallows. It is difficult to feel much sympathy for a man who boasted of having taken part in twenty-six duels, and one wonders why justice was so slow in catching up with him; but for Bristol the death of his sister's son under such horrible circumstances must have been a shocking blow, for during the intoxicating days of the Dublin Convention they had been on the best of terms and the Bishop had lodged in Fitzgerald's house.

Horace Mann, now eighty years old and near the end of his long life and his forty years' duty as British Minister in Florence, was able to be of service to the Bishop by keeping all news of the event out of the Italian gazettes 'knowing the prejudices of all Italy on such a subject'.[7] It was one of his last acts in the post he had held for so many years. Lord Bristol was thus able to continue his journey secure in the knowledge that this family tragedy was not public property in a country where his own eccentric behaviour had made him so well known a figure. Altogether this visit to Italy had not been a great success for the Earl-Bishop and his remaining months there were spent in uncharacteristic quiet. By February 1787 he was back at Downhill.

2

In November 1786, shortly before the Bishop returned to Ireland, a marriage took place which had his fullest approval. The couple consisted of his kinsman Henry Hervey Bruce (brother of Frideswide Mussenden) and Letitia Barnard, granddaughter of a previous Bishop of Derry. It was a marriage made possible only by Lord Bristol's generosity, for young Bruce's poverty had at first been considered by the bride's family as a permanent disqualification, despite the couple's devotion to each other. The young man had just left Trinity College, Dublin, and was destined for Holy Orders, but he had no other prospects or expectations. It seemed (in Lord Charlemont's phrase) as though 'two innocent bosoms were resigned to the horrid tyranny of despair.'

At this point the Bishop intervened very much like a *deus ex machina,* promising to keep a paternal eye on the bridegroom's future career in the Church and removing all immediate difficulties by settling on him an annual income of £400 a year (in those days a more than adequate sum upon which to begin married life and much more than the Bishop had settled on either of his daughters). The promise was well kept with regard to Bruce's ecclesiastical career for with Bristol's ever more protracted journeys abroad it fell to Henry Hervey Bruce to act as his agent and representative in the diocese of Derry. When Lord Bristol made his will in 1791 he left all his Irish property to Bruce whom he described as his 'dearly beloved cousin'.

We owe our knowledge of this business to Lord Charlemont who recalled it as an instance in the Earl-Bishop's favour when candour compelled him to record some of the more agreeable aspects in the character of his former political rival.

What was the motive behind this refreshing but apparently impulsive act of kindness to a very young and not-too-close relation? It is never easy to assess the motives of a man who, as Emma Hamilton later said of him, always 'dashes at everything', for like so many people who dash at things he often lacked the commitment or the interest to see them through. At the present moment he was at loggerheads with his eldest son whose conduct he found far from satisfactory (though he was using his influence to have him appointed to succeed Sir Horace Mann in Florence) and perhaps saw in Hervey Bruce everything that he would himself have wished for in an eldest son. He may well also have had some feelings of guilt after the death of Frideswide Mussenden and hoped to make reparation by providing much-needed help for her brother. It is certain that his infatuation with Frideswide was innocent enough, but the scandal that resulted from the libellous 'exposure' of their relationship must have caused her considerable distress. Her death so soon afterwards added to the tragedy though was in no way caused by it. Was his virtual adoption of Henry Hervey Bruce, like the dedication of the Mussenden Temple, a gesture to the memory of his charming *chère cousine*?

Less pleasing to the Bishop on his return was the action of a much nearer relation. He brought his youngest daughter a dress from Italy but it did not meet with the approval of that critical but neglected young lady, and she sold it – very possibly at the instigation of her no less neglected mother.

'Louisa has *sold* the beautiful gown I gave her because the shape was not *fashionable,* and I have redeem'd it and paid her the price,' he burst out in high indignation to Lady Erne. 'I think you wd not have sold my present at any era of yr life for Ten times its value – '*mais je suis fait a Tout.*' I strike against my heart and it hurts my hand, all but a corner of it which will not petrify – in the meantime I am stoick enough to find adopted children, brothers, everything, and can smile with ineffable contempt at the injuries and revilements I incur. In this country I am more popular and more courted than ever: yet I do nothing but build houses, plant forests, decorate villas, and live with my acquaintance as my inclination induces and my property prescribes.'

For all the bombast of the last sentence of this letter the Bishop was unable to disguise the feelings of hurt irritation bred in him by the conduct of his family and the political frustration that seventeen months of foreign travel had failed to eradicate. He needed a new outlet for his unwaning energies. Downhill was now more or less completed and no longer absorbed all his 'edifying' interests. He must start again on another project. In March 1787 he proudly announced to Lady Erne: 'I have begun a *new Villa* . . . the situation is beautiful and salubrious beyond all description.

'Imagine to yourself then, my dear Mary,' the letter continues in an enthusiastic description of the chosen site at Ballyscullion, 'a globular hillock of gravel carpetted with dry green grass whose declivity reaches at the end of half a mile to the Banks of the River Bann, or rather of Lough Beg, the small lake; this Lough Beg terminates at both ends in the River Bann – southward which you may be sure is the front of my house; the River again, after being decorated by Mr. O'Neill's new Bridge at Toome, ends in Lough Neagh, and this is finally bounded by an immense ridge of the conical Mountains of Mourne – such is my prospect to the South. On the East, which is the aspect of my Eating Room, the River Bann and the hills of the county of Antrim, together with a few hundred acres of my own estate, and a bridge which I am on the point of building will serve to amuse our eyes when we are not employing our knives and forks: but, on the West, that Phenomenon in the County of Derry, a woodland country with an elegant Village and the Mansion of Mr. Dawson together with a serpentine River of two miles length will decorate the view from my drawing room . . .'.

The position and surroundings of this new villa with the elegant vistas of hills, wood, and water, was in marked contrast to the bleak and austere site of Downhill, and shows the Bishop as an early votary of the new cult of the picturesque. Inspired with this ideal he would expend much energy in the forthcoming years in urging the patrons of the various churches within view of his new property to build spires, thus adding an architectural touch to what was already a masterpiece of nature. Five years later he could report a measure of success to Lady Erne. 'The Worshipful Company of Drapers in the City of London', he told her, 'have in the most obliging and flattering manner given me unanimously £100 towards building a steeple and spire at Ballynascreen, so that before the end of the year I hope to have 4 or even 5 spires in the sight of Ballyscullion built chiefly at the expence of other people to beautify the prospect.'[8]

As to the actual villa itself this, he told his daughter, was to be 'perfectly circular' in imitation of a house he had seen on an island in the Westmorland lakes. The house the Bishop had in mind is one of the most romantically placed of any in England. Standing on Belle Isle, the only habitable island on Windermere, it was built in 1774 to designs by John Plaw. The building is circular, a stone drum of three storeys surmounted with a dome and lantern, and entered by a pedimented portico supported on four unfluted Ionic columns rising to the top of the second floor. There are no outhouses or arcades as there would be in the Bishop's two houses that were modelled on it (for Ballyscullion was to prove the prototype for Ickworth), and the structure, on its green wooded island, has the simple character of a temple.

With the house at Belle Isle as their model, Bristol and Shanahan set to work upon their version of the design which was to be on a much grander scale with two sweeping curved arcades connecting the central drum with smaller pavilions at the extremities. The central building was in fact oval in shape and not 'completely circular' as the Bishop had at first envisaged it, and was 84 feet by 74, while the whole front elevation, including the two pavilions and the connecting arms, extended for 350 feet (as compared with 600 feet as would be the case at Ickworth).

The foundation stone was laid about April 1787, for in that month Shanahan wrote to the Bishop regretting that he would be unable to be present at the ceremony, adding that the tenants and all the neighbourhood had good reason to rejoice as 'they all know very well it is the only means to enrich them.'

By November 1789 the house was sufficiently complete for the Earl-Bishop (by then once more on his travels) to send a fairly detailed description of it to his eldest daughter. 'My House at Ballyscullion which you don't care a jot about and which I care so much about is finished,' he wrote with slight exaggeration, for in fact the house was never to be entirely finished. 'It is an Oval like the Pantheon, supported and surrounded with 22 Pilasters of the corinthian order, fluted and 28 feet high. The Portico has six columns 30 feet high of the same corinthian order. The Hall is 24 [foot] square, the Drawing and Eating room 36 by 24 and the Library 67 by 24. The stair case is a double cork-screw of Portland stone, lighted from above and the great stairs surround the back stairs so that the master and servants cannot see each other, tho' going up at the same time. The offices will be join'd to the House by a semicricular colonade like that of St. Peter's only closed, because of the Climate . . . I want some beautiful chimney pieces, pray tell Cardelli so.'[9]

It was for Ballyscullion that the scheme was first developed for hanging pictures that the Bishop hoped to perfect in his later plans for Ickworth. 'I shall have . . . Two Galleries,' he explained to Lady Erne, 'one for a series of German painters, the other for a Chain of Italian painters, and by good luck I have found at Sienna a picture of *Guido da Sienna* with its date upon it 30 years older than Cimabue, generally supposed to be the restorer of Painting in Italy: such an History of the Progress of Painting down to Pompeo Battoni can not but be amusing: and young geniusses who cannot afford to travel into Italy may come into my house and there copy the best masters.'[10] His later idea of hanging pictures according to schools and periods has already been referred to, but this is the first indication of the Bishop's interest in Italian primitives, a taste in which he was far ahead of his times.

Ballyscullion was a much more perfect and original design than Downhill which had become rather straggling and ungainly with its later additions. A visitor to the Bishop's new villa in 1796 left this description of its interior: 'You now entered upon a magnificent hall lighted . . . from the top of the dome. Around this hall ran two galleries one above the other, beautifully railed with bronze work, upon which opened the doors of the upper apartments. The reception rooms on the ground floor were segments of circles superbly fitted up as to paper and silk hangings, the walls covered with pictures. In the hall and on the principal staircase were sundry casts and statues. The underground storey was arranged with due attention to culinary convenience communicated by a vaulted passage with the offices then in progress of erection near the house. Off this passage were a variety of vaults which, I imagine, will still exist, and may furnish matter of speculation for the antiquary a century or so hence when the name of the Bishop shall have passed down oblivion's stream.'[11]

Around the exterior of the house the visitor noticed a Latin inscription immediately below the cornice which supported the lower balustrade. The text was from Virgil, 'the only alteration in the text being the substitution of the Bann for the Mincius of the Roman bard.' A translation of the inscription reads:

Here is a verdant plain:
I will place a temple of marble
Beside the waters where the vast
Bann strays in sluggish windings
And clothes its banks with tender reeds.

This beautiful and graceful house about which the Bishop wrote so eloquently to his eldest daughter was in fact to see very little of its episcopal builder. The house was habitable by 1789 but by then he was abroad. He did not return until November 1790. The next year was the last he spent in Ireland; he went away once more in the autumn and never visited the country of his adoption again.

For the remainder of his life the house stood empty and still unfinished, for the pavilions that were designed to hold his pictures and works of art were never completed. At his death it passed to Henry Hervey Bruce, but he preferred Downhill, and Ballyscullion continued to be untenanted, its contents removed to the other house, its rooms standing empty and desolate. Its ultimate fate was due to neither violence nor decay, which between them have accounted for not a few Irish mansions; it fell a victim to taxation, that enemy of so much enterprise and art.

In 1813 (ten years after his death) the Bishop's new villa at Ballyscullion was dismantled to avoid payment of the window tax. Its ruined remains stood for some years afterwards and were known in the neighbourhood as the Bishop's Folly. Only the portico has survived. It was rescued by another bishop, Dr. Alexander of Down and Connor, who re-erected it at the front of St. George's Church, Belfast, where it may still be seen.

3

When the Bishop set off on his travels again in the autumn of 1788 he had no excuse of ill-health for what was to prove an absence of two years from his diocesan duties. Perhaps he considered excuses no longer necessary; if he had any special motive for this excursion, which was to follow the familiar route through France and Germany to Rome and Naples, it was to collect pictures and marbles for his new house.

We can follow him on his travels from the letters he wrote to his daughter Mary who was for the moment in Florence staying with her eldest brother Lord Hervey, now established there as British Minister to the Court of the Grand Duke of Tuscany.

Early in November we find the Bishop taking part in a scene that might have been painted by Fragonard, though it took place less than a year before the storming of the Bastille, when he attended the Prince de Condé's hunt at Chantilly. The Prince and his suite were dressed in peach-coloured cloth laced down the seams in silver, and carried round their shoulders the characteristic French horns which the Prince and his grandson sounded from time to time. The latter was the tragic young Duc d'Enghien, then a lad of about sixteen years old, whose life was later to be sacrificed to the ambition of Napoleon and the wily schemes of Talleyrand.

The scene was a bit too formal for the Bishop's taste, the huntsmen's hair being 'as completely dress'd as if going to a Ball and their Jack boots the only emblem of hunting', though three stags were killed and the Prince talked of setting out the next morning with a pack of hounds to dislodge a wild boar: 'such are the Laurels worn by the descendant of the Great Condé'.

Meanwhile in Paris 'politicks are going forward at a great rate', but for his own part Lord Bristol declares that he does not yet believe in 'the *States General,* the Resurrection of the dead, the forgiveness of Sins nor Patriotism Everlasting'. With this flippant parody of the Apostles' Creed he dismissed the formidable forces gathering to overthrow the *ancien régime*. He saw no cloud on the horizon.

In taking this attitude the Bishop was not guilty in any particular lack of perception. One tends to regard the period just before the French Revolution as a sort of glorious sunset in which the old order, with a tired elegance, drifted from view to make way for the violent and bloodthirsty age that succeeded it. In fact, of course, Europe had known a good deal of unrest and revolt in the decades before 1789, and Bristol, coming from Ireland, saw nothing in the situation in France to cause him undue alarm. His reaction, indeed, was if anything one of a rather patronizing contempt for the manifestations of political ferment that came to his notice. Thus in December he writes to Mary from Bordeaux: 'The political tumult here is incredible and every morning relates some new debate of the preceding night. I only laugh at 'em, and say a Frenchman turning Patriot in imitation of an Englishman is the fable of the frog swelling to the size of an Ox – they laugh too, and talk on . . .'.

As a professed upholder of the rights of humanity Lord Bristol could afford to adopt his tolerantly amused pose, but like many an old Whig he found himself in a decidedly exposed position when caught in the full blast of liberty, equality and fraternity. At Montpellier in March 1789 he was writing in a similar spirit to that of his letter from Bordeaux: 'This Frippery Country is still the same, a skipping dancing tribe – they are fit only for themselves – and when the circling glass goes round they talk of Beauties which they never saw, and fancy raptures which they never felt. All now is commotion, and all soon will be sing-song, in the meantime the hot heads let one another's blood, the Clergy rise against the Bishops, and the laity against the Nobles.'

When the sing-song finally broke out in earnest, however, there were few people who liked its tune less than he did, and the man who had cried 'we shall have blood' in Dublin a few years before now found himself denouncing the whole French nation as 'grown more contemptible than ever', and could only liken them to 'a band of monkies who have burst into a shop of old china and are breaking all about them'. By the time the Republic was established they had become 'those doubly damn'd miscreants, first as French, secondly as *Reps*'.

In spite of all his rebellious attitudes in Ireland and his dark threats of civil war his objectives had never been revolutionary in any true sense. He wanted to bring some social justice to a deprived section of the community, but never aimed at the overthrow of society as it then existed. In fact he believed that if the Catholics and Presbyterians of Ireland were to be given their due the result would be to strengthen society rather than to weaken or destroy it. He saw revolution coming as a result of the rejection of the principles he stood for and not by their adoption. He was, in short, a reformer, at most a radical, but never a revolutionary except in the eyes of his enemies and detractors; and it was his rash and provocative behaviour rather than his ideas that encouraged them in this belief.

Now, like other men who have been tempted by the role of demagogue, he was to learn that the mob is only useful as an instrument of policy when it happens to be on your side. There were many points in the ideals of 1789 that, as an English Whig, he could readily approve of; but as the reforming movement progressed towards violence and revolt and seemed to lead only to anarchy his reaction against it became ever more determined. If it was a question of order or chaos he stood firmly on the side of order.

This hardening of his reaction to the French Revolution was a gradual progress. He spent the winter and spring of 1788–9 in the south of France passing his time very agreeably, staying 'with every Prelate and Laick whom we like or who likes us'. The main problem he had to resolve concerned not the future of France but whether or not he should himself go on to Spain, a country he had so far never visited. It attracted him, he had earlier told Lady Erne, for 'its climate, its manners, and its Natural History which is as yet *Vierge – parfaitement Pucelle*'.

In readiness for this expedition he had ordered five saddle horses. 'As soon as we pass Perpignan,' he wrote with enthusiastic anticipation, 'we shall find a perpetual sunshine, and such a succession of new objects as cannot fail to benefit the mind as much as the body. Our project is to coast it by land (*bien entendu*) by Gibraltar, Andalusia, peep into Don Quixote's country, return by Algarve, Lisbon, Oporto, Gil Blas, Salamanca and Ovideo, thro' Biscay to Bayonne and Bordeaux . . . I propose to myself great pleasure, great health, and great improvement by this excursion. All I want is a good Architect to copy the interesting buildings, and perhaps I may meet with such an one here.'

Unfortunately this interesting project came to nothing, and the Bishop was never able to add a Spanish note to his architectural taste. Tales of bad roads and worse inns put him off, as well they might a man already in his sixtieth year who was still accustomed to travel on horseback. But he did not give up hope of achieving his object one day in the future when there were better roads and better inns, 'for the Climate is superior to everything and the inhabitants as honest as Human Nature can be'.

As a consolation he discovered near Toulouse what he described to his daughter with characteristic exaggeration as 'the very greatest curiosity of All Europe'. This was the library of Count MacCarthy, 'an Irishman by birth and by taste and letters-Patent a Frenchman'. It consisted, he wrote, of 'Books not intended to be read but to be admir'd, old illegible Manuscripts illuminated in the most exquisite manner, and first editions of printed books which look like Manuscripts of the most beautiful handwriting, – all these either on Vellum or parchment, or such superfine paper you would take it for parchment – then the binding in Blue and Red and yellow Morocco so superbly gilt that the binding often exceeds the cost of the book, and every page lined so delicately with Red Ink that this article alone is worth more than an ordinary binding'.

He urges his daughter not to miss a visit to this curiosity if ever she had occasion to pass that way. But surely there is a note of irony in his description and the word 'curiosity' was carefully chosen. The Bishop was not really the sort of man to have much time for books 'not intended to be read but to be admir'd'.

4

Lord Bristol next turns up in Germany where he had planned to meet Prince Augustus of Saxe-Gotha, that friend of former travels who now summoned him dramatically to their old haunt of Pyrmont. '*Venez donc,* my lord,' the Prince had written in July 1789, '*entre les bras de votre ancien ami et Serviteur qui est si heureux d'avance par l'idée seule de vous voir et de vous assurer de vive voix de son tendre et inviolable attachement pour vous.'*

Whether or not the old friends met is difficult to say, for though Bristol was in both Hanover and Dresden, and suggested a rendezvous with the Prince in Frankfurt am Main (which the latter was unable to keep) there is no evidence to suggest that he visited Pyrmont on this occasion. His chief concern at the time was to procure the model of a pagoda belonging to the Duc de Penthièvre as he wished to erect a replica of it at Ballyscullion. Indeed, the pursuit of this elusive pagoda seems to have been the Bishop's main preoccupation during the period immediately following the storming of the Bastille by the Paris mob.

In fact he chose to pass this period, so crucial for the fate of the old order, almost exclusively in the society of princes or members of ruling families. He talks of travelling to Italy in the company of the sister of the Duchess of Courland, dances attendance on George III's sister the Duchess of Brunswick, visits his old friend the Duke of Würtemberg (nicknamed 'Déjà-déjà') and befriends his nephew during an illness, thus earning the gratitude of that young Prince's mother, a niece of Frederick II of Prussia. It was almost as though he had taken a perverse delight in associating with this glittering company over whose heads the clouds were beginning to gather, for few people had a wider or more varied circle of friends than he had and he might just as well have devoted his time to artists, men of learning, or anyone else who took his fancy. Of course, no one at that time could foretell the full consequences of the events in France, but none the less the wind that blew from Paris was decidedly chill.

Whatever was happening elsewhere the Bishop was thoroughly enjoying life in Germany. In November 1789 he wrote to Lady Erne in the highest spirits: 'You will wonder, my dearest Mary, at not having heard from me for so long a time, and still more at hearing from me at this time of the year from the centre of Germany, but the truth is, my dear Child, I am so occupied and so amus'd, so *fêté par tout,* that I cannot get on, and my curiosity is as insatiable as if I were five and twenty – this country is full of natural history and natural historians. The roads are so bad they give me full leasure to study the country; and the inhabitants so civil from the *Prince* down to the Peasant that nothing is hid from me. My common course is a Circle, and like a Planet, a vagabond star, I almost turn round my own axis whilst I make another revolution round the Sun. In a few days I shall arrive within a few miles of Ausburg, and then like a Comet strike off at a Tangent to Francfort where I expect to meet a Professor of Natural History whom the Elector has lent me tho' he was the Director of his Cabinet. From thence we go to Mayence, Manheim, to the dear Princess of Baden, so to Stuttgart – *déjà-déjà* – and at last to Augsburg – then dash into the Tyrol, and so for Italy – but when or where as yet I know not. If you have a mind to write to me direct à la Poste restante to Innspruck where I have business will keep me at least a week. The Blessed, says the Latin proverb, never count the hours, but I count neither days nor weeks, and whereas others lay their cares under their Pillows and resume them the next morning, I lay my *spirits* there to resume them at day-break; for this body of ours, my dearest Mary, is but a Fiddle, and the Soul a Tune which depends on the Rosin given to the Fiddle . . .'[12]

As though to banish the intrusion of any unpleasant thoughts of the disagreeable events taking place in France he concluded his letter by telling his daughter that the officer who had just dined with him had sent his regimental band which was playing outside his window as he wrote.

The letter gives a vivid impression of the Bishop's restless progress from place to place, like a comet or vagabond star as he himself described it. He remained as indefatigable as ever and had lost none of that feverish compulsion to rush about which he had shown on his first visit to the Continent almost twenty-five years before. Within a month of writing this letter he was in Rome, pausing in his 'dash' through the Tyrol to meet a fellow amateur of geology, Count de Brandis, a canon of Augsburg and Brixen; surely the only occasion on which a Count-Canon has met an Earl-Bishop.

In Rome the Bishop was still welcome at the house of Cardinal de Bernis though that prelate's position as Louis XVI's Ambassador was now directly threatened by the revolution. Lord Bristol, when he was back in Ireland, told how his old friend had responded to the demands of his country's new rulers. When letters arrived telling him that in the future appointment of bishops no regard was to be taken of the Pope, that all nobles were to return home, and that he himself must take the oath to the Civil Constitution of the Clergy, the Cardinal answered 'with a firmness worthy of an old Roman'. He had already, he declared, taken an oath to his God, his religion, and to his King, and he would take no other.[13] It was this spirited act of the Cardinal's that provoked Lord Bristol's outburst against the 'band of monkies'.

For the present, however, Rome presented very much the same untroubled face that the Bishop had known of old, and as before it was in the stimulating company of artists rather than ecclesiastics that he chose to amuse himself.

On this visit to Rome Lord Bristol met Madame Vigée le Brun and sat to her for the first of the two portraits she was to paint of him. This talented and prolific artist was also a woman of considerable beauty, charm, and intelligence. She had started her career as an artist when only fifteen years old, having learnt her craft in the studio of her father, a minor artist named Vigée. In 1779, when she was twenty-four, she painted a portrait of Marie Antoinette which established her reputation both as an artist and as a social celebrity. Many commissions followed, including more than twenty portraits of the Queen, but she still managed to lead a busy social life in which her husband, the artist, critic, and picture dealer J. P. B. le Brun, played a less important part. Her close association with the Court made it advisable for her to leave Paris when the Revolution broke out, and she made her way to Italy. This was the first move in what was to prove a triumphal progress, taking her to Austria, Russia, and Switzerland, before settling temporarily in London in 1802.

At the time she painted the Bishop's portrait Elizabeth Vigée le Brun was thirty-four or thirty-five years old, in the prime of her fame and beauty. That the Bishop himself was a little smitten by her charms is indicated by the fact that he persuaded her to make him a copy of her own self-portrait, the original of which now hangs in the Uffizi in Florence.

They met again in Naples early in 1790 when Madame le Brun was engaged, among other commissions, in painting Emma Hart, Sir William Hamilton's beautiful young mistress. Here she painted what is perhaps the best portrait of the Earl-Bishop. He sits on a balcony or terrace commanding a view of Vesuvius across the bay of Naples. One hand lies on his knee, the other arm rests on the balustrade with the hand dangling at an elegant angle. The Bishop sits sideways to the artist but his head and shoulders are turned in her direction and his face betrays a look of frank admiration. It is indeed a very delightful composition and catches the alert, almost youthful expression of face, and manages to portray the eager interest in life and irrepressible high spirits which were still the most characteristic features of this man now entered upon his sixtieth year.

Madame le Brun was certainly aware of the activity of this man who must otherwise have appeared quite elderly to her, for she noted in her *Souvenirs* that 'one may say he passes his life on Vesuvius, for he ascended the mountain every day'. Her own attitude was understandably less heroic; in order to enjoy life in Naples, she decided, one must first overcome the terror inspired by the volcano. After experiencing the outbreak of revolution in Paris she decided that she had had enough terror, and prudently returned to Rome.

When Bristol himself returned to Rome in 1790 he was to sit to another distinguished female artist. This was Angelica Kauffmann, who in 1769 had been elected in the first group of Royal Academicians, and was famous for her mythological and neoclassical paintings as well as for her portraits. Though a more varied and, at this period, a more experienced artist than Vigée le Brun her portrait was less successful.

The Bishop is depicted seated, his head resting on his hand in a posture of meditation, while a bust of Maecenas looks down on him from the top of a bookcase. The classical allusion was certainly appropriate but the effect was not happy. The Bishop looks weary and very much his age. The study lacks the animation and vivacity of the other portrait – perhaps because the sitter found the artist, a mature Swiss lady of forty-nine, less of an inspiration than the charming (and much younger) Frenchwoman.

It was on this return visit to Rome that Lord Bristol made his most important artistic commission. Sir William Hamilton, that tireless patron of British artists in Italy, had interested him in the work of John Flaxman, who had been living in Rome for the past three years. Bristol visited his studio and there discovered the man 'small in stature, slim in form' who 'walked with something of a sidling gait'[14] whom he was soon to proclaim as the modern Michelangelo, the artist who 'will probably rise to be the first sculptor in Europe – exquisite Canova not excepted'.

Flaxman at thirty-five had still to make his reputation as a sculptor though his work had been known to the more discerning patrons before he left England, and he had already done considerable work for Wedgwood. His marriage in 1782 had provoked Sir Joshua Reynolds to remark: 'So, Flaxman, I am told you are married. If so you are ruined for an artist.' At the time the Bishop visited him he was at something of a crisis in his career, uncertain whether or not to remain in Italy, which may account for the fact that he agreed to a sum of money which he later thought insufficient for the work involved.

All the same it was a challenging commission which Lord Bristol now offered him and was to result in the most ambitious work undertaken by Flaxman while he was in Italy. The subject was to represent the Fury of Athamas inspired by the description in Ovid's *Metamorphoses*. The group was to be based on the Laocoön and when completed showed Athamas, demented with rage, in the act of snatching the child Learchus from the arms of Ino while the infant Melicertes clings to her robes in terror. The sum agreed upon for the work was £600.

Work on this group was to cause Flaxman a great deal of trouble and he was said to have been out of pocket when it was completed, but at the time he seems to have borne the Bishop no grudge. To Sir William Hamilton he wrote: 'I have the honour to inform you at present with much more satisfaction that I shall be detained here three years longer by the noble patronage of Lord Bristol, who has ordered me to make a large group for him in marble of the fury of Athamas, from Ovid's Metamorphoses, from a small composition of my own . . . I cannot conclude my letter without telling you the liberality of Lord Bristol has reanimated the fainting body of Art in Rome; for his generosity to me I must be silent, for I have not words to express its value.'[15]

Whatever Flaxman may have thought in the long run of the terms agreed upon for the statue there can be little doubt, as his letter to Hamilton shows, that he was perfectly satisfied when the bargain was struck. As for Lord Bristol, he was delighted with the group when it was eventually finished, considering it to be 'the finest work ever done in sculpture' and boasting that it 'exceeded the Laocoön in expression',[16] an opinion which few people would now share, though the *Fury of Athamas* (now at Ickworth) is a splendid example of neo-classical art.

1. Frederick Hervey, Bishop of Derry, from the portrait by Pompeo Batoni. (By kind permission of M. A. Nicholson, Esq., Q.C.)

2. Downhill from the south-west. (Engraving by J. Ford.)

3. The Bishop of Derry with his eldest son and the Earl of Chatham, from the picture by William Hoare, R.A. (Ickworth, The National Trust.)

4. View of Ballyscullion, from the *Statistical Survey of the County of Londonderry* by G. V. Sampson, 1802.

Unfortunately the Bishop was not always inspired to quite such artistic heights in his patronage. It was probably on this visit to Rome that he commissioned another work based on a monument of antiquity which Lady Webster (later Lady Holland) was to see in its completed form five years later and describe as 'a lasting monument of Lord Bristol's bad taste'. This was a version of the *Infant Hercules* in which, according to Lady Holland's account, 'Pitt is represented as the infant Hercules strangling the serpents, the heads of which are the portraits of Mr. Fox and Lord North, the coalition. Pitt's head is of the natural size upon the body of an infant. The whole performance is like some of the uncouth decorations in the middle ages in our English Cathedrals.' This bizarre piece of sculpture, which was taken from a caricature, was, she tells us, the work of one Sposino, an Italian sculptor and restorer, as 'the English artists all to a man refused to execute this puerile conceit.'[17]

It was actions of this sort, resulting in a tactless and rather heavy-handed form of humour (on a par with the unpleasant and heartless practical jokes which the Bishop was still capable of playing on his unsuspecting guests) that showed up the least attractive side of his nature. It was this aspect of his personality that caused men like Lord Charlemont to say of him, when passing judgement on his character, that his genius was 'like a shallow stream, rapid, noisy, diverting but useless'. If the verdict was neither accurate nor fair there were none the less many occasions when an onlooker, knowing nothing of the more worthy side of the Bishop's quixotic nature, would feel himself inclined to agree with it.

Bristol had returned to Rome from Naples in March and it was in June that he sat to Angelica Kauffmann. By November of the same year he was back in Ireland. There is no record of the route he took but it seems probable that he avoided France and returned by way of Germany and the Netherlands, as there is evidence that he was in Amsterdam at this period. In the letter, already quoted, in which he described to Lady Erne the purchase of the picture by Guido da Siena he ends with the remark: 'My purchases three years ago from Mr. Hope of Amsterdam amounted in one morning to £3,000 and the next day I bought for £750 more; so that I have now little left to buy . . .'. These words were written in August 1794. The whole of the year 1791 was spent in

England or Ireland so that the 'three years ago' must refer to the autumn of 1790 when he was returning from Italy.

John Hope of Amsterdam was a rich banker and collector whose son, Thomas Hope of Deepdene, a generation younger than the Bishop, was to revolutionize furniture design by his severe neo-classical taste and be described by Sydney Smith as 'the man of chairs and tables – the gentleman of sofas'. Bristol unfortunately only tells us the price of his purchases, not the subjects, but we can guess that these were the 'series of German painters' intended for the never completed gallery at Ballyscullion. If this is so they would later have been transferred to the gallery at Downhill and perished in the fire of 1851 which did serious damage to that wing of the house.

5

On his way back to Ireland Lord Bristol passed through London and presented himself at Court. This in itself was an act of some imprudence for whatever people might think of him in Rome or Naples, in London he was still regarded (as the Duke of Rutland had described him to William Pitt) as that 'extraordinary English peer and more extraordinary Irish prelate' the rabble-raiser of 1783. Nothing that had happened in either Ireland or Europe since then, not to mention Paris which the Bishop was known to have visited so recently, had done anything to increase the welcome of a man with such a reputation at the Court of George III. The King, in fact, received him with scant ceremony. According to a contemporary newspaper report, when Lord Bristol approached 'the greatest personage' to solicit some favour, 'instead of receiving a gracious reply that personage turned short on his heel without deigning to make him any reply'.[18]

The Bishop, who as long ago as 1778 had proclaimed his amazement to Sir William Hamilton at the King's 'strange, indecorous and personal animosities . . . to which he had lower'd himself ever since his accession', held his Sovereign in no greater respect than that sternly moral Monarch held the 'wicked' Bishop of Derry, and the latter returned to Belfast looking 'as brisk, young, and blooming as ever' in spite of this resounding royal snub. His spirits were as high as ever and he was happily, if prematurely, prophesying a counter-revolution in France.

As though to compensate him for the rebuff he had received in London the people of Derry went out of their way to welcome their Bishop on his return. The same newspaper that had described the unfortunate episode at St. James's Palace came out with a fine tribute in his praise which showed that his manner of running his diocese was generally approved by the people even though he chose to spend so much of his time away from it. 'The Citizens and Corporation of Derry', the newspaper declared, 'are making preparations to honour the Earl of Bristol on his arrival among them from the Continent by every mark of esteem and affection; a deputation from both bodies are to wait on his lordship to learn the time of his intended visit, and to notify their intention. In every character in which this prelate has appeared, he has shone forth with a lustre which attends only on the conjunction of a good heart with fine talents. As a man, and a denizen of the world, the Earl of Bristol has been distinguished for his zeal in the cause of freedom, as a peer of Ireland he is honoured for his attention to her peculiar interests – interests which in the hour of trial his indefatigable exertions to secure and promote, shewed to be nearest to his heart; and as an Irish Bishop, Derry stands eminently distinguished by a *singular* line of conduct, a uniform promotion of *native* clergy to the benefices of his diocese. Since the See of Derry was filled by the Earl, every vacancy in the Irish Church has been filled – as every vacancy in the Irish Church ought to be – by an Irishman.'

The Bishop must have been particularly pleased by this public recognition of a policy he had followed ever since attaining the episcopal bench, a policy he had himself once defined in a phrase to the effect that no merit, however transcendent, would induce him to transplant a foreign plant into his diocese. He had been unable to bring about his other wise and humane schemes for reform because their enactment depended upon others whom he had failed to persuade or win over; but in his own diocese he could make his own rules, and this particular one he refused to modify or set aside even for his 'nearest friends and most important suitors'.[19] This fact alone, in the Ireland of the late eighteenth century, made a largely absentee bishop more popular and respected than many a resident prelate who remained constantly present in his diocese to the great advantage of his friends and relations.

Lord Bristol's reception in Derry was indeed a splendid affair. He reached the city on 30 November 1790, at about three o'clock in the afternoon and was received on the bridge by the Corporation and a company of the Derry Volunteers. A procession was formed, and with this mixed civil and military escort he was conducted to this palace in state. Here the city fathers and other notabilities grouped themselves on the steps and addresses of welcome were presented to which the Earl-Bishop made an 'elegant and most animated answer'. The Volunteers, who were under arms, had meanwhile formed up in front of the palace and after the speeches were over fired three volleys into the air by way of a salute to their episcopal colonel. This spectacle was greeted by the 'loud and repeated acclamations of the populace'.

In the evening the Bishop dined with the Corporation and more speeches were made. He was congratulated upon his safe return to Ireland and thanked for support he had given to the various schemes for the improvement of the city, of which the construction of the bridge, then nearly completed, was the chief. The Volunteers, who shared in the entertainment, were able on this occasion to express their admiration by words rather than by shot. Their spokesman announced the satisfaction they all felt in having his lordship as a member of their association and also in the knowledge that he was among the first to show approval of the principles for which they had taken up their arms.

The Bishop's answers to these moving addresses were in his usual style of highflown hyperbole which was no doubt very suitable to the occasion. He was constrained, in replying to the Corporation, to admonish the as yet unknown person who would in due course succeed him in the occupation of the See of Derry. Upon his grave, he informed his listeners, a 'silent but instructive stone' would remind this cleric of the salutary fact that 'the *softest down* in his pillow is the love of his fellow citizens, and their *applause* the *brightest jewel in his mitre*; that to *preserve* his *dignity* he must learn to waive it; and truly to *enjoy* his *wealth,* he must have the courage to *share* it.' Carried away by these lofty sentiments the Bishop went on to proclaim, in startling contradiction to the example of his own conduct, that the duties of an 'extensive and opulent prelacy' summon the holder of such a post to 'residence and discipline' as well as to a pious discharge of such duties as 'can alone vindicate, or insure, the splendid rent-roll annexed to this office'.

To those many people present at this entertainment who, in writing to their Bishop, had so often received replies dated from Rouen, Paris, Florence, Rome, Naples, Pyrmont, Dresden, Hamburg or any of a score more of foreign cities, this impassioned plea for the virtues of residence must have come as a considerable surprise.

Lord Bristol next turned his attention to the Volunteers. These excellent men received an assurance that he was 'as eager as ever to run the same goal with them' as when they had honoured him with an 'unlimited delegation' to the great national Convention in Dublin. He was, he now told them, as vigorous as ever to obtain the great objects they had in view, but even these solid and stalwart soldiers must have been a little incredulous when their Colonel-Bishop informed them that the praises of their association still echoed to the remotest regions of Europe.

The tumult of emotions inspired by this occasion must have carried the Bishop away and given wings to his fancy. Rarely had the contradictory aspects of his character been so glaringly displayed, for in fact, despite his protestations to the assembled Volunteers, he was to take no further active part in Irish political affairs; and as for the sacred duty of episcopal residence, he was to demonstrate his contempt for this great principle in just over a year's time by quitting his diocese for ever.

It was, however, a splendid welcome, and Bristol, who was guided so much more by impulse than by deliberation of mind, very probably imagined at the time that he had come back to settle in Ireland for a long period. Downhill stood waiting for him, rich with the spoils of his travels. Ballyscullion still had all the novelty and fascination of a new toy. If he had been shown the cold shoulder at St. James's his welcome back to Derry had been contrastingly warm-hearted and enthusiastic.

The rousing speeches captured something of the atmosphere of euphoria which had swept the Bishop along during the hectic days in Dublin seven years before and went no less quickly to his head. His popularity seemed to stand as high as ever; there was no reason why he should not start to lay plans for passing a serene old age in Ireland, for in the eighteenth century a man of sixty would appear older than he would today. For anyone other than the Earl-Bishop this would surely have been the case.

6

The bridge at Derry mentioned in the address presented to Lord Bristol, and just at that time nearing completion, had been one of his enterprises that had hung fire for many years. The first moves had been made as early as 1769, only a year after his appointment to the See. In 1770, while the Bishop was on his travels, Peter de Salis told his father, whose doctor had tended Hervey during his illness of the following year, that the Bishop of Derry, who had just visited him, had passed through France and Switzerland 'where he has made a collection of plans of the Bridges he has met with, particularly the wooden ones made by Piderman of Appengel . . .'

Whether this was on his own account or on commission from the city of Londonderry de Salis did not know, but he added that the Bishop 'has made an agreement with a foreman of this Piderman, who has engaged to make a Model of a Wooden Bridge of only one Arche of eight hundred and fifty two feet long, which is destined for the river Shannon. This model is to be made within eleven months and is to cost an hundred Louis d'ors. The possibility or impossibility of the execution of this model is to decide whether the Architect is to receive or not the sum agreed upon; and the Decision of this question is by mutual consent remitted to an Irish Architect in his Lordship's company, and another of Zurich.'[20]

It was not, of course, the Shannon but the Foyle that this single-arch bridge was intended to span. Delays of one sort or another prevented the work from getting under way; the Bishop's constant absences and absorption in architectural plans of his own possibly contributing to this unusual tardiness. More than fifteen years were to pass since he had ordered the model before anything was done, but in 1786 plans were at last drawn up and agreed upon. In 1789 the construction of a wooden bridge was started by a firm from Boston in New England, and it was upon this that Lord Bristol was received by the city fathers of Derry in November 1790 when it had just been opened for the use of pedestrians. In the following spring it was finally opened for vehicle traffic.

Lord Bristol's last year in Ireland was not notable for any particular event so far as his personal history is concerned. This was not so for the country of his adoption, for the years 1790–1 saw the emergence of Wolfe Tone as the leader of the Society of United Irishmen and his appeal to Catholics and Protestant Noncomformists to unite for the reform of a corrupt and unrepresentative Parliament.

As a recent Irish historian has written: 'The Union of Catholic and Dissenter had been advocated by the Bishop of Derry; it now became Tone's lifework.'[21] The Bishop might well have thrown the weight of his authority and popular appeal behind Tone's Society of United Irishmen, but in fact he remained strangely aloof, despite the protestations of patriotism and fervour for the great cause made to the Volunteers of Derry. Tone stood for almost exactly the same ideals as those the Earl-Bishop had advocated in 1783 and in whose name he had been prepared to go to the extreme lengths of public protest. Now the old fire seemed to have deserted him. Perhaps advancing years were at last beginning to make themselves felt (though he was soon enough to show himself in splendid form again when he resumed his travels); or perhaps his recent experiences in France had taught him a new caution in the conduct of public affairs.

Such interest as he took in politics concerned the world at large. The crisis between Russia and the Sultan over the Black Sea ports caused him to send his daughter Mary (his favourite correspondent among those members of his family with whom he was still on reasonable terms) a somewhat disjointed letter on the problems facing the Empress Catherine II, the 'Semiramis of the North'.

'I hope in God dear Mr. P[itt] will not think of War,' he wrote on 1 April 1791, 'as I dare believe he will not, as we have never been the richer nor the stronger for Continental connexions, and that I verily believe we could get more for driving the *circumcised Dogs* out, than for keeping them in, besides it is next to impossible but that, if Semiramis should go to Byzantium, she should lose either by intestine division or by foreign depredations the northern part of her empire; and then she would have to begin anew in the South what Peter the Great effected long ago in the North; and that in a country stript of inhabitants and so inur'd to slavery that they would never be capable of any exploit: add to this, the moment she should settle in Byzantium, Vienna and the near Eastern Empire, Sweden, and Prussia, would eternally be plucking her best feathers in the North and the maritime powers would be destroying her fleets as fast as she quipped them. But literature and the Arts and the sciences would gain rapidly by the culture of the descendants of Archimedes, Plato, Aristotle, Phidas and Praxiteles . . .'. As the Bishop grew older he was to indulge from time to time in schemes for the political reorganization of Europe – but these he confined to letters to his friends, of which this was an early example.

More agreeable than the problems, actual or merely conjectural, of Catherine the Great was the news that his old friend Sir William Hamilton was home in England on leave of absence from his post in Naples. The Bishop was at Ballyscullion when the news reached him and at once sent a cordial invitation for Sir William to join him in Ireland. 'My dear old schoolfellow,' he wrote, 'nothing shall ever excuse you either to my head or heart if you play me truant; I count so much upon your passing the Channel if you come to Wales that I would even send a warrant for you if I thought it would bring you. A month or two will repair you from the fatigues of your journey; you shall have musick every day or no day, you shall see the Giant's Causeway by sea and by land, you shall see extinguished volcanoes and almost burning ones, you shall have grouse-shooting or not as you please, you shall fish on salt water or fresh just as you like best, I will meet you where you please and bring you to the most romantick and perhaps the most sublime scenery you ever saw; only come, and do not disappoint your old friend and schoolfellow.'[22]

It was a pity that Hamilton's affairs did not leave him time to accept this pressing and charmingly expressed invitation. It would have been fascinating to read his account of the Bishop's houses and to know his expert opinion of the pictures and other works of art which his enthusiastic friend would have shown him. But Sir William had more pressing business on hand: he had come to England for the purpose of making an honest woman of his mistress Emma Hart, who had at last succeeded in persuading him to marry her.

Lord Bristol had sent Hamilton his invitation on 25 May. It was not until December that he learnt the true purpose of Sir William's journey home. The Bishop was well aware of the risk his old friend ran in marrying his mistress, and knew that raised eyebrows would greet the news in certain quarters. Society was not unduly intolerant, but Hamilton held an official position which it was considered impossible for his new wife to share, and there were bound to be snubs and difficulties ahead. Sir William himself must have experienced a certain apprehension as to how some of his friends would receive the news. He need have had no worries as far as Frederick Hervey was concerned. God Almighty, that prelate was later to affirm, must have been in a glorious mood when he created Emma Hamilton, and he now hailed the bridegroom, his old friend and contemporary, with a characteristic outburst.

'I congratulate you, my old friend, from the bottom of my heart, upon the fortitude you have shown, and the manly part you have taken in braving the world and securing your own happiness and elegant enjoyments in defiance of them,' he wrote. 'I was for a long time prepar'd to receive you both, and should have been too happy in contributing to unite you had Lord Abercorn been in Ireland instead of England; nobody mentions your decision but with approbation; no wonder provided that they have ever seen and heard Lady Hamilton; and now I flatter myself you have secured your happiness for life, and will enjoy your *otium cum dignitate,* and take your *dignitatem cum amoenitate* for the remainder of your days, and I shall claim my old Cabin at Caserta, that I may be a witness of that permanent comfort I so often wish'd you before.'[23]

By the time the Bishop wrote this second letter to Sir William Hamilton he was back in England. It was dated from Woodstock on 21 December 1791. His old wanderlust had returned, preceded, as so often in the past, by a bout of real or imagined ill-health. At some time late in the autumn of that year he left Derry in search of a mild climate. It is unlikely that he knew he was leaving Ireland for ever; his plans at that moment were uncertain, but we may be sure that he thought he would be returning at some time to Downhill and Ballyscullion. In fact he would never see his adopted country again.

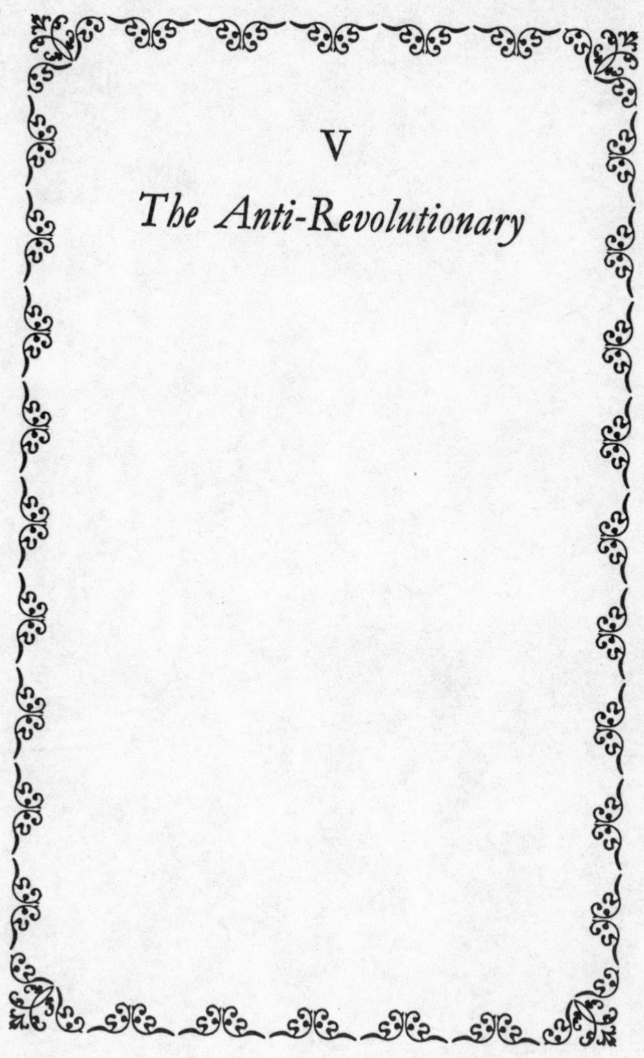

V

The Anti-Revolutionary

I

It was at some time in the early autumn of 1791 that the Earl-Bishop left Ireland for the last time. Once again his excuse for leaving his diocese was bad health and the need for change and a milder climate, though the latter reason does not explain why we next find him (in September) at Annan in Scotland. Here, in sight of the bleak stretches of the Solway Firth, he felt so very unwell that he decided to make his will.

This document, which is signed 'Bristol and Frederick Derry' is dated 17 September 1791. In it he assigned to his eldest son Lord Hervey all his property 'of every denomination whatever' in Great Britain; all his property in the Kingdom of Ireland (with certain minor reservations) was left to his 'dearly beloved cousin Henry Bruce, Rector of Aghadowvy in the diocese of Derry'. His remaining children were provided for in a somewhat arbitrary manner out of the £10,000 which the Bishop had himself been left by his eldest brother George, who had stipulated that this sum was to be divided in Frederick's own will among his children in such proportions as he chose.

The manner of his choice was nothing if not capricious. He confirmed that his two eldest daughters, Lady Erne and Lady Elizabeth Foster, must consider the £2,000 they had already received in marriage portions as constituting their shares in this fund, which left a residue of £6,000. This remaining sum was disposed of in a curt phrase: 'I give to my affectionate and dutiful daughter Lady Louisa Hervey five thousand pounds and to my undutiful and ungrateful son Frederick William Hervey I give one thousand pounds.'[1]

The cause of this discrimination against Frederick, then twenty-two years old, is not clear. He was a clever and promising young man who had already distinguished himself at St. John's College, Cambridge, where, in his mother's words, he had succeeded in his examinations 'with such wonderful credit and *éclat* that he was declared first of his year in every subject'. His father's distaste for taking part in examinations was notorious but this could hardly have been the reason for the discord.

There had been a dispute between the parents some four years before when the Bishop had wanted his son to visit the Netherlands with a tutor; Frederick had sided with his mother against the idea and between them they had prevailed against his father's wishes. It may be that the young man had declared himself too openly in sympathy with his mother in the rupture between his parents and thus earned his father's displeasure, though the Bishop showed no animosity to Louisa on this score.

By the premature death of Lord Hervey, Frederick was ultimately to succeed his father in the earldom so the gesture of 'cutting him off' with £1,000 came to nothing. He was later to be Under-Secretary of State for Foreign Affairs and was raised to the rank of Marquess in 1826. In his latter years he spent much of his time in Brighton where he earned a reputation for philanthropy and charitable works, gaining a very different image in the popular imagination from that enjoyed by his father. Certainly father and son were very different in temperament. They were to have more serious differences of opinion in the course of the decade that followed the Bishop's making of his will.

The lucky Henry Bruce was informed of his good fortune in a letter written from Annan on 5 October. The will, of which he would be one of the executors, was to be delivered into his keeping in case of the Bishop's death, 'which I still think not very remote', the writer added rather gloomily. 'If I acquire strength 'tis very slowly,' Bristol had informed him, 'and the gout which at present is in both my feet scarce allows me to walk, and the bed is too debilitating to be confined to it. My Physician is a man of ingenuity and tenderness, visits me twice a week from Dumphries and remains with me about a day and an half; his conversation is the best medicine he gives me.'

The doctor from Dumphries clearly knew his job, for nothing stimulated the Bishop so much as lively talk. By the end of the year he was well enough to be able to make his way south again. In December he stayed at Blenheim Palace, surely a house after his own heart (it was from Woodstock that he wrote to congratulate Hamilton on his marriage), and then continued on to Plymouth. The salubrious and mild climate of this naval port decided him to pass the winter there before going abroad.

His activities this winter, during which his health was fully restored, can again be traced in a series of letters addressed to his eldest daughter who was now back in London and living in Bruton Street. 'Amid the Chaos of letters which surround and almost confound me,' he wrote to her on 29 January 1792, 'I have only a moment to say that if your husband will not allow you a Coach in London your Father will – and tho' I never was more pinch'd for money, yet I beg you would do the thing handsomely and not only have the Comfort of going in your Coach but also the pleasure of being drawn by Pretty horses – and I will pay you either monthly or at the end of the Season as you like best. Adieu my dear Child, I really have not a minute to spare nor a Brain to resist such incessant calls upon it.'[2]

Though he now described the French as 'that nation of Baboons' he was seriously concerned with the plight of some of the refugees from the Revolution whom he met in the course of his wanderings in Plymouth and its neighbourhood. 'I am now busy, who would think it? in procuring lodging, diet and accommodation for two miserable French Exiles whom I met at St. Austell's in Cornwall,' he wrote in March. 'One is certainly a Bishop, the other I conclude his Grand Vicaire.' He asks Mary to see if she can find them 'one Room with two beds up two pairs of stairs in the neighbourhood of some good cook-shops where a man can fill his belly without much emptying his Purse'. He begs her 'if you are your Father's own daughter, and I doubt it not' to help him to extricate these unfortunate exiles from their present distress, and concludes: 'For my part *je déteste la France, mais quelque fois j'aime–non – je plains les François*.'

The next day he entertains her with his literary views: 'What books appear this year I like "The Loves of the Plants" immoderately, and think Townshend's travels thro' Spain not unentertaining. Has Whitaker's defense of Mary Queen of Scots come out? the beautiful and as he says "the Virtuous, the chaste Mary" – believe it who can? a Princess born in Edinburgh and educated in Paris – chaste! and virtuous – 'tis Hypocrisy against the Devil . . .'. When interest in reading flags there was always fishing, but 'what a coquette is this Plymouth Sound to me – here I am flirting with it perpetually – and not one single John Dory to be caught, nor even a Red mullet.'

Meanwhile there is his constant interest in pictures to keep him amused. 'Think what a lucky man is Lord Camelford,' he writes on 20 March, 'he has just bought 3 Claudes at one stroke. My own collection is forming from *Cimabue* thro' Rafael and delicious Guido down to Pompeo Battoni, the last of the Italian school – and in Germany from Albert Durer's Master down to Angelica [Kauffmann]. But I have no good Rafael, nor any satisfactory Guido, but a *Correggio* that is invaluable and two Claudes, sold to me by that Liberal, Gentlemanlike, excellent man Mr. Henry Hope of Amsterdam.'

He is now determined, he tells her, on acquiring some pictures that are about to be auctioned at Christie's sale rooms. 'I have set my heart on two . . . which I actually did buy in my last séjour at Rome and was jockey'd from by the Vendor pretending after 3 days receipt of my money that he meant Pounds sterling and not zecchins – *e che differenza, Mia Cara*!' The lots he is now after are all portraits, numbers 86 and 87 in the catalogue, or failing them number 102. He asks his daughter to make the arrangements for his bids to be placed, but he will not go higher than fourteen, or the most fifteen, guineas, for that was the price he gave for them in Rome.

Alas! the Bishop's price was not high enough. The three pictures, which have been identified as a portrait by Tinelli ('of wonderful effect and strength of colour in which this scarce and famous artist excelled'),[3] a *Venus and Adonis* by Schiavone, and a portrait of a Doge of the Raggi family by Capuchin Genoese, were sold respectively for eighteen, nineteen and a half, and thirty-three guineas. When the news that he had been outbid reached him Lord Bristol took his defeat philosophically: 'A thousand thanks to you dear Mary for all your trouble and sollicitude about my pictures. If they are truly sold they are certainly gone for more than they are worth.' The modern reader can only wonder that such pictures could have been sold for so little, but account must be made for the differing value of money. This was the age when a Canaletto could be bought for fifteen or twenty pounds.

The distraction of the sale room and the excitements of picture collecting did not prevent the Bishop from showing his usual interest in events in the world at large. Indeed, political matters could not be far from anyone's mind in the year 1792 which saw France declare war on Austria and Prussia and was to end with the trial of Louis XVI. The Revolution had moved into the offensive and many of its Whig supporters in England were beginning to undergo a change of heart which the French King's execution in January 1793 was destined to complete.

Bristol's hostility to France continued to be vigorous but did not blind him to the need for reform in his own country. Nor was he as insensible as some to the lessons to be drawn from the situation on the other side of the Channel.

By May 1792 he was back in London and from his house in St. James's Square set down, in a letter to his eldest daughter, some of his ideas on the political issues of the times. 'I own Mr. Pitt's politics and mine with respect to Reform differ greatly,' he confessed. 'I would call on Mr. Grey and Doctor Priestly for a specifick system of reform, as an *Ultimatum* beyond which no more was desir'd, and then canvass it fairly, as they do the African Slave trade, not as a Ministerial but as a Political meaures – for whilst all Reform is precluded by the high hands of Power, and so many of the very best Citizens think that some is necessary, what can we expect but an explosion like that in France which, had the *severity* of the *Bastille* been corrected, the *abuse* of *lettres de cachet* been restrain'd, the Nobility and Clergy tax'd like other citizens, had probably never *happen'd*. The Dissenters are becoming every day more numerous, the Clergy of the Church of England every day more remiss, more voluptuous, more Abandon'd, more dissipated, less learned and more contemptible – where can it end? In some great convulsion – I pledge myself *that* at no remote era.'

Though the Bishop was in no very strong position to criticize his fellow clerics in matters of voluptuousness or even of dissipation, he once again showed himself in advance of his times (or at least in advance of general 'official' opinion) in his assessment of the problems of the day. Pitt constantly postponed, and eventually abandoned, bringing in any measure of reform, partly on account of opposition from the Court, but chiefly because all his energies were employed in conducting the campaign against revolutionary France. Had a policy been followed on the lines sketched out in the Bishop's letter many of the problems that faced the country at the end of the long period of war (by which time both Pitt and the Earl-Bishop would have passed from the scene) might have been solved or avoided.

The Bishop was soon to leave England and these political

reflections, in line as they are with the views he had held for so many years, take on a valedictory note when we realize (as he at the time of writing them, did not) that he would never set foot in England again.

Before setting out for the Continent, quite undeterred by the storm of war and revolution that raged there, he had one more visit to make in his native country. He decided to go to Ickworth, which he had not visited once in the past ten years. The idea of building a house there had taken hold of him again and he set off during the summer to choose a suitable site for it. This was yet another example of the Bishop's inconsistent nature, for he had often professed a distaste for the place and had told Arthur Young that he particularly disliked it on account of the wetness of the soil, adding that he would never be such a fool as to build in so wet a situation.

It is interesting to speculate on the cause of this apparent volte-face, though admittedly it is difficult to accuse anyone of changing face who so rarely (except in his political beliefs) ever faced for long in the same direction. Was he now so disillusioned with the state of affairs in Ireland that he had decided not to return there; or was it merely that the urge to build had so possessed him that he must find a new opportunity to express his architectural ideas now that Ballyscullion was almost completed? The latter is the more likely, especially as he envisaged the house he would build at Ickworth more in terms of a great museum to house his pictures and sculptures rather than as just another country house to embellish with such overflow of works of art as could not be accommodated at Downhill or Ballyscullion. The house he now had in mind (though not as it was finally completed by his descendants) would combine the uses of the National Gallery with those of the British Museum; it was an entirely new venture.[4]

Ever since the break-up of their marriage Lady Bristol had been living at Ickworth Lodge. The Bishop now took care not to meet her. She had passed the late summer and early autumn with their daughter Louisa at Ramsgate. It was during their absence at this then fashionable seaside resort that Lord Bristol chose to visit his old home.

2

The Bishop left England in September 1792 accompanied by his chaplain. He was to remain abroad for the rest of his life. His ultimate destination was Italy but he first passed over a year in Germany, having avoided France because of the unsettled state of that country, which was soon to be at war with his own. As he had only recently referred to the French both as 'monkies' and 'baboons' and was to heap further imprecations on them at every opportunity, this decision was no doubt wise and indeed hardly surprising. What is surprising to the modern reader is the fact that his plans for travel were so little impeded by the general state of war in Europe at the time.

Pyrmont was once more his headquarters. The place was familiar, the climate agreed with him, and it was a good centre for excursions to other places of interest in the region of Hesse, Hanover, and Saxe Gotha. It is, in fact, in Cassel that we first hear of him, writing to Lady Erne on 9 October to say that Pyrmont has done him all the good he expected and the journey a good deal more, so that he wanted nothing but to perpetuate the health and spirits he enjoyed. Everyone who met him remarked how young he looked for his age. Alas! this could not be said for his old friend Prince Augustus of Saxe-Gotha. That kind and accommodating Prince was desperately ill. 'The cold dry air which fortifies me', declared Bristol, 'debilitates him, attacks his bowels, *et le mette à deux doigts du tombeau.*'

In Cassel Bristol was able to admire the splendid collection of pictures as well as the town itself which he considered to be the most elegant in Germany – 'a circus twice as large as that at Bath, a Square exquisitely elegant and spacious, one side of which is form'd by the façade of the museum, a repository of everything curious in Arts and Nature, and another side opens into the most beautiful country that wood, water, hill, and mountain can form, and in the foreground the publick walks and gardens.' Add to this an art gallery containing four masterpieces of Claude Lorraine, two landscapes by Rembrandt, 'exquisite Van Dykes, Holbeins, Berghems, and invaluable Teniers', and it will be seen that the Bishop was in his element.

As a background to this, however, the ominous rumble of revolution was not so very far away. Only the day before he had encountered Lord Findlater, 'that strange animal', in full flight, having been frightened out of Frankfurt by General Castine and some thousand French troops who were lurking in the vicinity. The great bankers and wealthy merchants of Frankfurt had left even before Lord Findlater. Perhaps to show his contempt for this panic the Bishop, in the next sentence, advises his daughter should she herself decide to come abroad to travel 'leisurely' through Germany.

He, at least, showed no disposition to change his plans on account of the warlike activities of the French. He continued to drink the waters at his favourite German spa where he had temporarily taken the lease of a villa. When in June 1793 he moved to Hanover for a month or so it was not to escape from any peril of revolution but simply 'to avoid the rains of Pyrmont'. He then intended to visit the Hartz mountains – 'thence to Gottengen, Cassel and so home – that is Dear Pyrmont'.

Nevertheless, his attitude to the Revolution continued to harden, especially after the execution of the King when the extremist elements in Paris began to take over. If he had previously attacked the 'establishment' who wished to maintain the *status quo* by force, he now equally attacked the revolutionaries who wished to overthrow it, as both appealed to force and not to reason.

He had a thorough horror of the Jacobins and all who supported them. In this category he included Charles James Fox, against whom he now directed the sort of remarks that had been thrown in his own direction when he had himself been playing the role of demagogue in Dublin ten years before. 'We are told here,' he wrote to Mary from Hanover, 'that nothing could be more eloquent or more logical than Mr. Pitt's speech in confutation of that execrable Demagogue and Rebel Charles James. I beg of you therefore to send me one or two of those papers that retail and detail the best. Fox seems to be in universal contempt both as a man and a Politician all over the continent, and his last mendicant pension has made his heart as contemptible as his mind.' It was much in the style that Horace Walpole had once used on the subject of the Bishop of Derry.

The Bishop had now a patriotic as well as an ideological reason for maligning the French, for on the first of February they had declared war on Great Britain, adding Spain to the list of their enemies the following month. France now stood out, in the eyes of Lord Bristol and of many others, as a general threat to civilization. The liberal, idealistic climate of 1789 was giving way before the advance of the Terror which was to establish itself in Paris in the very month in which the Bishop wrote his letter from Hanover.

All the same it comes as something of a shock to find this old champion of the rights of humanity applauding the second partition of Poland, which had taken place in May. 'The partition of Poland', he declared in this same letter, 'seems to me one of the wisest, the most just and the most humane strokes in Politicks that has yet been struck. 'Tis certain past all doubt that the French Democracy and Anarchy was on the point of being introduced not only into Poland but into Prussia, Pomerania, etc., and 'tis hardly possible to meet a man of any station whatever who is not imbued with those principles of Chaos. Clubs prevail in every town in Germany and such places as Pyrmont, Gismar, Meinberg, etc., and receive Committees where all these opinions are broached and where a stranger need only shut his mouth and open his eyes to be convinc'd of the Progress which the love of Anarchy has made in all this country.'

These alarming signs of danger and confusion, for which Poland was paying the price of her liberty and independence (the very principles the Bishop had bravely advocated for Ireland), did not prevent him from trying to persuade his eldest daughter to visit him in Germany. His letter of invitation from Pyrmont on 14 July also contained some startling revelations on the effects of tea-drinking as well as a curious remedy for seasickness:

'If ever the fancy should take you to visit me at Pyrmont, I think I could venture to protect you from sea-sickness – at least it always succeeds with me, tho' it is true I have not weakened my Stomach with Tea as you have, and with good reason, for the smallest cup of it will shrivel up my fingers as if I were ninety and give me cramps in my legs and soles of my feet, and bereave me of sleep during half the night.

'But to the ship – lash your carriage to the mast, and in the center you know is little or no motion, then let down the glass on the Windward as if it were winter, and keep yourself in a perpetual sweat. I have been twenty-two hours at sea and felt no inconvenience but a little mawkishness at times.... Tis the stoppage of perspiration is one of the chief causes of our Sickness – keep up that and we are safe.'[5]

Lady Erne, perhaps wisely, did not submit herself to the perils of sea travel or the scarcely more inviting hazards of war and revolution. She remained in England and her father continued his wanderings in Germany with only his chaplain, Trefusis Lovell, as companion.

Their travels, fortunately for posterity, took them to Jena, where an encounter took place between the Bishop and one of the most celebrated personalities of his day, an encounter which was to show them both in an interesting light. The author of *The Sorrows of Werther* happened to be in Jena at the same time; he had heard of this travelling prelate but never met him before. With the shrewd eye of a poet and novelist Goethe described the Earl-Bishop as follows:

'About sixty-three years of age, of middle or rather low stature, of slight frame and countenance, lively in carriage and manners, quick in his speech, blunt, sometimes even rude; in more than one respect narrow and one-sided, as a Briton, unbending; as an individual, obstinate; as a divine, stiff; as a scholar, pedantic. Honesty, zeal for the Good, and the unfailing results thereof, show everywhere through the disagreeable points of the above qualities, and they are balanced, too, by his extensive knowledge of the world, of men and of books, by the liberality of a noble and by the ease of a rich man. However vehemently he may be speaking (and he spares neither general nor particular circumstances) he yet listens most attentively to everything that is spoken, be it for or against him; he soon yields, if he be contradicted; contradicts if he does not like an argument, though made in his favour; now drops one sentence, now takes up another, while arguing throughout from a few chief ideas. Thus a great many pet expressions appear to be fixed; he will only admit that which the clear perceptions of the understanding can recognize, and yet in the argument it is noticeable that he is capable of much more genial views than he will allow even to himself. As for the rest, his manners seem careless, but agreeable, courtly and affable. Such is about the character of this remarkable man (for and against whom I have heard so much) as I met and observed him one evening.'

The Bishop began by attacking Goethe for the dangerous ideas he had expressed in *Werther* but (we have only Goethe's account of the episode) found that he received as good as he gave in the argument that followed.

'It was sometimes his whim to be offensive,' the poet later told Frederic Soret, 'but if one treated him equally offensively he would become perfectly amenable. In the course of our conversation he tried to preach to me about *Werther* and lay it to my conscience that by writing it I had tempted people to suicide. "*Werther*", he said, "is a completely immoral, damnable book." "Stop!" I cried. "If that is how you talk about the wretched *Werther*, what tone do you propose to take against the great of this world who with a single stroke of the pen send a hundred thousand men to war, eighty thousand of whom will kill each other and excite each other to fire and slaughter and pillage? And you, after these horrors, thank God and sing a *Te Deum*! And what about your sermons on the terrors of hell, which so frighten the feeble spirits in your congregations that they lose their wits and end their miserable little lives in a mad house? Or your orthodox dogmas, many of them untenable by any rational man, which sow the fatal seeds of doubt in the minds of your Christian listeners, so that these poor souls, who are neither weak nor strong, lose themselves in a labyrinth from which death is the only way out! How do all these things lie in your conscience, and what sermons do you preach to yourselves about them? And yet you try to call a writer to account and condemn a book which, owing to the misinterpretations put upon it by a few shallow minds, has at most rid the world of a dozen fools and idlers who had nothing better to do than blow the feeble remnants of their confused little brains out altogether! I thought I had done a real service to mankind and erned their gratitude, and now you come along and try to turn my little good feat of arms into a crime, and yet all this while your priests and princes are permitting yourselves such almighty liberties!"'

It was clearly a thorough trouncing in which the Bishop had to stand as whipping-boy for all the crimes of the whole sacerdotal profession. But in accusing this particular prelate of preaching on the terrors of hell Goethe was standing on flimsy ground; it was unlikely, indeed, that his opponent in the argument had preached on any subject at all for a very considerable period.

'This outburst worked on my bishop like a charm,' Goethe continued. 'He turned meek as a lamb and treated me from then on, during the rest of our conversation, with the utmost courtesy and subtlest tact. Thus I passed an extremely pleasant evening with him. For Lord Bristol, for all his occasional rudeness, was a man of some intellect and cultivation, and fully qualified to discuss a wide variety of subjects. When I left he accompanied me to the door and then sent his chaplain to do the further honours. The latter, when we reached the street, exclaimed to me: "Oh, Herr von Goethe, what a fine speech that was you made! You have quite won his Lordship's heart – how clever it was of you to hit upon the secret of pleasing him! If you had been a little less rough and forthright with him I am sure you would not be going home feeling so satisfied with your visit as you do now." '[6]

In fact they had hit on the secret of pleasing each other, for if the Bishop had not criticized *Werther* in the way he did he would not have been subjected to Goethe's tirade, the delivery of which so obviously delighted its author. Bristol, too, must have enjoyed it almost as much, for despite his meek looks he agreed entirely with the greater part of what the poet had to say. One cannot help thinking that he had made his adverse and outrageously tactless comments on the book on purpose to provoke the great writer. It would have been typical of his perverse sense of humour.

The Bishop's moves are difficult to trace after his encounter with Goethe in the summer of 1793. In the early autumn he was in Switzerland, his mind still preoccupied with the old problem of building steeples. He urges the patron of one of his Irish parishes not to employ an architect when renovating the church so that the money thus saved can be used on beautifying the steeple and spire: 'As to the church, I entreat you not to make it larger; the increase in our congregation is too problematical, and a small one in a large church is as uncomfortable as it is ridiculous. Let it decorate the country if it cannot receive it, and at least be a monument and an example to posterity how well the squire and the Bishop could draw together . . .'.[7]

After delivering this excellent piece of episcopal advice the Bishop disappears from view, to emerge in January 1794 in Trieste, from where he writes petulantly to Sir William Hamilton: 'This damned climate – cold, damp, and ungenial – ruins me.'

3

While Lord Bristol was wandering about northern Italy in the autumn of 1793 trouble was brewing for his eldest son in Florence. John Augustus, Lord Hervey, had been British Minister at the Court of the Grand Duke of Tuscany for the past six years, but recently his conduct had given rise to some embarrassment to his compatriots and considerable irritation to the Court and Government to whom he was accredited.

Lord Hervey had inherited a good deal of his father's arrogance and eccentricity without the saving virtues of affability and benevolence that distinguished the Bishop's character in his better moments. He had also a less firm command over his temper and emotions, both of which were strong and somewhat tempestuous. He was sadly ill cast for the role of diplomatist.

The whisper of scandal had first been heard in 1791 when a certain Lady Anne Hatton had received the cold shoulder from the female section of the British Colony in Naples (led by Emma Hamilton whose own recently acquired virtue still had the essence of novelty) when it was learnt that this lady had been 'living publickly' with Lord Hervey in Florence. The whisper soon became a shout when it was further discovered that he had been involved in a skirmish over the possession of this fragile beauty with no less a person than Prince Augustus, the sixth son of George III, who was visiting Italy in search of health and finding much else besides. Fortunately the tact and wisdom of Sir William Hamilton kept the situation from getting out of hand and saved the Prince and the envoy from undue obloquy.[8]

Hervey's conduct did not improve, however, and by the summer of 1793 matters had reached a head; his eccentricities were no longer confined to questions of purely private concern. 'It will not be possible to allow him to remain after his behaviour to the Grand Duke,' Lady Webster confided to her Journal. 'In those letters which he wrote remonstrating against the exportation of grain from Tuscany to France, he calls the Grand Duke a fool, and Manfredini [the Tuscan Chief Minister] a knave.'[9]

Lady Webster was travelling with Lord Holland, whom she

afterwards married. Holland's account of these strange events went into a little more detail. 'Lord Hervey', he wrote, 'had personally insulted the Grand Duke of Tuscany, and it was generally supposed, in the *maldicente* city of Florence, that resentment at the French Minister for having supplanted him in the good graces of a lady quickened his hatred of the French Republick, or at least gave it the turn of insisting on the dismissal of his rival . . . Lord Hervey's conduct was intemporate, indecorous, and violent in the extreme. . . . In a personal audience with the Grand Duke, on which he insisted in violation of etiquette, he intimidated that prince into a dismissal of La Flotte [the French Minister], and a breach of that neutrality which had been recognised and approved of by Great Britain herself. . . . No minister at the Court of Florence but the Russian agent co-operated with Lord Hervey in this measure.'[10]

By now evidence of the envoy's peculiar and very undiplomatic behaviour had reached England where it caused grave alarm both to the Government and to his family. His formal recall became inevitable and unavoidable. Lady Bristol had long lamented her eldest son's warmth of temper and dreaded the effect that this news might have upon him. She wrote to Lord Grenville, the Foreign Secretary, who assured her that her son had lost his post by his own indiscretion and not through the revenge of the Florentine Minister.

She then persuaded her second son Frederick to solicit an interview with Pitt and to urge the Prime Minister to allow him to go out to Florence and be himself the bearer of the sad tidings of his brother's dismissal. 'Fred saw Mr. Pitt this morning,' she wrote to Lady Erne in September. 'Nothing could be more gracious, open and condescending, with very obliging professions of regard to the Family, and concern for this unlucky incident. I find they have nothing in view for him but a pension – but we must try for some distinction.' In the circumstances Lord Hervey was lucky to get even a pension to soften what his mother described as 'this *fâcheuse pilule*'.

Frederick Hervey left England on 28 September, according to a later letter from Lady Bristol to her daughter: 'Fred's request to be messenger of *bad news* is so uncommon that I see it has struck Mr. Pitt very much, and he has behav'd with uncommon kindness to him. It is certainly a charming thing, and I think his going to

Hervey will mollify him and do a great deal of good. He sets out tomorrow . . .'. She had more than one reason for wishing Frederick to visit Italy at this time. It was not just a case of making Lord Hervey swallow his 'troublesome pill'. 'We must labour incessantly to bring some good out of all this evil,' her letter concludes. 'I sometimes think that dear Fred going over to Italy at this moment may bring about your Father's reconciliation – how happy that would make us – and if he *settles,* it will make England pleasanter to Hervey and may in the end reconcile him to all things . . .'.

This hope of Lady Bristol's was not to be fulfilled. Either because he was unaware of what was going on, or because he wished to have no part in it, the Bishop kept his distance from Florence and from his sons' problems and difficulties. As for the elder, 'he seems to dislike his recall,' Lady Webster noted, 'and talks of going again into the Navy, where, by-the-bye, he is very unpopular.'[11] The future did not look very bright for the intemperate Lord Hervey; nor did he meet with any success when, to console himself for his lost position as envoy, he made a passionate and startling declaration of love to Lady Webster herself. Already separated from her first husband and hoping eventually to find another in Lord Holland, she replied to his advances with the coldest of rebuffs. 'Surprise and embarrassment have completely overset me,' she recorded in her *Journal.* 'Oh! what vile animals men are, with headstrong passions.'

4

In Trieste Lord Bristol was again laid low by illness. 'I have been in bed these four weeks with what is called a flying gout,' he told Sir William Hamilton, 'but were it such it would be gone long ago, and it hovers round me like a ghost round its sepulchre.' He managed, none the less, to keep an eye on the movement of ships in the harbour and reported to the envoy in Naples that a whole fleet of transports and gunboats were under way for Venice which they hoped to reach in two days, though the wind was neither favourable nor strong.[12] He sent this for Hamilton's information in order that he could pass it on to '*la première des femmes – cette maîtresse femme*', as the Bishop gallantly described Maria Carolina, the masterful Queen who ruled Naples in the name of her inept and incompetent husband.

His letter to Hamilton was written on 15 January 1794. By February we find him in the mountainous region of Aosta, having travelled a distance of more than three hundred miles despite illness or at least convalescence. What caused him to make so arduous a journey when in fragile health is difficult to say except for his unceasing restlessness and the fact that he believed the fever he suffered from would be cured by breathing the thinnest air.

While he was in Aosta the Bishop drew up a codicil to the will he had made three years previously in Scotland. He made yet further bequests to his cousin Henry Hervey Bruce including all his 'pictures, Statues, Busts, Marbles, *Gesses* as well in Rome, Florence, Leghorn, to be disposed of as he judges best', and added to the Irish inheritance already willed to Bruce all his personal estate in England as well; that is, all that was not protected by entail. Two further bequests were to women: 'I give and devise to Madame De Scheven born de Praut the sum of fifty pounds a year so long as she shall continue to live separate from that scoundrel and Brute her husband,' and to Madame Diroff, wife of Senator Diroff of St. Petersburg, he left his portrait by Angelica Kauffmann. Who these two women were, and why they received these legacies in his will, has remained a mystery. The latter lady, unlike the first, does not seem to have been separated from her husband, as the Bishop made provision for the picture to be sent to her in Russia.[13]

By May the revolutionary armies had occupied the passes leading from France into Piedmont, and the Valle-D'Aosta ceased to be a suitable place of retreat for an elderly and aristocratic invalid; the Bishop therefore moved south, dividing his time for the next few months between Florence and Siena. In Florence he took the lease of a house and immediately set to work on adding a new storey to it, an undertaking that made him very popular at a period when the war scare was causing unemployment, but was none the less a characteristically reckless and extravagant act as he had only rented the house for a period of five years.[14]

In Siena he busied himself with buying pictures (it was here, as we have seen, that he purchased the Guido da Siena primitive) and in scientific speculations of a curious nature which resulted in a further exchange of letters with Sir William Hamilton.

Just before his arrival there, during a particularly violent thunderstorm, about a dozen stones of different shapes and sizes fell from the sky at the feet of various witnesses, men, women, and children. Bristol had at first tended to doubt the possibility of such a phenomenon, but there were so many eyewitnesses that he found it impossible to withstand their evidence. 'The stones are of a quality not found in any part of the Sienese territory,' he told Sir William, 'they fell about 18 hours after the enormous eruption of Vesuvius, which circumstance leaves a choice of difficulties in the solution of this extraordinary phenomenon – either these stones have been generated in this igenous mass of clouds which would produce such unusual thunder, or, which is equally incredible, they were thrown from Vesuvius at a distance of at least 250 [miles] – judge, then, of its parabola .. .'. The local savants were generally inclined to the first of these two theories but the Bishop was eager to know his friend's view, for Sir William enjoyed a European reputation on all matters to do with volcanoes and their eruptions.

A few days later one of the actual stones was sent for his inspection, which Bristol's 'blundering head' had forgotten to enclose with his first letter. 'All the philosophical world is in arms about this phenomenon, and all impatient to know your opinion,' he assured Hamilton. 'The chief point is whether in this eruption Signore Vesuvius has emitted such a sort of stone; next, whether it be chemically possible for such a stone to be generated in a thunderstorm.'[15]

Hamilton came down in favour of the theory that the stones had been generated in the thunderstorm. The chief supporter of this theory in Siena was Father Ambrogio Soldani, a distinguished geologist and ecclesiastic, a friend and correspondent of Benjamin Thompson, later Count Rumford. Lord Bristol went to Soldani's monastery to inform him that Hamilton shared his views, and while still there wrote to tell Sir William that the learned priest was 'in raptures at learning that you had even for an instant the same idea as himself about the formation of these stones, whose generation appears to him every day more and more incontrovertible'. Soldani he described as 'a most sensible, candid, unprejudiced and intelligent man, indefatigable in the pursuit of truth'.

He was eager to know whether Vesuvius threw up stones similar to the one they had sent to Naples, for 'such a circumstance would a little stagger his theory, which all the babbling of Siena – male as well as female – does not as yet effect.'[16]

Hamilton's reply to this last request has not survived, so whether Vesuvius confirmed or confuted the theory of these enthusiastic amateurs of science must, like the 'aerial stones' themselves, remain concealed in obscurity.

While still in Siena the Bishop wrote an ingratiating letter to the poet Alfieri who was living in Florence with the Countess of Albany, widow of Prince Charles Edward Stuart, a liaison that had started some years before the Prince's death and had caused great scandal. Alfieri's tragedy *Saul* had recently been produced. Though Bristol was perfectly fluent in Italian, of which language Alfieri was the acknowledged master, he preferred to address the poet in French, and began his letter: *'Comment se porte mon cher Dante, le Comte Alfieri?'* He assured the author, who was peculiarly susceptible to flattery, that he had 'devoured' *Saul* which had afforded him a higher view of the master's talents than ever before. Nor did he forget the Countess who despite her equivocal position as widow of a Pretender and mistress of a poet was not above assuming the grandest royal airs. *'Et l'adorable Comtesse,'* he asked, *'Comment se porte-t-elle?'*

When Lord Bristol followed up this letter with his own presence in Florence he was able to introduce another enthusiastic admirer of *Saul* to its distinguished author. A young French artist, François-Xavier Fabre, had been so struck by the tragedy that he had made a scene from it the subject of one of his paintings. The Bishop had recognized his talents on an earlier occasion and had offered his patronage to the artist. He now presented the handsome young man to the great poet and the mature but still vivacious countess. The situation was full of irony, for Fabre was not only to become the inseparable companion of this interesting couple, but after Alfieri's death was to succeed him in Madame d'Albany's affections, though he was nearly fifteen years her junior.

It was a situation which Bristol would have relished had he known the full consequences of so innocent an introduction. All that immediately followed was a splendid double portrait of the lovers, for it was the role of midwife of talent rather than the unconscious one of cupid that the Bishop had assumed in bringing the three people together. The Countess, for all her royal pretentions and affectations of taste, did not show much appreciation of the man she referred to dismissively as *'ce fou Bristol'*. Nor did Alfieri show much more discernment, though he had known the Bishop for some years. 'He is a madman,' he wrote rather patronizingly to a friend, 'but not without ability or culture.'

As a staunch Whig Lord Bristol had never taken the exiled Stuart Court very seriously and he had usually referred to the 'Young Pretender' with contempt during that unfortunate Prince's lifetime; nor did he show the slightest interest in the presence of Cardinal York during his many visits to Rome, though York, like Bristol, frequented the palace of Cardinal de Bernis. In the present instance it was the Countess of Albany's association with Alfieri, for whom the Bishop had a genuine admiration, rather than her past connection with the Stuart claimant, that made him dance attendance on her in Florence.

He was, in fact, able to be of some service to this pushing and self-important woman who so liked to retain the obeisances due to an exiled monarch while at the same time enjoying the notoriety of a much publicized love affair. As a former pensioner of the French Court the Countess was now in some financial straits, for the Revolution had brought an abrupt end to any supplies of money from that source. She had therefore decided, with a singular lack of tact, to approach the British Government in the hope of persuading the Ministers of George III to grant a pension which the *ci-devant* Ministers of Louis XVI, if any still survived, were no longer in a position to provide for her.

Lord Camelford, a cousin of William Pitt's, had agreed to act as intermediary but had most regrettably died at the crucial moment before matters had reached any conclusion. The Earl-Bishop then gallantly took up her petition and saw that it was forwarded to the Prime Minister. Nothing, alas, came of it, and the Bishop got no thanks for his efforts. Gratitude does not seem to have been a characteristic of this woman who, in the opinion of Horace Walpole, had 'not a rag of royalty about her'.

Bristol continued to patronize Fabre, encouraging his taste for large canvases on classical themes, a genre in which he was less successful than in his portraits. One such, which the Bishop commissioned, depicted Ulysses and Neoptolemus attempting to take the arms of Hercules from Philoctetes when he was on a desert island with a wounded leg, a subject, surprisingly perhaps to modern eyes, in full conformity with the contemporary neo-classical taste.

While still in Siena Bristol sent a letter to his daughter Lady Erne which showed him completely restored to his usual health and energy in spite of complaints about his nervous system. 'The warm weather, my dearest Mary,' he wrote on 10 August, 'had done me infinite service and the cool weather come in after the rains is going to do as much. I bathe every day at Noon in a whale of a tub, I sleep every night out of town at a Villa whose atmosphere is *senza paragone* and return in the morn to chocolate and company: never reprobate Italian hospitality! This villa with 10 handsome rooms on a floor is lent by a man I never saw in my life but hearing of my convalescence has given his mite to smooth it. We shall not move towards Naples till October, and then change from Cold Baths to sea baths, for my whole nervous system is so shaken that the interior of Calabria is not more so. . . .'

He goes on to talk about Ickworth and the villa he plans to build, saying that he hopes next year to pass the autumn there and lay the foundation stone of his new house. This, of course, was not to be the case, but the house was very much in his mind at the time. When he reached Rome early in November *en route* for Naples the first tentative moves were made towards appointing an architect and drawing up the plans.

A vague reference in Joseph Farington's diary suggests that the Bishop may have considered employing John Soane as his architect. On 23 December 1794 Farington wrote: 'Lord Bristol invited Soane from Rome to Ireland. . . . Soane went, but could not agree with that capricious character. He left him and returned to England.'[17] As we know, it was impossible for Bristol to have done this as he had not been in Ireland since 1791. It is possible, however, that he saw Soane in Rome and sent him (or at least suggested that he should go) to Ireland to look at the house at Ballyscullion which was to be the model for Ickworth.

On the other hand, apart from Farington's unspecific reference, it is not at all certain that Soane was in Italy at this time. Perhaps the diariest was confusing this with a previous encounter between the Bishop and the architect when the latter had been dazzled by 'the magnificent promises and splendid delusions of the Bishop of Derry'.

Soane was just over forty in 1794 and well established in his profession; he was no longer the eager young student who had travelled from Rome to Naples with the Bishop of Derry in 1778. It is not surprising that he found his would-be patron's ideas capricious, for Bristol had a very decided conception of what he wished his new house to be like. He wanted to find somebody who could interpret this plan in architectural terms, not someone who might have other ideas, however good or original, of his own. He was, in short, looking for someone younger, more amenable, and less set in their ways.

He found what at first appeared to be just such a person in Charles Heathcote Tatham who was in Rome measuring and making drawings of classical monuments. Tatham was only twenty-two, but he already knew Canova and Angelica Kauffmann and had met Sir William and Lady Hamilton, and any of these distinguished friends could have introduced him to the Bishop.

That the Bishop made an approach to him we know from a letter of Tatham's to Henry Holland written from Rome on 19 November: 'The Earl of Bristol Bishop of Derry, lately arrived in Rome, to my great surprise consulted me to make him a design for a Villa to be built in Suffolk extending nearly 500 feet, including offices. The distribution of the plan is very singular the House being oval according to his desire.' From this letter it is clear that Bristol had already determined on the chief characteristic of Ickworth, which was to be a much larger version of Ballyscullion. We do not know just why Tatham's plans were rejected, but perhaps it lay in this very fact, for the architect whom the Bishop finally selected two years later not only had the advantage of youth, but had also actually worked on the plans for Ballyscullion with Shanahan.

Lord Bristol did not stay long in Rome. Shortly after his arrival there his old friend Cardinal de Bernis died in the palace where the Bishop had so often enjoyed his splendid receptions and which now sheltered the two fugitive French Princesses Madame Adélaide and Madame Victoire, the aunts of Louis XVI. This unwelcome *memento mori* may have hastened the Bishop's departure. He also had a wild plan to put to Hamilton when he reached Naples, that the Ambassador should resign his post in favour of Lord Hervey and accept that disgraced diplomatist's pension in exchange; a plan which would hardly have received the approval of London even if Hamilton had thought of entertaining it.[18] In fact he showed no interest in it at all.

5

At the time of the Earl-Bishop's death the *Annual Register*, in paying a glowing tribute to his memory, declared that 'there is not a country in Europe where the distressed have not obtained his succour and the oppressed his protection. He may truly be said to have clothed the naked and fed the hungry. . . .' Ostentatious in so much the Bishop made a secret of his charities, but on one occasion at least a witness was present to record him in this agreeable light.

Bristol had just arrived in Naples and was in a hurry to take possession of the house he had hired for the winter when a man was announced bearing a letter of introduction from an Essex rector called Narcissus Proby. The stranger, Robert Broadstreet, found the Bishop 'surrounded with pictures he had newly bought' but was given a polite reception. 'An instance of his liberality that took place when I was there was pleasant enough,' this stranger later wrote in a letter home. 'A decent elderly woman came in to pay her respects and asked him how he did. "Like a Bishop", says he, and pointing to a pile of stuff – "look here," says he, "this is for you." The poor woman looked first at the stuff, and then at the Bishop, *da capo*, till at last she burst into tears, and began kissing his hand, saying she was not worthy to kiss his hand, and would like to kiss his foot. "No," says he, "I am no Pope, tho' I am a Bishop. I am a heretic and must be damned you know?" "Oh! No, No," says the woman with a tone of doubt and distress that was inimitable – and in Sterne's hands would have made an excellent companion for Corporal Trim doubting whether a negro had a soul or not.'[19]

It was during this visit to Naples that a real intimacy grew between the Bishop and Lady Hamilton, with all the exaggerated endearments and flattering phrases on his side that he was accustomed to bestow on the objects of his affections. She was his 'dearest Emma', his 'ever dearest Lady Hamilton', his 'sweet Emma' or his 'dearest dear Emma', and on one occasion he even dropped into doggerel to enquire

Oh Emma, who'd ever be wise,
If madness be loving of thee?

Once again it was a case of an *amitié amoureuse* that went no further than arch flirtation on the Bishop's part and an amused response from Emma who was both flattered by his compliments to her beauty and entertained by his sallies of wit. That there was often a gross element in his humour troubled her not at all, for like the Bishop himself she had a strong streak of vulgarity in her nature.

She was quite unalarmed by his irreverent and often outrageous remarks and by his complete indifference to the self-importance of others. 'Lord Bristol is with us at Caserta,' she wrote to her former lover Charles Greville on 18 December. 'He passes one week at Naples and one week with us. He is very fond of me and very kind. He is very entertaining and dashes at everything. Nor does he mind King and Queen when he is inclined to show his talents.'[20] Emma must have found something very refreshing in this after three years in the constrained atmosphere of an embassy. It was very delightful to receive the attentions of so eccentric and diverting an admirer, and the fact of his being sixty-four years old added a reassuring note of safety, for all that her husband was exactly the same age. In fact she had a good deal in common with the Bishop in addition to a boisterous and extrovert temperament. Both enjoyed the limelight, both had a superabundance of high spirits, both loved intrigue and were able to imagine themselves in the thick of affairs when they were able to pass on a piece of political gossip. It was a relationship that gave them each a great deal of pleasure without causing Sir William a moment's uneasiness. Hamilton had complete confidence in his young wife's conduct and in the conduct of his friend; nor, indeed, would anyone abuse this confidence until Lord Nelson appeared on the scene.

Emma Hamilton's comment on the Bishop's indifference to King or Queen when he wished to show his talents was certainly not without foundation. He had never at any time been a great respecter of persons. Very soon the decorous society of Naples was to be shocked by some examples of his startling manners and his total lack of deference to personages of royal blood.

It was generally held against the King of Naples that he spent all his time in hunting and other pleasurable pursuits and left the management of the country in the hands of the Queen. The accusation was indeed true, though the King hotly denied it and liked to give the impression (especially to influential foreigners) that he ruled as well as reigned. Thus it was that in conversation with the Earl-Bishop the King lamented the injustice of the charge, pointing out how he always heard Mass, discussed affairs of state with his Ministers, signed official papers and only then, when these disagreeable matters were dispatched, permitted himself to indulge in his favourite sports and amusements. 'Yes,' Lord Bristol replied, having listened patiently to the royal complaint, 'and so in other matters your Majesty distinguishes between public duty and private pleasure. You first, as a duty, wed her Majesty, and then for your pleasure make love to my daughter!'

The reference was no doubt to his daughter Elizabeth who had been in Naples some nine years before and had spent much time in Rome and other parts of Italy since. Angelica Kauffmann had then painted her in all the freshness of her beauty which would certainly have made a great impression on the susceptible Ferdinand IV. But to suggest that the King had made love to her was just the sort of exaggeration in which the Bishop so often recklessly indulged. Sir William Hotham, who recounted the story many years later, declared that Ferdinand never invited Lord Bristol into his presence again, which is certainly untrue. Perhaps the King, whose intelligence was limited, was so stunned by the audacity of the reply that he refused to believe that he had heard it.

A second episode concerned an English prince. At the time of Bristol's visit to Naples Sir William Hamilton was also entertaining George III's son Prince Augustus (later Duke of Sussex) then in his early twenties. Sir William's house was famous for its musical parties. His first wife had been a brilliant harpsichord player and he himself performed on the violin, while Emma, at very little urging, would entertain the company with her loud and full-throated soprano.

The Bishop was present at one of these parties when the celebrated English singer Elizabeth Billington (who had just appeared at the San Carlo theatre in an opera specially written for her by Bianchi) was engaged to entertain the guests. Bristol was devoted to music and had prepared himself for an enjoyable evening. He had not, however, made allowances for the Prince, whose enthusiasm took the rather strange form of adding his own voice, which was neither trained nor true, to those of the professional singers. The Bishop, we are told in Lady Hamilton's *Memoirs*, 'who was naturally impatient, endured all this for some time with only muttering now and then a peevish pish or two; but at length the interruptions became so annoying that he could contain himself no longer, and turning to the royal singer, said: "Pray cease, you have the ears of an ass".'

Instead of being silenced by this rebuke – and one has every sympathy with the Bishop – the Prince, with the insensibility of youth, continued his accompaniment of the singers ever more loudly, and later provided the company with one or two solo efforts of his own. These were received with sycophantic applause by everyone except Lord Bristol, who remarked very loudly to his neighbour: 'This may be very fine braying but it is intolerable singing.'

Lady Hamilton was at this period busily engaged in ingratiating herself with the all-powerful Queen of Naples. Maria Carolina, the formidable daughter of the Empress Maria Theresa, had been violently anti-French ever since the execution of her sister Marie Antoinette and found a natural ally in the Earl-Bishop who was so glibly amusing in his choice of derogatory epithets to describe that powerful and predatory nation. In the frequent notes that passed between the Queen and Emma there were often complimentary remarks directed at '*ce cher bon et bien faisant évêque*', and there would be pressing requests for Lady Hamilton to visit the Queen '*en compagnie de votre Mary*' (as her somewhat original French styled Emma's *mari*) '*et de l'Évêque*'.

The Bishop was equally enthusiastic for the Queen, to whom he would send his 'warmest wishes – physical, political and moral', but would sometimes express his ardour with a remarkable freedom of language. Having once failed to meet Lady Hamilton at the opera before she left for Caserta, the royal palace some sixteen miles from Naples, he sent after her an undated letter which, had it fallen into the hands of the Queen, might have caused her more surprise than pleasure.

Ever dearest Emma,

I went down to your opera box two minutes after you left

it; and should have seen you on the morning of your departure – but was detained in the *arms of Murphy* as Lady Eden expressed it, and was too late.

You say nothing of the adorable Queen; I hope she has not forgot me: but, as Shakespeare says, 'who doats, must doubt,' and I verily deem her the very best edition of a woman I ever saw – I mean, of such as are not in *folio* but are to be *had* in *sheets*. . . .

Ever, and invariably, dearest dear Emma, most affectionately, your

B.

You see, I am but the second letter of your alphabet, though you are the first in mine.[21]

It was altogether an unusual letter to receive from a bishop. But if we are to believe the scurrilous and unreliable *Memoirs of Lady Hamilton* it was not the first occasion upon which Emma had encountered the outrageous side of her new friend's character. At least once she had herself been the target for one of his devastating sallies.

She was engaged in conversation with the Bishop in her own house when a woman of notorious reputation was announced. Upon her entrance Lord Bristol immediately took up his hat and prepared to leave the room, but Emma detained him for a moment with the remark that she hoped their company was not disagreeable to him. 'It is permitted for a bishop to visit one sinner,' he is reputed to have replied, 'but quite unfitting that he should be seen in a brothel.'

It is charitable to all concerned to hope that this story is apocryphal, though it has an unpleasant ring of authenticity about it, for the Bishop could be quite merciless to anyone (even a friend) who was foolish enough to lay himself open to one of these unexpected and cruel attacks, which came like a sudden flash of lightning on a summer day. They were to become more frequent as he grew older. He would launch his attack with deadly aim irrespective of the rank or station of his victim; one of his later targets being no less a person than the King of Prussia.

6

It was while he was in Naples that Bristol's hatred of the new France and all it stood for reached its zenith; nor would his distaste for the principles of the Revolution abate for the remainder of his life.

The Queen and Emma shared his views to the full. Born a Habsburg and married to a Bourbon, with her sister and brother-in-law both victims of the guillotine, Maria Carolina's violent antipathy to the government then ruling France was understandable enough. Emma's dislike is more difficult to explain and rose, perhaps, from feelings of insecurity which she had not yet shaken off after exchanging the uncertain role of mistress for the more assured status of wife. Sprung, as she was, from 'the people', it might be thought that she would have had some sympathy for a movement which, for all its faults, was still at least officially dedicated to the principles of liberty, equality, and fraternity and stood for the general betterment of mankind. In fact her hatred was implacable and expressed in the most violent terms. Unlike her more liberal and easy-going old husband she seemed quite blind to the faults of the absolutist regime in Naples (personified in her beloved friend the Queen) and lost no opportunity in giving shrill expression of her detestation of all things French.

The Bishop's opposition to France was no less violent than Emma's or the Queen's. It is true that he was accustomed to expressing himself in superlatives and was not the sort of man who would react mildly to any situation; all the same it is difficult to see the old champion of the rights of humanity in the individual who could now find nothing good in the ideas that were fast sweeping over Europe. In spite of this, however, it would be wrong to see him as becoming a mere 'reactionary', one whose only wish was to see the old order restored everywhere. He still remained highly critical of the *ancien régime* in France, or at least of the princes who had formerly ruled in that country.

This became clear enough when he left Naples in the spring of 1795 and escaped from the immediate influence of these two baleful women. With the old rapidity which time had done nothing to diminish he dashed northwards through Italy and Germany, reaching Munich in July. From there he dispatched a letter to Lady Hamilton parts of which, at least, must have jarred on the ears of that enthusiastic votary of the House of France.

'Here is great news from England,' he wrote on the sixth anniversary of the fall of the Bastille. 'My letters of the 26 June assure me, seven thousand men are embarked for St. Pol de Léon, together with an immense number of Emigrés . . . that six sail of the line from Russia were in sight, and the pilots gone to conduct them – that in Amsterdam, and other towns of Holland, there is the greatest insurrections in favour of that fool the Stadholder. All this, however, can only tend to facilitate peace, but not at all to restore that despicable, odious family of Bourbons – the head of which is now at *Verona*, where we left him eating *two capons* a day; ('tis a pity the whole family are not *capons*!) and, what is more, dressing them himself in a superb kitchen – the true chapel of a Bourbon prince.'[22]

What this letter shows most of all, perhaps, is that it remained impossible to pin the Bishop down to any one point of view. Just as he appears to settle down to a consistent line of conduct or a decided course of opinion, off he shoots at a tangent much in the way that he continued his unpredictable progresses along the highroads of Europe, never resting for long in any one place. He was still the man whom Horace Walpole had dismissed with irritation a dozen years before as 'that mitred Proteus the Count-Bishop'.

VI
The Adorable Friend

I

During all these travels, whether the Earl-Bishop was in Rome, Naples, Munich or Pyrmont, the thought of the great house he hoped to build at Ickworth was never very far from his mind. It was to be his architectural masterpiece, though to his wife, living in disgruntled neglect in England, the whole idea appeared as no more than 'a stupendous monument of folly'.

That he had, from the very beginning, a clear idea of what the house would be like is evident from the commission he gave to Tatham in Rome in the autumn of 1794. A year later (September 1795) his plans were far enough advanced for him to be concerned with points of detail. 'My only difficulty now is how to get the basso-rilievos executed,' he wrote at this time from Germany to a friend in Rome. 'The upper ones must certainly be painted as Dear Canova suggested, being beyond the reach of the eye's accuracy, but the lower ones must be bold and I suppose in gesso. . . . As the extent of our basso-rilievos is immense we must blend Oeconomy with our Magnificence or we shall wreck the Vessel.'

At some point between rejecting Tatham's designs and writing about his basso-rilievos the Bishop must have settled upon Francis Sandys as his architect, or, more correctly, as the interpreter of his own architectural ideas. Not much is known about Sandys's early days, though he is described as a native of Kilrea in County Londonderry. It is probable that he was the son of an Irish architect of the same name who entered a design for the Dublin Royal Exchange competition in 1769 and who was later responsible for a gothic dining-room at Bellevue, County Wicklow. Sandys's brother Joseph was a clergyman who later held livings in the Derry diocese, and who also had some architectural knowledge, though it is doubtful whether he was qualified. His signature appears on some of the papers relating to Shanahan's work at Ballyscullion, and he was to collaborate with his brother Francis at Ickworth, acting as clerk of the works.

Francis Sandys met the Bishop in Rome and was there given his assignment. It is possible that Lord Bristol summoned him from Ireland especially for this purpose as he already knew of his work, through the connection with Ballyscullion. That the young architect received his commission in Rome we know from a note in Joseph Farington's diary for 1 July 1796, when he recorded that Flaxman had visited him in the company of Francis Sandys, 'a young man who left Rome the beginning of April, and is now employed, as he says, in beginning to build a Palace at Ickworth for Lord Bristol'.[1] The reference to the two men visiting Farington together is of special interest for Flaxman was responsible for designing some of the bas-reliefs that were causing their patron such trouble.

To describe the new house at Ickworth as a palace was no exaggeration. Though the basic plan was similar to that used at Ballyscullion the whole building was conceived on a much grander scale, the total length being 600 feet to Ballyscullion's 350. The central oval construction or rotunda was to be 160 feet by 120 (compared with 84 by 74 at the other house) and the height of the dome was 104 feet from the ground.

The central rotunda had two tiers of columns. Those supporting the entablature or cornice which surrounded the building at the level of the first floor (where the rooms were thirty feet in height) were of the Ionic order, while Corinthian columns rose from above this cornice to support the sculptured or bas-relief frieze which formed part of the entablature encircling the dome two floors above. Similar panels in bas-relief appear at the first-floor level between the columns, forming a band above the windows and just below the entablature. The reliefs were in terracotta and represented scenes from the *Iliad* and *Odyssey* of Homer after Flaxman's designs. They were the work of the Carabelli brothers who took five years modelling them.

The projecting portico, similar to that at Ballyscullion, but reaching only to the height of the first floor, stands at the front of the house. It has a pediment, though an earlier design of Francis Sandys's shows a flat-roofed portico supported on six pillars in front (instead of four as in the final version) and with the curving corridors that join the rotunda with the flanking pavilions connecting with the portico and not projecting from the side of the rotunda as in the final design. These curving enclosed corridors (which at Ballyscullion the Bishop compared to the piazza of St.

Peter's at Rome) again follow the Irish design, though the pavilions were planned to be very much larger and were again intended to house the collections of works of art. Though the rotunda was completed to the level of the roof at the time of the Bishop's death the corridors had only risen a few feet from the ground, while work on the pavilions had barely started. In this sad and desolate state the house stood until the Bishop's son and heir Frederick finally completed it (with various modifications) in 1830.

Ickworth presents a unique and splendid aspect with its extraordinary pillared and domed rotunda, its delicate neo-classical bas-reliefs, and its wide embracing corridors leading to the two pavilions, each the size of a substantial country house. The interior rooms with their lofty ceilings and each with one curving wall, are on the same magnificent scale, nor is there much evidence of their creator's 'oeconomy'. Lord Bristol intended to live in this part, keeping the pavilions as galleries for pictures and sculpture. His son, when completing the house, used the rotunda only for state occasions and confined his living quarters to one of the pavilions, the other remaining a shell.

It is strange to think that the Earl-Bishop never saw this house which is such an expression of his personality and occupied his thoughts ever increasingly during his last years. It would be difficult to find any other house which had been so closely and fastidiously supervised from so great a distance, or that was so intimately associated with the man who never set eyes on it. It is almost impossible to realize, when visiting it, that the Bishop never so much as set foot in a single room. Yet it obsessed him to such an extent that in one letter to his daughter Elizabeth written from Naples (and from his sick-bed) in which the problems of this brainchild keep intruding like a recurring theme of music, the letter ends, after a brief reference to the Neapolitan monarchs, with the strange cry of 'The House – The House – The House.'

It was in this letter, written on 6 March 1796, that he explained his method of hanging pictures to his daughter, with his quaint assessment of Raphael as being among the minor poets of painting. But before this he had something to say about the construction of his new house: 'You beg me on your knees that Ickworth may be built of white stone brick. You know my dear, what Ranger says to his Cousin, and upon my knees I beg you too. What! Child, build my house of a *brick* that looks like a sick, pale, *jaundiced* red brick, that would be red brick if it could, and to which I am certain our posterity will give a little rouge as essential to its health and beauty? White brick always looks as if the bricklayers had not burnt it sufficiently, had been niggardly of the fuel; it looks all dough and no crust. I am even looking out for its crust too, so my dear, I shall follow dear impeccable Palladio's rule, and as nothing ought to be without a covering in our raw damp climate, I shall cover house, pillars, pillasters with Palladio's *stucco* which has now lasted 270 years. It has succeeded perfectly well with me at Downhill on that temple of the winds, as well as at my Casino at Derry – that temple of *Cloacina*. It has resisted the frosts and the rains of Vicenza – *c'est tout dire* – and deceives the most acute eye till within a foot.'[2]

Another friend who was to receive some letters on the subject of the new house was John Symonds, the Cambridge professor who had been a member of those convivial evening parties at the old house shortly after the Bishop had succeeded to the title and estates. Symonds, who lived at Bury St. Emunds, had the advantage of being a close neighbour and so could keep an eye on the work of the young architect and his brother who were endeavouring, in the face of a flood of letters and instructions from Italy or Germany, to interpret the ideas of their exigent but often bewildering patron.

'An old friend claims your opinion of his new house,' the Bishop wrote to Symonds on 16 July 1796, from Pyrmont, 'for altho' he has a very high opinion of it himself, yet your judgement would highly raise it. I wish to make it quite classical, to unite magnificence with convenience and simplicity with Dignity. No redundancy – no superfluity – not one unnecessary room, but the necessary ones to be noble and convenient. To have few pictures, but choice ones, and my Galleries to exhibit an historical progress of the art of Painting both in Germany and Italy – and that divided into its characteristical schools – Venice, Bologna, Florence, etc., etc. The gentleman I present to you is Mr. *Lovell*, my Chaplain . . . no bad artist, and a connoisseur of merit. Accompany him to Ickworth, as he can better explain to you my architectural ideas than even my Architect himself, and I flatter myself they are both Pure and Noble. When that house is finished I hope to make some residence at Ickworth, tho' its vicinity offers nothing but yourself worth cultivating. Adieu, and be certain that neither time nor absence has abated the sentiments of your sincere friend Bristol.'

A few months later, on 5 October, the Bishop wrote again, commenting a little complacently on his architectural plans, and once more outlining his now familiar ideas on how a collection of pictures should be exhibited.

'A thousand thanks, my worthy old friend,' the letter begins, 'for all the attention you are so good as to give to my Architects and architecture. Your opinion has great weight with them and your experience as well as taste fortifies your opinion. In all Europe I have not seen a style of building with which I am enamoured as with my own. It has not a room too much or too little: it has no littleness in any corner nor any disproportion in any part: it will be both cool in summer and warm in winter. . . . The idea I have struck out of showing the historical progress of the art of Painting in all the *five* different schools of Germany and Italy I deem both happy and instructive. Galleries in general are both confused and uninstructive. Mine, by classing the authors under the different schools, will show the characteristick Excellence of each, instruct the young mind and edify the old.

Venice – Coloring, Titian.
Bologna – Composition, Guido.
Roman – Sentiment, Rafael.
Florence – Drawing, M. Angelo.
Naples – Extravagance, Salvator Rosa, Polimea . . . ?

'I have been if possible more fortunate as well as more copious in the German than even the Italian School, having by means of the King of Prussia acquired master pieces of Wohlgemuth, instructor of the Divine Homerican Albert Durer.'

Some eighteen months later (29 March 1798) Symonds is called in to settle a disagreement between the Sandys brothers—'my young Hounds' as the Bishop calls them – who are in dispute over the dimensions of the galleries. 'One brother', he is told, 'deems that a gallery of 115 feet long will drown my mansion and eclipse its splendour – the other *computes* that less than 115 feet in the length of each gallery will not leave sufficient Room in the square of each office yard for Larders, Laundries, etc., etc., suitable to the Mansion and the family that must inhabit them. Who shall decide when *Doctors* disagree – 'tis I, my dear friend, who make you a judge in Israel, therefore

"*Assume the God*
Affect to nod
and Truly *shake their spheres*"

'You on the spot like a true friend examine with your judicious Classical eye the relative proportions of this puzzling animal. Let it be, neither a bustard with wings too small, nor yet an heron with wings too large that drown or eclipse the Body – take if possible Arthur Young with you, that soul of fire, – and be good enough to report to me your deliberate candid advice, by which I order *The Adelphi* hereby to decide. . . .'

This letter gives some conception of the sort of problems Francis Sandys and his brother had to contend with in working for a patron who was so exacting in his requirements and yet who never visited the site where the work was taking place. Everything had to be done, as it were, by remote control. That they contrived, between them, to create a masterpiece of architecture (albeit a unique and curious one) by this difficult method is in itself an achievement of some magnitude. In order to facilitate matters to some extent Joseph Sandys made a complete model of the house in papiermâché on a scale of one inch to twelve feet, and this was sent out to the Bishop in Italy.

So much was still incomplete of the interior arrangements of Ickworth at the time of Lord Bristol's death that we are left guessing about many of the details as he himself would have had them. His pride in the ingenious double spiral staircase at Ballyscullion makes one think that he would have conceived of something similar for the rotunda at Ickworth, but no plans have survived. His heir never completed the staircase design, substituting a plain wooden stairway to the first floor which remained until the present one was built to Sir Reginald Blomfield's designs in 1907. But there is at least a hint that the Earl-Bishop had something very much grander in mind. 'Tell Mr. Sandys,' he wrote from Naples to his archdeacon, 'that I highly approve his drawing for the Iron rails of the staircase, but that in order to save expense I apprehend they ought to be of *Cast Iron* and gilt afterwards. Could they be of Cast Copper they would look infinitely richer, as I have witness in the Royal Staircase at Brussels.'[3]

Of his scheme for the decoration of the rooms we know little for the same reason, though among the works of art looted by the

French from his collection were mosaic pavements as well as marbles and pictures, all, presumably, intended for the embellishment of his new house. The great height of the ceilings of the main apartments arose from the Bishop's curious belief that he was unable to breathe properly in small rooms. His lungs, he was convinced, always played more freely and his spirits spontaneously rose much higher in lofty rooms than in low ones where the atmosphere was tainted with the disagreeable odour of our own bodies.[4] It was for this reason that the ground floor rooms at Ickworth were thirty feet high.

Ickworth was the crowning achievement of Lord Bristol in his role of 'edifying' bishop; it also established the reputation of Francis Sandys, for all that he had to leave his work unfinished when the news of his patron's death reached England in August 1803 and all work on the building was stopped. Sandys later designed the Assembly Rooms at Bury St. Edmunds and various other country houses in Suffolk, as well as in Sussex and Cambridgeshire, and exhibited at the Royal Academy between 1797 and 1809. Whether he lived to see his 'Palace at Ickworth' completed it is impossible to say as the date of his death, like that of his birth, is not known.

2

We left the Bishop in Munich in the summer of 1795 from where he sent Lady Hamilton his unflattering picture of the Comte de Provence busily devouring two capons a day. It was in this city that he embarked on the last, and in many ways the most ludicrous, of those attachments to women very much his junior in years that were such a feature of his life after the final separation from his wife. Though the lady in question could hardly be called young (she was a voluptuous and very experienced woman of forty or so) it must be remembered that Bristol himself would enter his sixty-sixth year that August, and so was a least a quarter of a century her senior.

His new *chère amie* had been born Wilhelmina Encke, was known as Madame Ritz, and would very soon become Countess von Lichtenau. For the past twenty years or more she had been the mistress of King Frederick William II of Prussia who already had two wives and at least one other official mistress, not to mention his more casual liaisons. Madame Ritz had presented her royal lover with two children who were known as Count Alexander and Countess Mariana von der Mark. The name was also used in the French form of de la Marche. The son had died young and at the time of her encounter with the Earl-Bishop in the Bavarian capital only her daughter survived though she appears to have had a son by some other union, perhaps by the mysterious Ritz.

Wilhelmina Encke's career had much in common with that of Emma Hamilton whose acquaintance she was soon to make in Naples. Both had very great beauty and fascination; indeed, it was said of the former that her appeal was such that no man could resist her. Both were of obscure or humble origin. Both had been taken under the protection of men older than themselves who had supervised their upbringing and education. Both professed a great enthusiasm for music and the arts, though while Emma's knowledge in these fields was never more than superficial, Madame Ritz seems to have been a woman of genuine culture and strong intelligence. Both women enjoyed meddling in politics, though here, again, Madame Ritz had the advantage, for she was the mistress of a reigning monarch and could meddle to some purpose. At this period, though her influence over Frederick William was as powerful as ever, their relationship was no longer a passionate one. A bond in this relationship was their daughter Mariana for whom the King had a strong paternal affection.

On the whole it is no very great surprise that so susceptible a man as the Earl-Bishop, who had recently basked in the warmth of Emma's affection, should now fall a slave to the charms of Wilhelmina. Furthermore he enjoyed meddling in politics quite as much, if not even more, than either of the two sirens of Naples and Berlin.

When she met the Bishop in Munich Madame Ritz was on her way south hoping to study the art of Italy and find distraction after the recent experience of an unfortunate love affair. In Berlin she had met a young Irish peer, Lord Templetown, and fallen in love with him. As her own union with Ritz had no legal authority behind it she seriously thought of marrying Templetown, for all that he was fifteen years younger than she was. The King of Prussia, who was both apathetic and tolerant, had been quite unperturbed at the thought of an affair between his friend and the young Irishman, but as soon as a marriage was hinted at he fell into a panic. The thought that Wilhelmina might leave the country for ever was more than he could contemplate or allow. A quarrel between the lovers gave him his opportunity and Templetown was banished from Berlin. The danger thus conveniently removed he graciously allowed the distracted woman to travel to Italy (on the condition that she write to him every day) there to regain her composure and that serenity of mind upon which he so much relied.

Lord Bristol first met her, as it transpires from one of his later letters to her, at a concert in Munich. Madame Ritz had beauty and intelligence, a combination which he always found irresistible in a woman; her well-known connection with the King of Prussia gave the added promise of an interesting field for political intrigue, and her famous charm did the rest. Once again the Bishop had found a subject for those extravagantly phrased outpourings of devotion at which, considering his age and his cloth, he was so unexpectedly adept.

Though there was always a certain amount of play-acting in these relationships he seems, for a while at least, to have been genuinely fond of his '*adorable amie*', as he was soon calling her. But there can be no doubt that, from the very beginning, he was as much attracted by her political influence as by more tender emotions, for at this time he was obsessed by the political ferment of Europe and was constantly sending notes full of military and strategic information, as well as backstairs political gossip, to Sir William Hamilton in Naples.

The Bishop lost no time in suggesting a further meeting. 'Dear friend,' he wrote, 'if the weather is fine tomorrow, make it more so for me by your dear and valuable company on Lake Stanberg. People say that it is all that is most beautiful in the surroundings of Munich and you, who love pictures so much, should not neglect a picture painted by Nature – that painter to whom you owe so many favours, possessing such attractions as to make the head whirl of whomsoever has the audacity to contemplate them. Do not, dear friend, refuse the first favour which I have dared to ask of you and which, indeed, I should hope to have the opportunity to repay . . . and reckon amongst the most devoted of your admirers the Earl of Bristol.'[5]

There was little opportunity at these first meetings for the friendship to develop or for any favours, of whatever sort, to be given or repaid. Madame Ritz was merely passing through Munich on her way to Italy and the Bishop, on the move as always, was in fact heading in the opposite direction. He was bound, by way of Pyrmont and Hanover, for Berlin, the city Madame Ritz had just left after parting from her young Irish lover. But there was time for him to discover her plans in Italy and for him to show how useful he could be to her there; and no doubt Madame Ritz, for her part, prepared the way for the Bishop's favourable reception at the Prussian Court.

As to her response to the more ardent passages in his letter, her parting from Lord Templetown was too recent and too sudden for her to have been in any mood for a new attachment. If she welcomed Lord Bristol's advances it was simply as a distraction, though his own personal charm (which was considerable when he was in a good humour) and his cultivated and amusing conversation obviously appealed to her. No one was better able to make himself agreeable to a charming woman, and this must have been flattering, even to a king's mistress.

There was, however, never at any time anything to suggest that she was in love with him, and less to suggest that they ever became lovers. She certainly esteemed him, until a change in her circumstances showed her how fickle even a bishop can be, but only in the eyes of contemporary gossips were they ever anything more than 'dear friends'. Before leaving Munich on their respective journeys they agreed that they would meet again in Naples.

In Berlin the Bishop was able to do at least one favour for Wilhelmina. In discussing their travels she had told him of her wish to visit Naples where the remains of antiquity no less than more recent treasures of art had a special appeal and interest for her. The Bishop's circle in that city revolved round the Court and the Palazzo Sessa where Sir William and Lady Hamilton had their official residence. For Madame Ritz to join this exclusive circle it would be necessary for her to be presented to Maria Carolina; but here a problem presented itself. The most rigid Spanish etiquette prevailed at the Neapolitan Court and Madame Ritz had no more chance of being presented there than had Lady Hamilton when she still went by the name of Emma Hart. If, on the other hand, the Prussian King could be prevailed upon to issue a patent of nobility in her favour then all difficulties would be brushed away and the dust of an equivocal past conveniently swept under the carpet. Things were still arranged in this way in Berlin and Naples while France was enjoying Year Three of the one and indivisible Republic.

The fat and indolent Frederick William was easily won over. Perhaps he had a twinge of conscience for the manner in which he had settled the affair of Lord Templetown and wished to make amends to his beloved Wilhelmina. Lord Bristol was certainly responsible, in part at least, for the King's act, and it was as Countess von Lichtenau that Madame Ritz in due course made her curtsy to the sister of Marie Antoinette. But if the Bishop had done his *chère amie* a good turn it was to prove of only a temporary effect. The Prussian nobility had put up with Wilhelmina Encke or Madame Ritz without any bother; it was by no means the first time that a mistress had held influence at Court. But when she was raised to the nobility they saw it as an affront to their caste, and it was for this reason as much as any other that she was arrested and thrown into prison at the time of the King's death.

If the Bishop had made his point with the King on the question of their mutual friend's title he saw this as no reason to temper his abrupt manner or to curb his unruly tongue when he was in the royal presence. Earlier in the year Frederick William had signed the Peace of Basle with France, and since then Prussia had occupied the place of a neutral in the war against the Republic which the Earl-Bishop of Derry so cordially detested. He chose to show his repugnance for this treaty at a most inopportune moment when the King was entertaining the Duke of Brunswick at a dinner at which several other German princes were present. Lord Bristol was offered some capon, but refused it. When the King of Prussia asked him if he disliked the dish he answered: 'Yes, Sir: I have an aversion to all neutral animals.'[6]

3

Before he left Berlin the Bishop became alarmed at rumours that the newly created Countess was lingering in Tuscany and the Veneto and not proceeding towards Naples with the speed and energy that characterized his own mode of travel. For a moment the fear assailed him that perhaps she was not going to keep her promised rendezvous with him in Naples after all.

'I learn this morning with great pleasure that your charming person is in Pisa,' he wrote on 2 November, 'but with great displeasure that you are thinking for an instant of breaking faith with me and going to bury yourself in the swamps of Venice instead of enjoying with me the earthly Paradise of Naples with its perpetual Spring and the most beautiful sky that Nature has ever created; where you are awaited with the greatest impatience and where I would have attended upon you most diligently and where we would have spent whole superb days listening to the divine Paesiello, the inimitable Cimarosa and the delectable Hamiltons. Show me this infidelity if you dare and Apollo and all his Muses will second the maledictions that I shall call down upon you for having permitted me a sip of your charming society and then having dashed away the cup. It is as though at dinner you had allowed the little pâtés to be tasted and then sent away the main course. Oh fie! dear lady, that would be truly vile and unworthy of your heart. Do you know that this morning I spent two really delightful hours admiring your superb setting[7] – your elegant bed from which only the sleeper was missing to render it perfect, and above all your magnificent *salon*. Everything there bears the stamp of impeccable taste and there remains nothing to wish for in that fairy palace but the presence of its mistress . . .'.

Lord Bristol himself rushed southwards to Italy in close pursuit of this letter, and by 25 November he was in Bologna. Here he ran into the ubiquitous Lady Webster who not so very long before (according to her own account) had been resisting the amorous advances of his eldest son in Florence. Her feelings towards the Hervey family were not warm, and she particularly disliked the Bishop for his attacks on the character of Charles James Fox, who was the uncle of her friend and future husband Lord Holland. This was the occasion when she described him as 'a clever, bad man', and a few years later she would go even further and call him 'that abominable, wicked old fellow Lord Bristol'.

The Bishop's opinion of Lady Webster has not been recorded, which is perhaps fortunate for her. In later life (as Lady Holland) she was not greatly liked outside her own immediate circle and was a formidable character within it; there was therefore little likelihood of there being much love lost between them. All the more strange, then, that he should ask her for a copy of her portrait. In Bologna they were both staying at the same inn; Lord Bristol, so Lady Webster tells us in her *Journal*, accompanied by some wretched dependants. 'He dines with me one day . . .', she wrote. 'He asked me to let him have a copy of my picture, the one by Fagan, and belonging to my friend Italinski. I hesitated much, and implied, without giving it, a refusal.'[8] There was to be a curious sequel to this episode in Naples.

The picture had been painted in 1793 by the Irish artist Robert Fagan, and though it showed the subject sitting on a terrace with a view of Vesuvius in the background it had in fact been painted in Rome, for the artist did not visit Naples until 1797. No doubt Bristol had seen it in Fagan's studio, for the painter was a friend of Gavin Hamilton and Thomas Jenkinson, the leading figures in the circle of British artists and art dealers in Rome and both well known to the Bishop, and he shared with him an interest in archaeology as well as in paintings. He was later to be responsible for shipping some of Bristol's pictures to Malta with disastrous results, for they were all ruined by being stowed where the salt water could get at them.[9] His picture of Lady Webster is a charming work of art, though the Bishop's interest in it, as we shall see, probably sprang from other reasons.

Bristol reached Naples in December. Wilhelmina had not yet arrived so he set about finding suitable accommodation for her, at the same time dashing off a letter to Rome where his friend still dallied. It is clear that she was by no means so impatient as he was for their reunion; a further indication, in addition to her own emphatic statement in her *Apologie* that she considered it horrible to accuse a man of his age of physical love, that their relationship was never more than platonic. None the less the Bishop found it difficult to contain his eagerness to set eyes on his adorable friend again.

'For heaven's sake, *chère Comtesse et adorable amie*,' he wrote on 29 December, 'do not continue to moulder in the mire of that unhealthy town of Rome, of that city without citizens, those Senators without a Senate, of that sky, half water, half air: but come and enjoy this earthly paradise and increase its charms, its pleasures and its attractions by your presence.' The first place he had inspected on her behalf, he tells her, had no rooms to let – and punning on the words *boudoir* and *boude* assures her that there was not even 'the tiniest boudoir which, in fact, is a very superfluous item for my amiable and well-beloved Countess who is never sullen or pouts at anyone.' He had, however, found her rooms elsewhere in which surroundings he is convinced she will regain her health and gaiety and 'forget a certain damned Irishman (*ce fichu irlandais*) and replace him by a holy Bishop made worthy of your attachment through that which he has for you, and by the unaltered esteem which your virtues and your talents have implanted in the very depth of his all too susceptible heart.' He cannot wait for the moment when he will be able to show her all the sights of Naples, and ends his letter: 'Dear Countess, adieu until that blessed moment; leave as soon as possible – do not delay your happiness and mine.'

The Countess at last arrived in January 1796. The Bishop showed his enthusiasm for her by appearing in society wearing her miniature round his neck on a chain and by addressing her always with the familiar '*tu*'. The miniature added a further note of eccentricity to a costume which was already sufficiently bizarre, for during his latter years in Italy it was his custom to go about dressed in a white hat edged with purple, a coat of crimson silk in summer or of velvet in winter, a black sash spangled with silver, and purple stockings.

Wilhelmina's reputation, not as Countess von Lichtenau but as Madame Ritz, was well enough known in Naples for her association with the Bishop to cause a good deal of scandal. Few people considered their relationship an innocent one and the English community especially (except for the Hamiltons who knew their old friend too well) were very embarrassed to see the astonishingly dressed prelate always in the company of this notorious beauty, though they were ready to acknowledge her charm and good sense.

Sir Walter Scott's friend John Morritt was in Naples at this time and recorded seeing the Countess, whom he describes as 'a left-handed wife and long a favourite Sultana of his present [Prussian] Majesty'. The account he gave of the Bishop and his lady-friend probably reflected very accurately the general opinion in which Lord Bristol was held at this time by those of his fellow countrymen who were not personally known to him or ready to make allowances for his eccentric behaviour.

'We see her frequently,' Morritt wrote of the Countess von Lichtenau, 'and dine there sometimes as she gives very agreeable parties and is, in fact, a very pleasant lively woman, the innamorato people attribute to her is a curious one, viz. Lord Bristol, the Bishop of Derry, aged sixty-two [in fact the Bishop was sixty-five] with whom she is very intimate and travelled part of her tour. Now, as she is young and also rich, I think the affair may admit of doubt; though as to my Lord he is the strangest being ever made, and with all the vices and follies of youth, a drunkard and an Atheist, though a Bishop, constantly talking blasphemy, or indecently at least, and at the same time very clever and with infinite wit – in short, a true Hervey. As he courts every young and every old woman he knows, I suppose like the Irishman who was half married, that in the case of Madame de Ritz he has his own consent.'

The charge of drunkenness, as has already been pointed out, was a most unfair one; but the Bishop's behaviour, from the point of view of any outside observer, did everything to encourage a belief in the most unepiscopal conduct. For a man of his sacred calling ('*un saint évêque*' as he ironically described himself to his Wilhelmina) he managed to convey the impression of living a life that was both profligate and profane. As he did nothing to correct this impression, and a good deal to aid it, it is no surprise to find that it was generally accepted and believed. His association with the Countess, played out to its last grotesque endearment on the very public stage of Naples (a favourite resort of travelling Englishmen at this period) did more than anything else to confirm in the public mind the already widely held belief that Lord Bristol had become nothing more than a godless old reprobate.

January passed in idyllic fashion with the Bishop dancing attendance on his charming friend. She quickly established cordial relations with Emma Hamilton and was given a gracious reception by the Queen. Then suddenly, towards the end of February, tragic news reached the Bishop which completely prostrated him, coming, as it must have seemed to his sterner critics, like divine retribution. He learnt that his eldest son had died at sea. Lord Hervey had not been killed in action but had died, according to the account given out at the time, from the more prosaic cause of going on deck too lightly clad at night and catching a fatal cold.

The news had been received in England on the twelfth of the

month but we do not know just when the sad tidings reached Naples. The letter which the bereaved father sent to inform Lady Hamilton of his loss is simply dated 'Wednesday'. 'My dearest Emma,' he wrote, 'the very unexpected intelligence, which Prince Augustus has most delicately communicated to me, of poor Lord Hervey's *decease*, has quite *bouleversée* my already shattered frame. I would not allow your friendly mind to learn an event so interesting to me from any other hand than that of your affectionate and devoted friend, Bristol.'[10]

The letter suggests that the Bishop had already been unwell before the news reached him, but soon afterwards he was so ill that his own life was for a time despaired of. He lay in bed many weeks, reduced to a shadow, his pulse no more than a thread, 'scarce to be felt' as he told his daughter Elizabeth. From the public in general he received little sympathy; his conduct before his illness had outraged too many people. 'He has been nearly dying, and I am sorry to say is better and likely to recover,' was Morritt's laconic comment when the invalid at length began to improve.

It was during this almost fatal illness that Lord Bristol made his second attempt to borrow the portrait of Lady Webster, which was by then in the possession of Count Italinski, the Russian Agent in Naples. 'As soon as the physician declared him in danger,' Lady Webster wrote in her *Journal*, 'he sent to Italinski for my picture, adding that though he had refused him a copy, he could not deny a dying man anything. Italinski was embarrassed, but sent the picture. As soon as it came he had it placed upon an easel at the foot of his bed, and round it large *cries d'église*, and for aught I know to the contrary he may still be contemplating my phiz. What makes this freak the more strange is, that it is not from regard to me, as he scarcely knows me, and never manifested much liking for me; probably it reminds him of some woman he once loved, and whose image occupies his mind in his last moments.'[11]

People have long been puzzled by the Bishop's curious and seemingly inexplicable desire to gaze at this picture or to possess a copy of it. It was a natural deduction, considering his reputation for philandering, to assume that the picture recalled the image of some former lover to the sick man's mind. But in fact it is probable that a much more natural and commendable emotion was inspired by Fagan's portrait of Lady Webster. If the picture is compared with Tischbein's portrait of the Bishop's daughter Elizabeth, painted in 1778 when she was twenty years old (Lady Webster was twenty-two when she sat to Fagan), it will be seen that the two faces bear a striking resemblance to each other. That this daughter was in his mind at the time we know from the long rambling letter he wrote to her from his sick-bed on the subject of 'The House' while still far from recovery.

If it was indeed his daughter's likeness that he saw reflected in the features of the sitter, then there is something infinitely touching in the thought of the Bishop placing the portrait at the foot of his bed and surrounding it with wax tapers. Of course, Lady Webster's own theory cannot be ruled out, but the suggestion that it was simply the aesthetic beauty of Fagan's picture that inspired his request seems unlikely.[12] Bristol had a large collection of works of art with him in Naples, many by great masters. He might well have wished to include Fagan's picture, or a copy of it, in his collection; but he would hardly have made a request – almost a demand – to see it when he was virtually *in articulo mortis* on mere grounds of connoisseurship. Whatever the reasons may have been for his placing Lady Webster's portrait on an easel at the foot of his bed they were certainly personal ones.

Lord Bristol recovered in due course and the picture was returned to Italinski. If he took the opportunity to have it copied no such copy has survived. He made no further reference to it and never asked to see it again. The death of his son, which came as such an unexpected blow, turned his mind once more to his family and, it is possible to think, to the picture which so closely resembled his younger daughter. As to his younger son, now his heir, as convalescence proceeded towards complete recovery a luminous idea occurred to the Bishop with regard to the new Lord Hervey's matrimonial prospects which was to possess his mind for the next year or so to the great embarrassment of the young man in question.

4

It will be recalled that the Countess von Lichtenau had a daughter by the King of Prussia who went by the name of Mariana von der

Mark. This girl, now seventeen years of age, was blessed with three advantages that easily offset the unfortunate accident of illegitimate birth; she had youth, great beauty, and considerable wealth. She was, furthermore, a favourite with her royal father who was said to love her above all his other children, even those born in lawful wedlock. It now occurred to the Bishop that she would make an excellent match for his son Frederick, heir to the family honours and still unmarried.

Lord Bristol, in spite of his Whig beliefs, was clearly dazzled at the prospect of a union with the royal House of Prussia, albeit on the wrong side of the blanket, and he began to indulge in extravagant dreams of the advantages which would accrue to his own family from so splendid an alliance. The Countess, for her part, saw equal benefits for her daughter in a connection with the family of the obviously very wealthy and influential Earl-Bishop, whom she probably regarded as having a position in Great Britain not dissimilar from that occupied by a Prince-Bishop in Germany.

She joined enthusiastically in the scheme, and as her period of leave from the Prussian Court was drawing to a close began, before Easter, a leisurely journey north, intending when she eventually reached Berlin to secure Frederick William's approval and support for their plan. She left a convalescent and inconsolable Bishop behind her in Naples. 'The good and kindly Lord Bristol is in despair without you,' Emma Hamilton wrote to her after she left, 'and awaits you with the same ardent desire as the Jews the Messiah.'

It was in fact that good and kindly nobleman's intention to follow in pursuit and join up with the Countess in Rome. 'Be sure, my dear Wilhelmina,' he wrote to her on 9 April, 'that the first use I shall make of my regained strength will be to go to Rome. Tomorrow I am going to make a first sortie by paying a short visit to Paestum. We return on Saturday and the following Tuesday, cost what it may, I shall hasten to Rome. When the Mountain refused to go to Mahomet the good prophet went off to the Mountain, which would not budge. . . .' He was, however, being too optimistic about the rate of his recovery, and it was at least a month before he was well enough to leave Naples.

When he reached Rome in May the Countess had already left. She had received disturbing news of the King of Prussia's state of health and decided to continue her journey back to Germany without waiting for the Bishop. As for Lord Bristol, before continuing northwards himself he took the opportunity to commission a couple more pictures. One was to be by the English artist Philip Reinagle, the other by the Antwerp-born Simon Denis. He wrote to Sir William Hamilton asking for passports for 'these two superlative artists' to go to Sora in the Kingdom of Naples. 'Lose no time, I entreat you', he urged Sir William, 'as time is precious, and I expect two of the very finest pictures ever painted.'[13]

Enthusiasm, rather than aesthetic taste, presumably inspired this opinion; for though both artists were admirable painters, the Englishman later specializing in hunting scenes, neither could exactly be compared with the great contemporary masters or be expected to produce anything more than competent and pleasing compositions. It shows, at least, that neither age nor illness had diminished his passion for art, and that the artists of Rome still had every reason to be glad at finding their eccentric patron in the city once again.

The Bishop did not remain long in Rome. On 26 May, shortly after his arrival, he sent another long letter to the Countess on the subject of their plan in which he included a flattering description of his son, the same young man whom he had denounced as ungrateful and undutiful in the will he had made little more than two years before: 'The prolongation of my convalescene, dear friend, has given me time carefully to weigh our plan; the more I think, the more I dream of it, the better I augur of it. He is to come to meet us at Pyrmont – and I have no hesitation in saying that you will be captivated and really enchanted by him. He is a perfect man of the world – versed in literature, conversant with politics; a handsome countenance, beautiful features, a striking face – natural eloquence – charming manner, English modesty and reserve; with a pride worthy of his father and forebears.

'In the meantime, I should like you to write from Venice to Graft, the Dresden painter, telling him to go at once to Berlin and there paint a full-length portrait of your daughter. Let her be standing, wearing a perfect informal dress and above all nothing on her head – let her elbow be leaning on a very beautiful chimney-piece as if she were speaking to someone. In that way we shall have her expression, her face, her figure, her carriage and all that is necessary for considering her at leisure. You will then be good enough to have this portrait conveyed from Berlin to Pyrmont from whence, having waged our campaign, we could if you agree, all at leasure return to Berlin chez-vous.

'How rapidly our friendship has grown since the concert in Munich! Everything has been in unison – true harmony ever since – *chère amie*, farewell.'

In arranging for his son to meet them in Pyrmont the Bishop had exposed the weak spot in the plot he had woven so dexterously. It had never occurred to him that Frederick Hervey might not wish to marry the Countess Mariana; that he might even have plans of his own about whom he should make his wife. If Lord Bristol thought such a thing possible then he must have imagined that the advantages of his own scheme would quickly change his son's mind and bring him to a satisfactory state of filial obedience. Here he underrated the strength of Frederick's character. In point of fact the young man had for some time been in love with Elizabeth Upton and had no intention of marrying anyone else. And here fate added a strange touch of irony to the whole enterprise, for Miss Upton was the younger sister of Lord Templetown, the *fichu irlandais* who had captured the heart of the former Madame Ritz in Berlin.

Of course it was some time before Lord Bristol became aware of his son's opposition, and even longer before he abandoned all hope of securing Mariana von der Mark as his daughter-in-law. Every pressure would be put on Frederick in order to make him change his mind, and the Bishop only gave up in defeat when it became clear that Frederick would marry no one else.

Meanwhile Bristol made his way towards Germany in happy ignorance of Miss Upton. Constant letters and notes were dispatched to his dear Wilhelmina. He left Rome early in June; at Civita Castellana he stayed at the same inn the Countess had occupied some time before and found her 'dear precious name' traced with her own hand on the chimney-piece in his room. This sent him into ecstasies. He mentions a whole list of presents he has sent to her house in Berlin and asks in return if she will give him a watch of her own choice: 'I have not worn one for ten years, having given mine successively to children and grandchildren and having the curious fancy not to give myself such baubles! but from your hand how dear it would be to me. . . .' In another letter he informs her that the wind is in the north and at each step he tells himself that perhaps the gust comes from her – 'has passed over her rosy lips, has mingled with her zephyr breath, and I shall believe that I am inhlaing at least a few atoms of the breath of my dear Wilhelmina.'

The journey was not wholly passed on this romantic note. In July, finding himself in an area of military activity, he was able to have some talk with General Count Wurmser, the commander of the Austrian troops in Italy, who in the following month was to find himself face to face with General Napoleon Bonaparte at Castiglione delle Stiviere and suffer a severe defeat. An account of this conversation was at once sent off to Sir William Hamilton.

'I have had a long conference with that spirited, active, zealous Marshall Wurmser,' the Bishop wrote. 'He entreated me to press you to make the Neapolitan troops penetrate into the Romagna as far as Ferrara – that the fate of Italy depended on it – that if they did but shew themselves he would profit from it to attack the French, who could not possibly face both armies, that he would cut off their retreat by Milan and Tortona, whilst the King of Naples might harass them at Bologna and Ferrara, and make 'em disgorge all their plunder. That if the Neapolitan troops do not advance, the French may possibly pour in more troops than he can resist, and the event must be very uncertain, but terribly bloody; in short, that Italy depends on it. Your impression, dear Sir Wm., must be on the Queen, no other has a soul, no, not me.'[14]

To this 'curious but true' report, as Sir William called it, there was no response from the Neapolitan Court, where indifference, undue optimism, or sheer panic seemed in turn to govern the councils of the irresolute King and the determined but often misguided Queen.

When the Bishop reached Pyrmont in August he found an eager trio waiting for him in the person of Countess von Lichtenau, the King of Prussia, and their daughter Mariana. Frederick William was in a deplorable state of health, dropsical, lethargic, and immensely corpulent, but ready and willing to signify his consent to his daughter's marriage. Frederick Hervey alone had made no appearance in answer to his father's summons, nor did he offer any hope of doing so.

Faced with this unfilial revolt the Bishop wrote to his daughter Elizabeth Foster whom it would seem had acted as an intermediary and broken to her father the unwelcome news of Miss Upton's prior claim on her brother's heart. The letter shows for the first time the extent of Lord Bristol's ambitions, both for himself and for his son, as a result of this much desired union.

'Dearest Elizabeth,' he wrote, 'though I would not for the world itself disappoint your poor Brother's hopes, if his noble generous heart be really engaged, nor even diminish of one obole the allowance I should be able to make him, which is exactly the same I gave your poor dear eldest brother, yet I must confess it would half break my heart to see his fixed on any other than the beautiful, elegant, important and interesting object I have proposed to him. At least, dearest Eliza, if you have any interest with him, induce him, beg him, my dear, not to decide before he is able to choose. She would bring him into our family £5,000 a year, *besides* a principality in Germany, an English Dukedom for Frederick or me, which the King of Prussia is determined to obtain in case the marriage takes place – a perpetual relationship with both the Princess of Wales and her children, as also with the Duchess of York and her progeny – the Embassy to Berlin, with such an influence and preponderance in favor of dear England as no other could withstand. Add to all this the King is so bent upon it from his great partiality to me, that I doubt not his doubling the dot in case F desired it, which indeed I should not. . . . In short, nothing could be more brilliant, or flattering, or more cordial than his reception in case he can think with us; and indeed, Dearest Elizabeth, the example he has before his eyes in and within his own family ought fully to determine him against a love-match; 'tis so ominous a lottery, so pregnant with blanks, so improbable of success. . . . All I desire of him is not to resolve against us, not to throw away a Pearl, richer than all his tribe; let him but see before he decides, let him weigh all we offer to his ambition, his ease, his comfort, his taste, and his pocket.'

It is curious to find a bishop pressing a marriage upon his unwilling son and urging at least three of the seven deadly sins as reasons in its favour, not to mention the argument he deploys (telling as it was with regard to his own family) against marrying for love.

Another letter followed comparing the relative merits of the two young ladies. The Countess Mariana he declared to be the prettiest, sweetest, most delicate and innocent as well as accomplished little woman he had ever seen (not to mention her being endowed with £100,000 down), while *She*, which is as near as he can bring himself to naming poor Miss Upton: '*She* has little or no fortune – your brother by the last act of settlement can make no provision for either her or her children and if he should die within five or six years – which the perturbed state of his mind might easily produce – what must be the consequence to his widow and her orphans? Once married and the first heat of passion allayed, what must be the state of an anxious debilitated mind?'

The Bishop appears to have convinced himself that if illness has not actually caused his son's unfortunate predilection for Elizabeth Upton, then the most dire illness will certainly be the result of it; an illness rising from 'black and melancholy ideas' for which, he is quite sure, 'medicine would be the more ineffectual as the malady would be in the mind'. He begs his daughter to persuade Frederick to come out to Pyrmont and to accompany him herself. The King of Prussia has personally written to the Directory at Paris asking for passports to be issued for Lord Hervey and his party.

This plea, together with one to Frederick, received no answer. On 16 August, his patience exhausted, the Bishop wrote angrily to his daughter calling her a nasty little imp of silence. 'What are you doing that one can hear no more about you than if one did not care for you, and yet who do I care for more?' he asks. 'I wrote your brother that he might bring your ugly face with him, and we would all go to Naples, where I have, without exception, the handsomest and best-situated house there; fourteen rooms on each floor all hung with Rafaels, Titians, and what not . . .' and off he goes again about the marriage he has planned: 'Oh! if I can accomplish my heart and soul's desire to join your dear brother's hand with la Comtesse de la Marche – £5,000 a year down, £5,000 more in reversion, an English Dukedom, probably Embassy to Berlin – *per Dio che Piacere*. . . .'

When there was still no answer anger (or mock anger) gave way to sheer bewilderment. 'Are you alive or dead?' he wrote on the twenty-seventh, 'or are you on a journey? or peradventure she sleepeth? If so, at least dream a little, or walk in your sleep, or talk in your sleep, for I have no patience with your long, very long, silence. . . .' Poor Elizabeth Foster must have been embarrassed by these letters, knowing her brother's determination to marry according to his own choice. She was quite unable to encourage her father's ambitious plans and perhaps sought refuge in silence.

When she did reply still more letters reached her setting out the advantages to be gained from a marriage with the young Countess; tables were drawn up comparing the two alliances much to the detriment of poor Miss Upton: 'No fortune' and 'wife and children beggars for want of settlement' compared with the showers of money, dukedoms and royal connections which the other alternative offered.

In September the offensive was renewed. 'And now, my dear child, for poor dear Frederick's affair,' he wrote to his daughter on the eleventh after first discussing her own concerns, 'and it amazes myself when I recollect the object the nearest to my heart for these last twelve or fourteen years – I thought I could be content to vegetate for the remainder of my *green old age* among painters and sculptors, masons and bricklayers, and was not aware of the very deep interest this warm, sensible heart of mine was likely to take in any project whatever; but I own to you the idea of fixing a son of your brother's superior and pre-eminent qualities, both moral and intellectual, in a station worthy of him and of us all, has kindled anew the almost extinguished sparks, the very embers of my expiring and effete ambition.'

So it went on until December, by which time even the Bishop began to show signs of exhaustion. It was a pity that he could never bring himself to see Elizabeth Upton as being quite so worthy of his son's high qualities (which he was generally, if not always, ready to admit) as was the young German Countess who, in a revealing moment, he once described as 'a real Cornucopia'. The great prize slipped through his fingers. Even before his own son finally married Miss Upton (which he did in February 1798) Lord Bristol had the mortification of seeing the rich and beautiful Mariana von der Mark married to another Frederick when in the spring of 1797 she became the wife of Count Frederick von Stolberg.

5

While carrying on these abortive matrimonial negotiations the Bishop had not forgotten the war which was being waged on so many fronts. 'Nothing can equal the déroute of the damned

Blackguard, pilfering, plundering, pillaging Republicans,' Elizabeth Foster was informed on 14 September 1796. 'Neither Minden nor Rosbach can compare with it; all their Artillery, all their baggage, all their waggons loaded with contributions, all taken. We have here two Officers and the son of our apothecary just arrived from Frankfort, who not only confirm all this, who were ocular witnesses to these ourang-cutangs running like themselves without shoes, stockings, or breeches, and the exasperated peasants knocking them down, like real monkies, their prototypes, with bludgeons, pitchforks, staves, all that came to hand – "*furor arma ministrat*" – 12,000 dead on the road or the field, 900 waggons loaded with wounded, that is 9,000 wounded and the Austrians in Frankfort before the rear-guard left it.'

These heartening accounts of the military successes of the Archduke Charles helped to restore the Bishop's spirits after his own reverses in his private campaign on behalf of the Countess von der Mark. Indeed, to many people other than the Bishop the defeat of Moreau and Jourdan seemed like a turning point in the war. At the end of September he visited Frankfurt and Cassel to form his own impressions on the spot. The Archduke and the Prince of Orange he found 'idolized by their armies and amply supported by their courage'. He was full of statistics of killed and wounded and declared with elation that 'if the Austrians can carry the fort of Kehl, Strasburg, entirely commanded by it, must fall, and then France will begin to feel the iron hand of Austria.'

From Cassel Lord Bristol dispatched another account to his daughter Elizabeth which was to see some of these hopes fulfilled. 'I am now returning to Pyrmont from my military expedition, for you know, child, we have Church militant as well as Church visible – Low Church and High Church,' he wrote on 30 September. 'The *affaire* at Alten Kirchen near Dittembourg which is near Marbourg was *bien sanglante*. The Ourang-Outangs or Tyger monkeys lost the few breeches they had. That modern hero, Prince Frederick of Orange (observe, my dear, all the great men of this country are Fredericks) this hero, who united the phlegm of Hannibal with the activity of Scipio, cut them to pieces like a sailor's biscuit. They have recrossed the Rhine, and evacuated Dusseldorf. On the Upper Rhine the bravery of the Austrian soldiers had taken Fort Kehl, which commands Strasburg; and the stupidity, indiscipline, and rapacity of the natives lost it.

They were plundering the stores when they ought to have been raising the drawbridge – *quelles bêtes* – Landau is known to have only 600 men and boys in it. The Arch Duke marched with 13,000 men to take it, and here ends my budget and letter, and so adieu dearest Eliza.'

As a commentator on these warlike scenes the Bishop was a lively correspondent. When it came to solving the problems of peace he was no less vivacious, and allowed his mind a wide sweep in reorganizing the frontiers of Europe to his taste. He liked to put forward plans, sometimes fantastic but rarely dull, as to how things should be arranged in a final peace treaty, the whole object of which, in his view, should be to weaken as much as possible the power of France, whether royalist or republican.

An example of the Bishop in this Olympian frame of mind, calmly setting the world to rights, was sent to this same daughter from Dresden later in the year. The letter is dated 28 December 1796.

'My idea', he begins grandly, 'is to annihilate *Holland* as a blackguard, mean, low, shabby, rival power, and sink her, as she was formerly, into the 17 provinces of Braband, etc., etc., then give them altogether to Bavaria, and the Palatinate to the old Elector, an ignorant enthusiast, and a Papist whose nonsense, as Bishop Burnet says, suits their nonsense. Brabant will at length have a Resident Sovereign. The Palatinate east of the Rhine I would give to a young branch of our Royal family as being Protestant; but west of the Rhine, and including all the iniquitous, profligate, debauched bishopricks, and their infamous chapters, I would cede to the Republick on condition, and for this condition I would spend the last drop of blood and money, that they cede all the Provinces south of the Loire to Louis XVIII. Here is France as a maritime and commercial nation sunk for ever; the two governments eternally at war together, and doing the business for England; but if France is to remain entire – Oh! judge of her future energy by her past, and dread the fatal moment when that restless people, having recruited her strength, pour all upon England: at all events, dear Elizabeth, I hope your *torpid* friends, for such I must call them, will not forget to secularize the two very lucrative but tyrannical bishopricks of Paderborn and Hildesheim in favour of two younger sons of our Royal family. The Bishops expect it, the people pray for it, and all Westphalia applaud it.

Perhaps that *log* Lord Grenville does not know that they exist nor has ever heard of the secularization of the opulent bishoprick of Magdeburg in favour of the house of Brandenburg after the 30 years [war], for, by all accounts from my diplomatic friends, a more ignorant blockhead does not exist. . . . The act of secularization depends entirely on the Emperor, who can refuse England nothing. The Chancellor of Hanover assured me that, to his knowledge, that corrupt, abandoned scoundrel, Lord Bute, had the offer of a secularization in 1762, but refused it. 'Tis supposed he pocketed £20,000 for this infamous refusal, and the younger sons in the consequence remain a burden to England. Oh! if your brother were now Minister at Berlin what a blow he might strike! . . .'[15]

It would be a mistake to take this panacea too seriously, and it could be argued that Bristol's very idiosyncratic plan was weighed altogether too heavily in favour of Great Britain, with its aim of 'sinking' the commercial rivalry of Holland and setting up tiny principalities with little object beyond relieving the British taxpayer from the burden of providing for the younger sons of the royal family. This narrowly nationalistic view comes as a surprise from a man of the Bishop's cosmopolitan outlook.

Also his idea of containing the belligerency of France by dividing that nation in half and creating a permanent rivalry between the two portions was hardly a realistic solution of the problem; though in apportioning the northern part to the Republic it shows that he realized, despite his distaste for the 'monkies' and 'ourang-outangs,' that the republican principles had taken root and could not be disposed of by the simple expedient of placing a Bourbon back on the throne. The only really practical idea he had to offer was the suggestion of an independent Brabant under a resident sovereign, an idea that would be accepted by the powers only some thirty-five years later when the independence of Belgium was recognized.

In addressing these views on foreign affairs, not to mention his unflattering opinion of Lord Grenville, the Foreign Secretary, to his daughter Elizabeth he had, of course, his eye on a wider and more influential audience; for his daughter was now very firmly established at the centre of the Devonshire House set whose influence in Whig affairs was powerful and far-reaching. Indeed, the *ménage à trois* which existed between Lady Elizabeth Foster and the Duke and Duchess of Devonshire was in its own way no less extraordinary and notorious than was her father's much publicized liaison with the Countess von Lichtenau.

6

Before leaving for Berlin and Potsdam in October the Bishop sent a letter to the Countess (who was already in the Prussian capital) which suggests that there had been some slight disagreement between them. 'See, *chère et très chère amie*,' he wrote, 'how I devote myself to you! Then do not reproach me with infidelities that I do not commit, that I shall never commit, neither from taste nor out of inclination or caprice, nor seduced by other charms.' Though his heart was wholly devoted to her she must not think that she had exclusive rights over it. 'I grant you willingly dominion over all my feelings but it is necessary that I should have regard to others – you have, for example, no rights over my charities nor benevolence – none over my friendly hospitality nor any authority over my gratitude. My heart is a large – I dare call it – a vast castle, whose main building is entirely yours and yours only! each apartment furnished with your name and your charming face adorned with your tender and worthy expression. But, dear friend, in the apartments of this castle I have the right to lodge men and women who love me . . . it is the guest-house of a convent where the lame, the deaf and the blind may find shelter.' To soften this rebuke he tells her of all he has been doing at Pyrmont against her return; laying a gravel path for her afternoon walk, making a wide carriage road for her to drive with the King and her daughter, and he hints at the prospect of buying a property for her in England.

While *en route* for Berlin news reached the Bishop that the King of Prussia had been taken seriously ill again. Any misunderstanding that might have existed between himself and the Countess was quickly brushed aside by the thought that his dear Wilhelmina might not find herself properly provided for in the event of the King's death. From Hanover, where he heard the bad news, he sent her a dramatic and, it must be assumed, sincere offer of help should an emergency occur.

'Dear, adorable friend,' he wrote on 22 October, 'the rumour of our dear, amiable and honoured King being abed and in extremis affects me deeply. I tremble, I shudder. What a privation for you should an accident happen – you, so accustomed to all the pleasures worthy of your elegant mind and great heart. What privation for you, dear, too disinterested friend! In any case I offer you my house in England, and all my houses in Ireland. Willingly will I share my purse with the friend who monopolises my heart and all my affections.' His house at Naples is also placed at the disposal of the King, for in Bristol's opinion only the '*l'atmosphère vernal de Naples*' can be hoped to effect a cure.

Meanwhile, though he comes to Berlin solely to bring her the consolations of a friend, he assures the Countess that during the crisis of the King's illness he will stay at an inn and not at her house so as not to add to her burdens. The King, however, must have made a considerable recovery before the Bishop reached Potsdam for there is no mention of his illness, nor indeed of Frederick Hervey's marriage, in the letter dashed off to Lady Elizabeth Foster from the palace of Sans Souci.

'At last on the 30th October – Sunday noon – here I am, truly worthy of this Philosophic Mansion – without care and almost without thought, so consummately am I Germanised,' he wrote enthusiastically, 'nothing, no nothing, not even the plains of Thetford or of Brandon can equal the aridness of this situation, nor even the Terrace of Weybridge surpass the beauty and luxuriance of the prospect. Hesperian gardens surround the house: grapes worthy of our best hothouses, pine apples as plenty as crabs in Devonshire or apples in Herefordshire. We can eat 12,000 in a year, and every week at Pyrmont we receive a dozen or more. Then for game the Basscourt at Chatsworth does not supply more fowl, ducks, geese and capon than we have – but alas! Tomorrow we enter the eve of November, and I have those accumulated Purgatories the Alps to pass before I can enter that earthly paradise Naples. . . .'

The Bishop remained just under a month in Berlin. It was a period of great diplomatic activity at the Prussian Court and Bristol, with his usual love of intrigue, meddled as much as he could between the King and the British envoy who was trying to bring Prussia back into the struggle against France. He was also, so the Countess assures us in her *Apologie*, in constant correspondence with Pitt at this time.

His handling of Frederick William, whose guest he was at Potsdam, seems to have been very far from tactful. According to a certain Colonel Dampmartin, a French *emigré* who had acted as tutor to the Countess's children, the Bishop told the King flatly that if he did not make provision against Wilhelmina being one day exposed to want and dependence then he would himself give her a very pretty castle and property worth £2,000 a year in rents. Audacious as this seems it was quite in character with the Bishop's way of doing things and tallies with what he had promised the Countess in his letter from Hanover. If Dampmartin's account is to be believed the threat resulted in Frederick William lavishing gifts of land and money on his mistress though he was hurt and annoyed at the Bishop's officious interference in his affairs.[16]

Even his mode of taking leave of the King was singularly lacking in graciousness. 'Sire,' he said, 'I am returning to dear Naples where the moon has more warmth than the sun at Berlin.' It is not surprising to learn that the King was beginning to get a little tired of Lord Bristol's company and saw him depart without much regret; none the less he presented his guest with a magnificent breakfast service in Dresden china decorated with medallion portraits of the Prussian sovereigns.

This extraordinary trio were to meet once again in Pyrmont in the following July. There was no longer any talk of family alliances, for Mariana von der Mark had already become Countess von Stolberg, though Frederick's marriage to Elizabeth Upton did not take place for another six or seven months.

The King's health had by now seriously deteriorated. The Bishop described him to Sir William Hamilton as being 'shatter'd to the very foundation, wasted to a skeleton and his long body and powerful frame bent almost double, looked like the bow of Ulysses'. The excellent air of Pyrmont, in which Lord Bristol had so much faith, brought on a temporary improvement: 'In a few days he grew erect, yet *stiff* everywhere but where he *should* be; his appetite returned, his sleep restored seems to announce good stamina and a full resurrection; his physician, however, was not deluded by what misguided common by-standers and declared . . . that the temporary dispersion of clouds did not insure fine and lasting weather. In fact some days after a silly excess at board, for at bed he could not trespass if he would, threw him back again, and he is now fruitlessly working up his lee-way.'[17]

Frederick William II survived only another four months; he died on 4 November after his return to Potsdam. It was then that the unfortunate Madame Ritz had to pay the price for becoming Countess von Lichtenau, a dignity which Lord Bristol had done so much in helping to secure for her. She was arrested and thrown into prison. The Bishop's comment on this event when the news reached him in Trieste was callous almost beyond belief. Writing again to Sir William Hamilton he simply states: 'Poor Madame de Ritz is in Spandau after playing the fool and some say the knave these last eleven months; she was arrested the day after the death of that old Porc d'Epicure.'[18] So much for the adorable friend and the dear, amiable King!'

The reason for Bristol's cold and unfeeling comment was that the Countess had been accused, among other crimes, of taking bribes from the French. He had reasons, satisfactory at least to himself, for believing the accusation to be true, and so turned violently against her. He does not seem to have considered the fact that she was also accused of the quite opposite offence of intriguing with himself on behalf of Great Britain. Though the Countess was liberated and her character cleared three years before his death, the Bishop made no attempt to see her again, nor did he put in any plea for the mitigation of her sentence. Poor Wilhelmina had to learn that there was another side to the personality of the charming and affable Earl-Bishop, and that it was both self-centred and heartless.

VII

The End of the Journey

I

When Bristol set off from Berlin in November 1796 his intention was to head once more in the direction of 'dear Naples' and its warm, welcoming sunshine. In fact he would not see that famous bay again until the winter of 1799.

In the meantime he would travel from place to place more restlessly than ever. Between December 1796 and April 1798 we find him in Dresden and Munich, then across the Alps to Venice and Trieste; back again over the mountains to Germany for Pyrmont and his last meeting with the Countess von Lichtenau and the King of Prussia; over the Alps once more to Trieste, then on to Padua and Turin, back to Venice and so on to Milan; three separate negotiations on horseback of the Alpine passes in a period of sixteen months when he was between sixty-seven and sixty-eight years of age and constantly complaining of ill-health. No wonder that he referred to these steep and dangerous passes as 'those accumulated Purgatories'.

His cavalcade jogged along the dusty or muddy roads with the Bishop and his attendants on horseback. His vast travelling carriage was so lumbered with all the baggage necessary for such an endless peregrination that one observer described it as looking like the cart of a quack-doctor. His cook rode on in advance so as to have a splendid meal all prepared and ready each evening for a master who declared that he arrived with the appetite of a curate but expected to find a dinner fit for a bishop.

It was now some five years since he had last set foot in his diocese and there was little to indicate that he had much intention of returning to it at any foreseeable date. The scandal of his long absence caused deep concern among the clergy, though some of the more ambitious were heartened from time to time by reports of illnesses that hinted at an imminent vacancy in Ireland's wealthiest See. About this time three of his brother bishops took it upon themselves to remonstrate with him over his refusal to reside in his diocese, a derelection of duty which they considered unwarrantable. To this rebuke the Bishop replied in his own peculiar way; he put three peas in a bladder and sent it to the Archbishop of Armagh together with two lines of doggerel in his own handwriting signed 'Bristol and Derry'. The lines read:

Three large blue-bottles sat upon three blown bladders;
Blow, bottle-flies, blow. Burst, blown bladders, burst.[1]

There is no doubt that his eccentricities became more pronounced as he grew older. One of the most extraordinary and inexplicable examples of this took place in Siena, at a time when other parts of Northern Italy were in the hands of the French revolutionary armies.

The episode took place during the Corpus Christi celebrations and was recorded by the traveller Pryse Lockhart Gordon. 'In one of his journies from Rome to Florence,' Gordon wrote in his memoirs, 'he halted at Siena, and when sitting down to dinner, the procession of the Host happened to pass under the window of his hotel. It would appear that his Lordship had a particular aversion to the tinkling of bells. Probably without thinking of the consequences, he seized a tureen of *pasta*, and the sash being open, threw the contents in the midst of the holy group! Such a sacrilegious profanation of the most sacred of ceremonies, I need hardly observe, occasioned the greatest dismay among the priests and their assistants, as well as the spectators, who assailed the house *en masse*, determined to wreak vengeance on the perpetrators of so monstrous an outrage. The bishop, however, had fortunately made his escape by a back way along with his valet, and by an ample distribution of his gold found the means of concealing himself until night, and of procuring post-horses to transport him from the Tuscan territories, never stopping until he reached Padua, at that time garrisoned by French troops.'[2]

Gordon assures us that he was told this story by the British Minister at Florence who knew Lord Bristol well. The Bishop claimed that he had no idea that the procession of the Blessed Sacrament was passing the window when he threw the pasta out, though to anyone who has witnessed a similar religious occasion in Italy such unawareness would seem most unlikely if not impossible; but even so, to hurl a tureen of hot spaghetti out of a window, whether anyone were passing by or not, was hardly the sort of behaviour to be expected from a distinguished nobleman and prelate. The Bishop's temper, like his sense of humour, could be very unpredictable, and it was probably a sudden outburst of rage rather than a premeditated act of discourtesy to a religion he had always respected that caused this very rash and impetuous action.

Another episode, though it happened later in his life, shows that the Bishop's more cruel or thoughtless sallies of wit did not always escape from retaliation. He had never cared much if he hurt the feelings or outraged the susceptibilities of his victims, and towards the end of his life he became less aware than ever of the effects produced by his free-and-easy sort of talk in the serious-minded and somewhat self-righteous atmosphere that prevailed in society during the revolutionary period at the end of century.

The incident was trivial enough but was indicative of the changing times. About 1800 Bristol had taken a young German artist, a patriot in the new spirit of the age, under his protection as a patron of the arts. They walked, rode, and passed the hours pleasantly enough together, and the artist dined at the Bishop's table. Upon one occasion when there was some company present one of the guests asked the young man what country he came from, but using the popular phrase of the day, enquired after his fatherland. Bristol, who had already described his young friend in his usual exaggerating way, and much to the latter's embarrassment, as a universal genius, an arch-cosmopolitan and a Jacobin, now answered for him: 'He was, and is, a man who has no fatherland. He is at home everywhere.'

The artist could not perceive that the Bishop intended a compliment in describing him as a cosmopolitan. He was deeply hurt in his patriotic pride and replied gravely that he had indeed a fatherland of which he was not ashamed and which he trusted was not ashamed of him: he was a Prussian. 'Prussian,' the Bishop answered, 'it's all the same to me if you are a Russian!' Upon this the artist rose from the table and left the room.

The next day the Bishop received a letter informing him that if he had been thirty years younger his guest of the previous evening would have demanded satisfaction; as it was he had earned nothing but his contempt. This letter, we are told, made its recipient hold his sides with laughter. But a malicious caricature by the same hand which was soon doing the rounds of Rome in which Lord Bristol appears to have been depicted as a 'long stretched-out pig' was not quite so easy to laugh off. There was, however, something to be said for being a cosmopolitan, or at least a man of the world, for when taxed with this crude caricature of himself the Bishop replied: 'He has revenged himself like a man of genius.'[3]

The world was indeed changing and the Bishop had found himself confronted by a new spirit. The old, leisured, enlightened (within its own narrow limits) yet privileged and exclusive society in which he had moved for so long was now fast disappearing from the scene. To be cosmopolitan was no longer the fashion. In its place was a new order, brash, arrogant, fiercely nationalistic, and narrowly doctrinaire. To the young political puritans nothing could be more irritating than Bristol's easy-going disregard of their idealistic ideas or his gibing use of the term Jacobin (which in fact he used with great inaccuracy). To these men bred in the spirit of the French Revolution, who looked forward to the nineteenth century as an age of progress, it was difficult to understand this old prelate who had known Voltaire and who responded to their new ideas with an irreverent and infuriating mockery.

It was not the least of the Bishop's eccentricities that he should think of going to Egypt, yet this scheme was one of his main preoccupations in the early months of 1797 and for a year or so afterwards.

The idea (this was before his break with the Countess von Lichtenau) was that his 'adorable friend' should leave the King of Prussia safely in Naples to recover his health and then join the Bishop on his expedition to Cairo and the valley of the Nile. He planned to take a large party which would include artists, authors, archaeologists, and scientists. His imagination was soon fired by visions of pillars, obelisks and sphinxes to be acquired for little more than the cost of their transportation and destined to add an exotic, oriental flavour to the landscapes at Ickworth, Downhill, and Ballyscullion.

After the death of Frederick William II and the eclipse of the unfortunate Countess he hoped to entice the young naturalist Alexander von Humboldt to accompany him. To a brilliant young man of twenty-eight or twenty-nine it was a tempting offer. 'I was aware that it was not easy to live at peace with him,' Humboldt wrote to a friend, 'but I can leave him at any time if he should oppose me too much. Besides, he is a man of genius, and it would have been a pity to have lost so excellent an opportunity. I might do something for meteorology. . . .'

They would visit Egypt and return by way of Constantinople and Vienna. It would have been the most ambitious of all the Bishop's schemes of travel and might, unlike his projected trip to Spain, actually have taken place but for the unexpected intervention of another and much more formidable traveller obsessed with the same idea. On 19 May 1798, while the Bishop's own plans were unavoidably in suspense, Napoleon Bonaparte embarked at Toulon for his expedition to Egypt. After this, of course, no more was heard of Lord Bristol's enterprising plan.

2

Since leaving Berlin with the King of Prussia tottering on the brink of the grave, though not yet quite fallen into it, and with the Countess still at liberty the Bishop continued to press his plan for the partition of France. Wilhelmina was sent a long and detailed letter on the subject in January 1797 which was intended for the eye of the King. The dangers to Prussia of the proximity of a powerful republic were again explained a month later in a further letter adorned with many examples both classical, biblical, and modern to emphasize the point.

'A powerful republic is always more active, more restless, more ardent than a monarchy,' the Bishop declared. 'I appeal to Rome, Carthage, Athens, Tyre and Sidon in ancient times, to Tunis, Algiers, Holland in the last century, and to France at the present. Every time a tyrant wishes to disentangle himself from opposition he plunges his country into war as did Alcibiades, Hannibal, Sylla, and de Witt. How then to emasculate a people? By a Pompadour, a Maintenon, a Cardinal Dubois, a Richelieu and so many others. My system then is to divide France and to weaken her. . . .'

The examples of Madame de Pompadour and Madame de Maintenon as lessons of how the bad influence of a *maîtresse en titre* can help to weaken and enfeeble the life of a nation were hardly tactful ones to draw for the benefit of a woman who herself notoriously occupied the same place in the life of Frederick William II as these two celebrated favourites had held in those of Louis XIV and Louis XV, but the Bishop, carried away by his pet theme, seemed unaware of the embarrassing parallel he was drawing. 'What a dose of politics for you, my dear Wilhelmina, to you who are nothing less than political,' he concluded with unintentional irony, 'but for me, *Sénateur Anglais*, I dream of nothing else – unless it be of you, dear, amiable, excellent friend.'

Having failed to secure the well-endowed Mariana von der Mark as his daughter-in-law Bristol had now set his heart on having his son Frederick appointed as British envoy to Berlin. With his son accredited to the Prussian Court, with Madame von Lichtenau at the King's ear and with his daughter Elizabeth busily pulling strings on his behalf among her influential Whig friends in London, the Bishop began to see himself controlling a vast spider's web of intrigue. A copy of his proposal for the dismemberment of France was forthwith dispatched to London. 'Dear Elizabeth,' he begged his daughter to whom it was sent, 'make your friend [the Duke of Devonshire] speak out if possible to the purport of this Memorial – read well yourself, read with Frederick – state the objections. At Dresden and Berlin the idea has more than pleased, perhaps the magnitude of the objects deters. It would not have deterred Lord Chatham, but, alas, he did bestride this narrow world like a stage Colossus and these petty men do but peep between his legs.'

Meanwhile the situation in Italy grew ever more menacing for a man so inured to travel as was Lord Bristol. On 4 January, just about the time he was explaining how he proposed to settle the problem of France, General Bonaparte won a crushing victory over the Austrians at Rivoli, and a month later Mantua surrendered to the French. The whole Italian peninsula lay at the mercy of the revolutionary army and it must have seemed to many people that the Earl-Bishop's plans of partition were a little premature. For the moment it appeared much more likely that France would dismember the rest of Europe rather than that she should herself suffer division at the whim of an eccentric English nobleman.

Even the Bishop's robust optimism was hardly a match for the daily bulletins of bad news that began to reach him in Venice that February. On the twelfth he had written to Sir William Hamilton in his usual jovial frame of mind asking his friend to get the King of Naples's permission for casts to be made of the famous statues of Claudius, Agrippa, Nero, and Hadrian in the royal collection.

The letter ends with heartening news of a French defeat at Trent.

Nine days later he writes from Klagenfurt in Austria in a more chastened mood, having been driven north by the unexpected French victories which had prevented his proposed journey to Naples. This time there is no good news to record and the letter is full of gloom. 'Nothing can excede the venality of the Austrian officers except their *lasciviousness*, many of whom are in bed with their whores when they should have been in the field of Mars instead of Venus,' he tells Sir William. 'I tremble for Naples once the monkies are able to reach Rome, but Naples missed the moment last autumn when *their* army could, by joining Wurmser, have annihilated the French. What the Hungarian recruits can possibly do no one knows, or ventures to guess, but *raw* troops seldom made *raw work*. Naples can yet save and recover Lombardy, but England must *save* and *cover* Naples. Are these orthodox politicks or not? . . .'

The Bishop, so used to telling people what were orthodox politics rather than asking their opinion (even in jest) seemed for a moment to have lost his habitual self-confidence. He concludes his letter on the same questioning note: 'Adieu, do you advise me to hire my apartment for next year – yea or nay? My best and kindest love to dear Emma. Does the Queen ever name me to you or to dear Emma – yea or nay?'[4]

Lord Bristol's movements are particularly difficult to trace at this time. He does not appear to have continued on from Klagenfurt northwards into Germany for in the spring or early summer of 1797 we find him back in north Italy again – though by July he was once more at Pyrmont for his final encounter with the Countess and the King of Prussia.

In an undated letter to Hamilton replete with political gossip he complains of having been in bed for fourteen days with jaundice at Padua. This letter must be read against the background of the tremendous events which were happening in the north of Italy at this time following in the wake of Napoleon Bonaparte's whirlwind campaign. In June the victorious young French General had founded the Ligurian Republic in Genoa and the following month the Cisalpine Republic had been proclaimed, comprising the former territories of Milan, Modena, Ferrara, Bologna, and Romagna.

A French commissary 'well dressed as usual and better mounted on two English horses of £50 each' had alighted at Bristol's inn for dinner. 'I sent my compliments to beg the news of the day,' Sir William was informed. The news was far from comforting either for the Bishop or for the Ambassador to whom the account was sent. The commissary confessed that his business was to find quarters in Ferrara for 12,000 French troops, the first contingent of a column of 25,000 destined to march on Rome and there affirm the sovereignty of the Roman people. Having achieved this purpose they would then proceed to subdue 'Rome's vassal' Naples with all its revenues and wealth.

'Since that day I have heard no more of the 12,000 men,' the Bishop continued, 'but it is certain that 4,000 cavalry are sett out from Ferrara for Rome, with that avowed impudent, audacious purpose; and moreover, that all the innumerable bodies of the new requisition from Lyons and the South of France speak publickly the same language. The Cisalpini in the meantime is crumbling fast, the municipality of Ferrara is dissolved, and a military Government for all justice established in its stead. An English family that stopt at Mantua, have just told me its ramparts are totally dismantled – not a gun left in the place, not a soldier in the town, not a zecchi in anybody's pocket after rigidly shutting up the gates for four days. . . .'

A light is cast on the general feeling of disillusion and discontent in that part of Italy by a conversation Bristol records at the end of this letter as having taken place with his physician at Ferrara. The doctor assured him that if the cabinet of Vienna had the good sense to establish a reasonable government in the Venetian territory with a sovereign and two Chambers, then within a month his country would accept it – but if not, then one despotism was as good as another. '*Verbum sapienti*' was the Bishop's comment on this.[5] He knew enough of the Vienna Government, however, to realize how forlorn a hope it was.

Rome in fact did not fall to the French until February 1798, some six or seven months after this letter was written. The Government of the Directory in Paris had certainly ordered an advance on Rome to 'punish' the Pope, but for the present Bonaparte was more concerned with the Austrians and before Rome fell he would have returned to Paris, leaving the proclamation of the Roman Republic to others. At this time Bristol's movements were being closely observed by the French and his correspondence was no doubt intercepted and read. Perhaps the obliging commissary, so ready with his information, purposely misled the Bishop, even though the general purport of what he had to say was true.

Certainly the Bishop showed no discretion at all in his letters, either in the military information he passed on to Hamilton, the plans for disposing of French territory he discussed with his daughter Elizabeth and the Countess von Lichtenau, or the general abuse of the republican 'monkies' which he bestowed on all and sundry. It never seems to have occurred to him that the avid curiosity he took in any military matter or diplomatic talk, the searching questions he addressed to the merest acquaintances or even to complete strangers (like the French commissary) on political or strategic matters, might make his activities highly suspect to the conquerors who now surrounded him. He remained quite unconscious of the danger of his position; for it must have seemed very unlikely, if not frankly improbable, to any official of the new republican governments then springing up in Italy, that a man calling himself both Earl of Bristol and Bishop of Derry could be acting in an entirely private capacity. In the general atmosphere of uneasiness and suspicion that prevailed the Bishop's curious and eccentric behaviour came more and more under the hostile observation of authority.

Very soon after writing this undated letter Bristol must have started out on his journey to Pyrmont which he reached some time early in July. Here, at this salubrious place which had so many pleasant memories for him, he escaped for a while from the turmoil of affairs in Italy, though thoughts of that country were never very far from his mind. His plans to return there were outlined to Hamilton on 14 July, which cannot have been long after his arrival: 'I hope to bring a beautiful cabinet to beautiful Emma, almost as fair as her skin, and as elegant as her form, and propose to leave Pyrmont on this first of September in order to reach Italy in its delicious autumn; but indeed all, all is autumn with her, her leaf is in the seer, and I doubt her returning spring is very distant, for she was rotten to the very core. . . . Adieu, old schoolfellow, let you and I be young still, for with all these games and gambols we may once more go to school, and not be the wiser; at least, you and dearest Emma will learn nothing new in the cordial assurance of my friendship and esteem.'

This was the letter in which Bristol described the deplorable state of health of the King of Prussia. Altogether his visit to Pyrmont this year cannot have been as pleasant as usual with the royal invalid so obviously in a critical condition. The Countess was naturally anxious about the future, for though she could hardly have foreseen the violent reaction against her that would come after the King's death, yet she must have realized that her happiness and security depended so much on his survival that the prospect of his imminent dissolution can only have filled her with despair.

The Bishop, of course, was still on the best of terms with her and as fulsome as ever in the endearments he lavished on her; there was no indication of the fickle nature of his attachment. When they parted company to return respectively to Potsdam and north Italy arrest and prison in fact awaited the Countess. The ordeal would be a shattering experience for her. She would have to face false charges as well as a matter of years in confinement, and the knowledge that her one-time friend and devoted admirer had accepted the accusations brought against her without question and turned his heart against her.

It is hardly an excuse for Bristol's callous rejection of the Countess to know that he was again in very poor health when the news of her arrest reached him in Trieste. 'I may certainly *die* out of Naples this winter, but I certainly cannot live out of it,' his letter to Hamilton began, 'for the gout has already assailed me in this pestiferous climate, and laid me 3 weeks on my *back*, and that you know is not the natural attitude for a man.' The news about 'Madame de Ritz' (for he no longer even uses the title he had been instrumental in securing for her) is thrown in with the rest of his political tittle-tattle as though she had never meant anything to him at all. 'Here many private letters mention that Buonaparte was arrested at *Strasburg* on the 30th,' he continues as though the one (in fact false) report meant no more to him than the others. 'Barras and he are reciprocally afraid of each other. He has got his mistress and now wishes to get his place. Adieu, my best and constant love to dearest Emma. . . .' What the recipient of this constant love thought of the Bishop's once no less constant love for the Countess is not recorded.

All the Bishop's thoughts at this time were fixed on the conduct of the war to the exclusion, it would seem, of everything else. Less than ten days after telling Hamilton, in a bare aside, of the terrible fate of the Countess we find him again sending military information to Naples.

Hearing for certain that there was a British fleet in the Mediterranean he wrote on 26 December to tell the envoy that French warships 'chuck full of all the plunder from Venice, incapable of resistance, like the fat alderman gorged with turtle and venison' were in port in Corfu 'under the rotten canon of a rotten fort'. A further twenty-five merchant ships, loaded in a similar manner, hovered near the port of Zara in Dalmatia where the inhabitants refused them entrance. '*Che boccone*, Sir William!' – 'what a mouthful,' he declares. 'The Russian Consul, a nobleman of Corfu, assures me that a thousand stand of arms dispersed among his countrymen will enable them to massacre every Frenchman in the island, for the whole garrison of the misterable fort consists only of 1,700 raggamuffins, *sans culotte*, *sans bas*, *sans souliers*. If you could forward this intelligence to our fleet, be it where it will, you yourself better than I can judge of the important service you will do both to the publick and individuals. Why, man, ten Spanish galleons are scarce richer, and then the men-of-war for Government. *Che Boccone*, *ti dico*!'[6]

So, having calmly dismissed the once adored Wilhelmina and her misfortunes from his mind, and plunged in the political intrigue which was still the breath of life to him, the Bishop ended the year 1797 in happy ignorance of the blows fate was to deal him in the year that was to follow.

3

While Lord Bristol's energies were so absorbed by the state of war in the area of the Mediterranean, the situation in Ireland, which he had last seen in 1791, was rapidly going from bad to worse. All the evils which he had tried in vain to remedy at the height of the Volunteer movement in 1783 continued and grew worse in their effect, though there had been some relief for Catholics in 1793 when they were given a measure of representation though they continued to be debarred from sitting in the House of Commons. The Irish Parliament, still unreformed, had little authority left and would soon make its submission to the British Parliament at Westminster.

Among the masses of the people the advent of the French Revolution had given rise to a new cause for hope, while to Dublin Castle the possibility of a French invasion added a new anxiety and fear to the task of government which was answered by increasing the establishment of troops. As a result of this from 1796 onwards Ireland had been virtually under martial law. The feelings of hostility to the Government and ruling classes among the unrepresented majority, inflamed and encouraged by the indiscipline and brutality of the troops, created a situation of extreme danger. By the beginning of 1798 the country was on the verge of rebellion.

Though the Bishop had remained closely in touch with his diocese through his agents, and in particular through his regular correspondence with Henry Hervey Bruce, he no longer identified himself with the Irish cause in the way he had done in former years. True, when signs of trouble made the Government bring more troops to Ireland in 1797 he had written a strong and vigorously worded letter of protest when he heard that soldiers had occupied his palace at Derry, and blamed his agent for not putting up a resistance; but his ever increasing hatred of revolutionary ideas put him out of sympathy with the leaders of the rebellion that was soon to break out.

On 16 January 1798, in a long letter to Thomas Pelham, chief secretary to the Viceroy Lord Camden, he accused the Government of attempting to stop the fever rather than cure it: 'In all my diocese, the very *foyer* of Rebellion, Mutiny and Insurrection, the embers are still warm, nay hot and ready to burst out again "and warm the Nations with redoubled Rage", but a good Physician, like you, will not content himself with the blisters and bleedings that have been applied, you will for the sake of the patient, as well as your own medical reputation, endeavour to extirpate the fever and finally destroy the seeds of it.'

The diseased body of Ireland required a radical antidote to prevent it from bursting, but the remedies he suggested merely emphasized how long he had been away from the country and how out of touch he had become. Ireland had passed beyond the point where things could be improved by an ecclesiastical reform in the administration of tithes on the lines of a plan he had proposed as far back as 1774. Yet this, and the suggestion that all religions should come equally under the patronage of the Crown, was all he had to offer by way of remedy, and the latter only so that the Government could 'be certain of the people they appoint and the doctrines they would teach'.

The fact of the matter was that for some years now Bristol had had no interest in Ireland beyond the limits of his diocese and the administration of his property there. He had become very much like any other absentee landlord. When rebellion broke out in earnest in May 1798 he was in no position to show his opinion one way or another, for he was himself detained in a Milanese prison; but his attitude to revolutionaries in Ireland would be no different now from his attitude to similar rebels anywhere else. He looked upon them as a menace to civilization.

At the time of the Volunteer Convention in Dublin the Bishop had been a fervent believer in the necessity for a thorough reform of the Irish Parliament, for he saw that legislative independence, so recently won, depended for its survival upon a strong reformed parliament which could hold the respect of the people it governed. With the failure of the movement for reform the decline of his interest in Irish politics began; it would reach its nadir in 1800 when Pitt's Act of Union came before the Parliament in Dublin. As a member of the Irish House of Lords he would vote by proxy in favour of the union.

4

Though so much of the Bishop's time and energy was spent in political intrigue and military espionage of a rather open and amateur sort, his main preoccupation in Italy remained the collection of works of art. Wherever he went purchases were made: pictures, busts, marbles, mosaics, urns, and antique fragments to adorn the great house he was building at Ickworth which he planned to be a veritable museum of European art both ancient and modern. As he moved about so constantly these treasures were for the most part stored in Rome against the day when they would all be shipped to England.

A portion of his treasure, however, was lodged much further north, at Leghorn. It consisted among other things of his collection of Italian primitives, a genre then very much out of fashion and of which he spoke somewhat slightingly, though he had the taste and perspicacity to acquire a number at a remarkably low cost. As the danger of a French invasion into the very heart of Italy grew more menacing the Bishop (taking his warning, perhaps, from the volumble French commissary he had met at Padua) decided to remove these valuables to a place of greater safety. Instructions were accordingly sent to his bankers at Leghorn to have all his effects there shipped at once to Corsica.

The bankers decided that Corsica was in more danger than Leghorn and ignored their instructions, but upon the approach of the French army they got into a panic and without consulting the Bishop hired a ship for the exorbitant sum of £1,800 in order to transport to Naples goods which the Bishop himself only valued at less than £800. Not knowing what had happened to these treasures on their arrival in Naples, whether they were in the hands of his agents or still in the Dogana, the Bishop sent a brief cry for help to Sir William Hamilton on 6 January 1798. This he followed up ten days later with a more detailed account of what the cargo contained.

'Now this freight of £1,800 from Leghorn to Naples', he wrote, 'is for pictures, busts, some Carrara statues and other marbles to the amount of £750, more or less. [In the first letter he had put the value at £670.] The pictures are chiefly of Cimabue, Giotto, Guido da Sienna, Marco da Sienna, and all that old pedantry of painting which served to show the progress of the art at its resurrection, and so, had they been even left to the mercy of the French, might have been redeemed for a *trifle*, being, like many other trifles, of no use to any but the *owner*. . . . Your advice, therefore, on how to proceed in the recovery of these goods, and information whether Sir J. Acton [Prime Minister of Naples], upon proof of these facts and my paying the usual reasonable freight from Leghorn to Naples, can relieve me from this fraud and rapine, is what I submit to your experience, your knowledge, and your friendship – certain, very certain, that what can be done will be done by you.'[7]

The Bishop was still himself trying to get to Naples but in the troubled state of the country it became more and more difficult to plan a journey of such length, passing, as would be necessary, through territory occupied by enemy troops. On 19 February he wrote to Sir William from Padua: 'Tomorrow I sett out for *Naples*, not being able to endure the damp of this part of Italy, which lay me up in bed for above the day, deprive me of my appetite, sleep and spirits; nothing but Naples can restore me, but how to reach it? If you know any magical means pray suggest it. . . . Oh! how I long to stretch myself in my garret at *Caserta* and hear all your excellent anecdotes and dearest Emma's Dorick dialect, eat woodcock pie and quaff humble port, till when, adieu.'[8]

In spite of his assertion that he would leave for Naples the next day he was prevented from doing so, for a month later the Bishop was still in the Venetian territory which since the Treaty of Campo Formio in October 1797 had been under Austrian control. His wrath was now directed against the new Austrian rulers who received almost as much of his scorn and invective as had previously been reserved for the French. 'Poor Venice is tumbling out of the frying-pan into the fire,' he wrote to the British Minister at Florence, 'those beastly brutal Austrians are establishing such a despotism that already the populace at Padua have begun to tear down the Austrian flag'.

It is to Lord Bristol's credit that he did not distinguish between friend and foe in his hatred of despotism, for in this respect at least he still retained the ideals that had guided him in the old days of the Volunteers. In March 1798 he wrote begging Sir William Hamilton and the Prime Minister of Naples to use all their influence (for the Queen of Naples was aunt to the Austrian Emperor) to prevent the Government in Vienna from 'playing their cards as ill as they do'. 'Tell our friend Sir John Acton, that philosopher as well as statesman, what I *almost* see with my own eyes, the imperial arms, erected with so much enthusiasm, torn down again at Padua and Vicenza with the same spirit, in consequence of the horrid despotism they are establishing in that country, yet have they given noble and respectable privileges to all Dalmatia which stands at the very door of Venice, and therefore is the great insult.'[9]

While Bristol was criticizing the conduct of the Austrians in Venezia the French were dealing him a crushing blow in Rome. His great store of treasure there, the bulk of his purchases over the past five or six years, was seized and impounded by order of the French military commander.

The fate of this collection in the years following its confiscation is extremely difficult to trace; more than once the Bishop had a chance to redeem it, but something or other always prevented the deal from being struck, either a dishonest agent or a sudden change in political fortunes. The ultimate fate of the collection is unknown; possibly it was disbanded or sold by the French; certainly it never returned to Bristol's possession despite all his efforts to secure it. As there does not seem ever to have been a list or catalogue of the collection it is impossible to trace any item from it or to know precisely what was lost, though, as will be seen, it consisted of many works by contemporary artists as well as old masters and other unspecified works of art.

The Bishop was never very accurate or exact in estimating the value of his possessions. He was as irritatingly casual and offhand in this as he was in keeping lists of what he bought or in providing detailed descriptions of his canvases. In this case he counted his loss as being between £18,000 and £20,000. In attempting to realize the value of this in terms of present-day money it would be necessary to multiply these estimated figures by ten or twelve times at least.

The first indication of his loss comes in a letter to the British Minister at Florence written on 10 March. The Bishop is full of rumours: he has heard that the Kingdom of Naples is arming in mass, that their troops to the number of 35,000 are advancing on Rome, that General Massena has been defeated and has fled to Ancona for reinforcements. 'For God's Sake,' he continues, 'enquire of the Neapolitan Minister or others, and write me what you can of it, as *it interests me deeply*; for they have confiscated all my immense property there; but having most nobly offered me to ransom it at a decent price, remains for me to know whether Massena is likely to remain *there* to receive the ransom.'[10]

The Bishop had been sadly misinformed on all points except the loss of his collection. He was unable to ransom it, and the Neapolitans would wait until November before advancing on Rome. Their brief occupation of the city at that time would again raise his hopes, but King Ferdinand was destined to leave Rome as quickly as he had entered it only this time with a French army at his heels. Soon afterwards he had to flee from Naples itself to Palermo in Sicily under the protection of Nelson's fleet.

The offer of ransom was withdrawn within a few days. A new idea, as extraordinary as it was original, then flashed into the Bishop's mind. 'Dearest Elizabeth,' he wrote to his younger daughter on 20 March, 'now or never perhaps may you most essentially serve me. All my effects at Rome are under sequestration to the amount of £20,000 at the very least. Could Mr. Pitt be induced to send a Minister to congratulate the Roman people on their emancipation, and appoint me to the Embassy, he would do himself and me a most essential service: me, because I should save all that immense, valuable, and beautiful property of large mosaick pavement, sumptuous chimney pieces for my new house, and pictures, statues, busts, and marbles without end, first-rate Titians and Raphaels, dear Guidos, and three old Carraccis – *gran Dio! che tesoro*; and himself, because such an embassy would wrench the Republick off the hands of the tyrant's dispoiler and merciless taskmaster, restore us the ports of Ancona and Civita Vecchia for our manufactures and codfish, and lay the foundation of a treaty of commerce, the most beneficial perhaps of any in Europe. Now, if either your friend, Lord Spencer, or, above all, your great friend, the Duke of Devonshire, or the Duchess, would effectually join in this lottery, you see, dearest Elizabeth, I should literally get the £20,000 prize. Dear girl, do what you can for me . . . I am on thorns till I hear from you. A ransom was offered by General Berthier, but that is now suspended.'[11]

A moment's reflection might have told the Bishop how inopportune, not to say impossible of execution, was his ingenuous plan. To send an ambassador to compliment the Roman people upon what was, beneath the republican masquerade, a French strategical victory, was hardly likely to commend itself to the British Prime Minister while his country was at war with France. Nor would his Catholic allies in Austria and Naples be particularly edified at the sight of a Protestant bishop congratulating the people of Rome on their emancipation from the sovereignty of the Pope. That Bristol did not pause for reflection shows the extent of his exasperation at this unfortunate turn of events. The letter is perhaps most interesting for the tantalizing but all too inadequate glimpse it gives us of the contents of the collection.

In Rome itself the confiscation of the Bishop's property caused great consternation among the artistic community. Though many of the artists themselves personally sympathized with the new and short-lived Roman Republic they respected the Earl-Bishop as a man and connoisseur and remembered his lavish patronage with gratitude. It was not so many years since Flaxman had recorded how Lord Bristol's liberality had reanimated the fainting body of art in Rome; now artists living and working in the city from as many different places and countries as France, Holland, Russia, Germany, Savoy, Naples, Venice, the Tyrol, England, Scotland, and Ireland, as well as Romans born and bred, totalling altogether to more than three hundred, petitioned Citizen Haller, the financial administrator of the Army of Italy, to restore the confiscated property to its owner.

Their petition, a copy of which later appeared in England in the *Gentleman's Magazine*, read as follows: 'Citizen Administrator – Among the effects belonging to the English at Rome, upon which seals have been put, are different objects of Art collected by the Bishop of Derry Lord Bristol. The Artists who are at Rome conceive that they may venture to represent that this generous Irishman, having for these forty years past spent the greatest part of his income in employing artists of all nations, may be considered as a valuable and useful character to the fine arts which the French Republic protects. The pictures and statues which he had purchased during the period, form a collection of the most choice works of the first painters and sculptors of our time; unique in its kind and worthy of being preserved entire. But a more direct motive, Citizen Administrator, ought to induce you to reinstate Lord Bristol in the possession of these effects; and this is that these articles are the works of men of which a number of the first artists, many of whom are French and Republicans, have been able to subsist during years of War little favourable to the fine Arts. The important benefits which have been lavished upon the Artists of all nations indifferently by a generous and impartial patron, induce them to present this petition; and the protection which the French Government and the French Armies bestow upon the fine Arts encourages them to hope that it will be attended with effect.'[12]

A similar petition, signed by 323 artists, was sent to the military commander General Berthier, a copy of which Lord Bristol sent to his friend Professor Symonds with the comment that it did equal honour both to them and to himself. In this letter he gives the value of his 'immense property there of marbles, pictures,

Mosaick pavements' as £18,000, slightly less than the figure quoted to his daughter.

The petition, alas, had no effect. Berthier was sympathetic, but he was about to be transferred to another command. It remained with Citizen Haller, a man notorious for his greed and rapacity, to decide on the fate of the collection, and no more was heard of the artists' request for the Bishop's property to be restored to him. Indeed these well-meaning men had sadly misinterpreted the role adopted by the French Government and Army as protector of the fine arts. As the Treaty of Tolentino, concluded the previous year, should have made clear to them, the policy towards works of art of the French Republic was to appropriate as many of them as possible and send them to Paris where, since 1793, the former royal palace of the Louvre had been opened as a public Art Gallery. Here masterpieces from many Italian collections were soon to be displayed as trophies of conquest.

At one period at least the Bishop's collection came fleetingly within his grasp, but only to be snatched away once more by the avaricious French. When the new Pope, Pius VII, returned to Rome shortly after his election in 1800, it was agreed that the French should relinquish the works of art they had seized. Lord Bristol looked forward to seeing his treasures again, but in April 1801 he was informed by Cardinal Consalvi, the Secretary of State, that his property was 'required' by the French Government, an order, presumably, that the Cardinal was powerless to resist, despite the Bishop's angry protests. The order came, on this occasion, from General Murat, at that time Governor of the Cisalpine Republic, a formidable and predatory neighbour whom the Pope could ill afford to offend. According to the General's ingenious interpretation of the treaty the agreement to restore works of art merely meant '*laissés en dépôt*'. A month later the Bishop had to report that 'the Sequestration was most insolently effected and still remains on my immense and precious property.'

This complaint was made in the course of a long letter to Lord Liverpool, whose son Lord Hawkesbury had married the Bishop's youngest daughter Louisa. The letter was started in April but abandoned for a month on account of a 'violent, sudden, unexpected and . . . unmerited attack of the gout, the most direful sugar-plumb of all Pandora's box'. In it Bristol revived the idea he had put to Elizabeth Foster three years before – that he should be appointed Ambassador to Rome – but with the rather fundamental difference that this time he should be accredited to the Pope instead of being sent to congratulate the Roman populace on their deliverance from him. The reasons he puts forward in favour of his suggestion were 'our Millions of R. Catholick subjects in Ireland' as well as the fact that 'all our property as well as our Persons here, for want of such an asylum as an Ambassador's house, is totally unprotected.' Perhaps to encourage Lord Liverpool's mind to similar thoughts, or perhaps by the merest chance, the next paragraph of the letter reads: 'As to pictures I have a Gem of Guercino's – a Roman Charity, too small for my Gallery, which I beg you to accept,which waits only for a Courier for Vienna, to send to you; and a *Tintoret* of the first class, but I fear too large for the same convenience.'

The Bishop was no more successful with Lord Liverpool than he had been with his daughter Elizabeth or her influential friends in getting himself appointed envoy in Rome. Nor did he have any success with 'that arch-plunderer' Murat. It does not appear to have struck him as at all inconsistent that he should apply for an ambassadorial post to the same city under such different circumstances, or that he should call for the restitution of an embassy that had not existed since Queen Elizabeth I had recalled her Ambassador from the Court of Pius V. All that he was concerned about was to regain the possession of his pictures and works of art.

5

In April 1798 the Bishop set out from Venice for Rome. His ultimate destination was Naples but no doubt he hoped that by going to Rome he might be able to discover a little more on the spot about the chances of ransoming his collection. At a small village between Ferrara and Bologna called Pedo he was compelled to take to his bed through illness and it was here, while still on his sick-bed, that he was arrested. The exact nature of the charge has never been specified, but as he had at no time disguised his contempt for the republican armies, and had lost no opportunity to spy on their activities and report his findings to their enemies, it is not very surprising that the authorities of the Cisalpine

Republic (in other words the French) decided to curtail his liberty when he crossed over into their territory.

He was treated with consideration and allowed to remain at Pedo under the inspection of a Council of War for eighteen days until he was well enough to be taken to Ferrara. While he was still lying ill at Pedo he had a visit from General Berthier, and if we are to believe his report a very remarkable conversation took place.

'Do not believe, my Lord,' the General began, 'that I or Moreau, or your friend Marion, or Delmas himself, serve from liking or principle or by choice this execrable Directoire, this pack of thieves, or this same charlatan Bonaparte.' He then went on, according to the Bishop, to give him some highly treasonable information about the present state of France for the information of '*votre grand Pitt*': '*Faites remarquer à votre cabinet que depuis Marseilles, Montpelier, Carcasonne et Bordeau jusqu'à Paris il ne se trouve une seule fortresse.*' Many Frenchmen he declared ready to take an oath of fidelity to Louis XVIII as a constitutional King, and finally, on the restoration of peace, he suggested a plan identical in every detail to that put forward by the Bishop himself for the division of France, the north for the Republic and the south for the King.[13]

The account of this conversation which contained much military and political information, was written in a letter to Sir William Hamilton in April 1799, a year after it took place, though the Bishop claimed to have jotted down in writing the substance of what was said as soon as Berthier was gone, asserting that the General had pronounced his declaration 'with an amazing spirit of revenge, antipathy and hatred to Barras, Buonaparte, and indeed the whole French nation'.

Though the period immediately before the fall of the Directory and the establishment of the Consulate under Bonaparte was a period of deep disillusion for many Frenchmen it seems extraordinary that Berthier, the future Prince of Wagram and devoted chief of staff to Napoleon, should have talked to a hostile foreigner in this strain, especially considering the situation in which Bristol stood at the time. If we are to believe the Bishop almost all his captors, especially Marion, an artillery general who dined with him every night at Pedo, were 'decided Royalists' and openly hostile to Barras and his fellow Directors. One should bear in mind, however, that Bristol was a great believer in the infallibility of his own arguments, and like many self-centred people easily convinced himself that everyone else held his own point of view, despite strong evidence to the contrary.

Though the Bishop mentioned General Delmas as featuring in Berthier's conversation he did not actually meet him until later when the General had rooms immediately below him during his confinement in Milan. They had many conversations there and according to the Bishop both Delmas and Marion were 'determined on the first occasion to give full proof of their abhorrence of the present execrable system of iniquity' in France. A great deal more talk of the same kind passed between Delmas and Bristol in Milan but it does not appear to have occurred to the latter that perhaps the general was leading him on. In fact Delmas's loyalty, like Berthier's, never seems to have been in doubt and he died fighting for France at the battle of Leipzig in 1813. If Bristol hoped to learn something from the free talk of his captors they certainly believed that they had something to learn from him, and no one talked more freely than the Earl-Bishop of Derry when given a little encouragement.

After his recovery the prisoner was taken to Ferrara and then on to Milan. In the latter city he was confined in the castle or fortress, presumably the Castello Sforzesco. His imprisonment, which lasted for nine months, was not unduly severe; he was able to write letters, order his own food and entertain friends. He also had free use of his money, 50,000 francs of which were paid to the Governor of Milan, General Hullin, as an inducement to secure his liberty after he had been languishing for four months behind bars. The General pocketed the bribe but failed to get the prisoner released.

Another attempt to gain his liberty with less costly but more tragic results was recorded by Lady Webster, though it is not confirmed by any other authority. 'That abominable, wicked old fellow, Lord Bristol', she wrote in her *Journal* on 18 December, 'is still kept prisoner at Milan. I believe, even in his confinement, he has contrived to make some miserable. He bribed his guards to let him escape, and when the moment was ripe for flight, he was unable to move, and several who were involved in his scheme were instantly shot upon being detected.'[14]

Certainly rumours of an attempted escape were current at the time and must have come Lady Webster's way. The artist Denis, whom the Bishop had befriended in Italy and who was now settled in London, had heard something to this effect which he passed on to the Countess von Lichtenau, herself a prisoner. 'Poor Bristol is still in the castle of Milan,' he wrote to her in November 'and his detention is grown more rigorous in consequence of an attempt to rescue him. His health is very feeble; he writes to us from the depth of his prison when ever he is able. It is rumoured in Germany that he was arrested for looking into his papers on your account to see if he had any traces of the money placed by you in England. *Quel triste changement pour notre ancienne société! Le Roi mort, Bristol à Milan, vous à Glogau. . . .*'

If the Bishop's imprisonment had anything to do with his former association with the Countess then it would help to account for his having turned against her, especially now that he shared her unhappy fate. It must be remembered, however, that Denis was only relating the gossip he had heard, and was writing from London, far away from the actual scene or from contact with anyone who could have given him accurate information. It is also a fact that though the Bishop had often warned Wilhelmina to place some of her money in safety in England she had always declined to follow his advice.

Whether or not Bristol attempted to bribe his guards he certainly made the best use of his opportunities while in prison to continue his indiscreet questioning and interrogation of any French officers he met, in spite of the fact that this habit of his was largely responsible for landing him in his present plight. It was a dangerous game, but he played it with some success as may be judged from a letter he sent to Lord Nelson after his release.

The letter was written from Trieste on 3 May 1799, two months or so after his captivity had ended. 'It was my hap, my Lord,' he began, 'during nine months confinement at Milan to make an intimate acquaintance with two of the many discontented officers in that Garrison. The first was a Captain Dalby, chief engineer to Buonaparte whose avarice led him to employ this man in composing an atlas in 30 sheets of his excellency's marches and victories but whose avarice tempted him to defraud the poor Engineer of one half of his Profits. . . . The second is Captain Vignon of the *gens d'Armes* who was frequently upon guard with me during a week at a time, din'd of course at my table and partook largely of my wine such as his miserable pay did not allow him to procure himself. He had often been at the foot of the Guillotine but as often escaped by the means of favor, protection, bribery, dexterity, but, what whetted his Revenge, he owed his danger to one of his comrades and his escape to himself. Captain Dalby is a *natif* of Geneva married to an Englishwoman educated from her infancy in Geneva – this was my first recommendation to the confidence of her husband. The General in Chief La Prune was ordered to Toulon soon after the departure of Buonaparte. I persuaded Captain Dalby to accompany him under the pretence of correcting errors in his Maps and by a large supply towards the expences of his journey, I engaged him to make me a return of the state of Port la Margue, the batteries of the entrance, etc. On his return he assured me the Garrison was composed of a few hundred Invalids – the guns of old bad Iron, on rotten carriages, and that neither in the Town nor Fort was there a supply of 20 rounds of either Powder or Ball. That of the miserable batteries at the entrance into *The Rude* there was not a single gun or carriage fit for use and that he was sure the Cannon must burst at the very first explosion. Captain Vignon some weeks after was ordered to conduct some galley-slaves to Toulon. I gave him the same commission and the same supply for his expences. At his return he assured me of the same facts, and added that he had narrowly observed the fort and nothing could be more practicable than a Coup de Main. . . .'[15]

Bristol had, of course, no way of checking the information he was given and it is possible that he was duped by these two officers; but whether this was so or not he showed a remarkable courage in engaging in this sort of espionage while he was actually a prisoner of the French. It was typical of the recklessness that had always been a characteristic of his personality but was none the less brave for that, for he cannot have been unaware of the fact that detection might well have proved fatal to him. Fortunately for him these highly dangerous undertakings remained undiscovered by his jailers, who would certainly have shown him no mercy, and some time in February 1799 he was given his freedom.

If the Bishop's incarceration was intended to teach him a lesson in discretion it cannot be said to have succeeded, for after his release he carried on in exactly the same way as he had done before. Indeed, his reputation for irresponsibility was such that he received very little sympathy at the time of his enforced stay in the *castello* of Milan. Many people in England thought that he had got no more than he deserved, and the general attitude was perhaps best summed up in a dispatch from Sir William Hamilton to Lord Grenville dated 29 May 1798, a month or so after the Bishop's arrest: 'We know little more about the Earl of Bristol's arrest and present confinement at Milan than was (as I see by the last newspaper) known in England the 29th of April, but we all know that his Lordship's freedom in conversation, particularly after dinner, is such as to make him liable to accidents of this nature.'[16]

A letter written to Lady Hamilton from prison suggests that Bristol had tried to enlist Sir William's help in procuring his release. It was, however, a time of crisis in Naples, as in most parts of Italy, with preparations well advanced for the disastrous invasion of the Roman Republic, and the Ambassador had little enough time to spare for his own affairs, let alone his old schoolfellow's.

'I know not, dearest Emma,' the Bishop wrote on 24 November, 'whether friend Sir William has been able to obtain my passport or not; but this I know – that, if they have refused it, they are damned fools for their pains: for never was a Malta orange better worth squeezing or sucking; and if they leave me to die without a tombstone over me to tell the contents – *tant pis pour eux!* In the meantime, I will frankly confess to you, that my health most seriously and urgently requires the balmy air of Naples, and the more balmy atmosphere of those I love, and who love me; and that I shall forgo my garret with more regret than most people of my silly rank in society forgo a palace or a drawing-room. But I will augur better things from the justice of my neighbour; and that they will not condemn, against all rules of probability, one of their best friends, unheard: especially one who, if he be heard, can say so much. . . .' After outlining the plans of travel which he hoped to undertake on his release, including another visit to Dalmatia, his letter ends: 'Sweet Emma, adieu! Remember me in the warmest and most enthusiastic style to your friend, and my friend, and the friend of human kind. If Sir William does not contrive to send me my passport, I will – I will – excommunicate him, and send him to the devil before his time.'[17]

By the time Bristol was released the Hamiltons had fled to Sicily with the Neapolitan royal family and were temporarily unable to offer him either help or hospitality; in fact he would not see either of them again. Meanwhile over the Bishop's 'dear Naples' there now flew the flag of the newly created but short-lived Parthenopean Republic.

6

After his release the Bishop made his way towards Venice by easy stages. At Padua he heard the news of the French General Jourdan's defeat by the Archduke Charles at Stockach. Nothing could have been better calculated to cheer the heart of a man just freed after nine months' detention as a prisoner of war. As soon as he reached Venice he dashed off a jubilant note to Lady Hamilton at Palermo:

'Hip! Hip! Hip! Huzza! Huzza! Huzza! for dearest Emma! Those doubly damn'd miscreants, first as French, secondly as *Reps* have thrown *doublets* and within these few days been beat—ay completely beaten twice. General Lusignan arrived the night before last at the Golden Eagle at Padua where I had been lounging away a month among Greek and Latin professors. The General, according to his age and dignity, had gone to bed tired, but I saw his Aide-de-Camp who, like all others of his rank, preferred supper to sleep, just as my aides-de-camp, vulgarly called Chaplains, usually do after a journey of seventy or eighty miles. . . .'

After describing the battle he characteristically asks Emma to procure from the Queen of Naples ('our dear invaluable Queen') a short letter of introduction for himself to her victorious nephew the Archduke as he considered that he had 'matters of great moment and character of great importance to communicate to him', and he again trots out his theory that nearly all the French he encountered at Milan, 'all the officers but one . . . and all privates without exception are zealous Royalists and execrate the Directory.' Indeed, all his imprisonment seems to have done was to have inculcated in him this very improbable hypothesis which he continued to believe in until his death.

A letter of the same date (28 March) to Sir William had more details with some rather exaggerated hopes attached: 'Yesterday,

Wednesday morn, just as I was mounting my horse arrived an Officer express from the Army of Legnago, with the glorious news that the Austrians had totally beaten those execrable highwaymen the French between Legnago and Bevilacqua, taken above 5,000 prisoners and laid 3,000 of Messieurs les Perruquiers *dead* on the spot, and were pursuing the rest. In this case you can expect the universal revolt of all the Cisalpine, since, as I came from Milan to Verona, nothing could be more loud, clamorous, or general, than the discontent of all ranks of men – not a single recruit could be obtained.'[18]

These letters show, if nothing else, that the Bishop had emerged from prison unrepentant and unchastened. He was back at once at his old game of transmitting military and political information to an ambassador who perhaps grew a little weary of these over-enthusiastic bulletins, for to judge by Hamilton's comments in his dispatch to Lord Grenville on the subject of the Bishop's arrest he did not set a very high value on these reports from his old and excitable friend.

Bristol's last years were spent in continual movement. The old roads, upon which he was such a familiar figure, were transversed once more. In April 1799 he was in Trieste, writing to Sir William about an idea for constructing a route from Manfredonia to Vienna. First a few hours by sea (as he had done it in 1772) and then on by way of Dalmatia from Spalato to Zara or Fiume, the road to be financed by a system of barriers or turnpikes. In the early summer, having abandoned the idea of further explorations in ancient Illyria, he crossed the Alps again to spend August in Pyrmont, unaffected by the notable absence of the Countess von Lichtenau. While there he entered his seventieth year with undiminished enthusiasm for the adventure of life.

The Bishop spent some months in Germany, for on 2 November we find him writing to Lord Liverpool from Regensburg in Bavaria where he found himself surrounded by *chouans*, the fanatical royalists who had put up a violent resistance to the French republican forces in their native Brittany. Bristol, as may be imagined, quickly caught their enthusiasm and assured Lord Liverpool that the appearance of a British army 'especially so large an one as 30 or 40,000 men' in their province would, with the volunteers who would join it as well as those it would release from prison, have 'the great probability of reaching Paris itself'.

It was certainly a more practical idea than some of his other schemes, and Liverpool promised, in his reply, to communicate the suggestion to his colleagues.

By the winter the Bishop at last managed to get back to Naples, the city he had been longing to see again since before his imprisonment in Milan. While he had been in Germany the Parthenopean Republic had been overthrown and the rule of King Ferdinand restored. In July the King had returned in a British warship with Lord Nelson and the Hamiltons. He had remained in the bay until early August but prudence or timidity had prompted him to stay safely on board ship and he had returned to Palermo without venturing to go ashore among his liberated subjects.

Bristol must have come back to Naples with mixed feelings. The Hamiltons had been obliged to return to Sicily with the Court and were no longer able to welcome him to his garret at Caserta. Their Villa Emma at Posillipo had been plundered and at the Palazzo Sessa Sir William's apartments had been destroyed by a bomb. In the city itself a cruel terror prevailed as the royalists took their revenge on the defeated republicans. The Bishop makes no reference to his own treasures in Naples, the 'Rafaels, Titians and what not' he had mentioned to Lady Elizabeth Foster. It is very probable, however, that they survived only to meet a worse fate later on; for these must have been the cases of pictures which Robert Fagan (who acted as Henry Hervey Bruce's agent after Bristol's death) admitted as having been ruined when they were placed in the hold of a ship where the salt water was able to penetrate and destroy them.

In the summer of 1800 Bristol travelled north again and spent some time in Florence and Siena. At the former city he had another encounter with the Countess of Albany, the widow of Prince Charles Edward Stuart, and commissioned a picture from Fabre who was now living in a *ménage à trois* with the Countess and Count Alfieri. The Countess noted that the Bishop was always falling off his horse, though fortunately without breaking his head; she hoped that he would remain in one piece until Fabre was paid for his picture.

In December 1800 the long deserted Lady Bristol died at Ickworth Lodge in the shadow of the 'stupendous monument of folly' her husband was raising near by. There had never been any reconciliation between them and their relationship remained cool until the end. During the previous August Elizabeth Foster had visited her mother and found her low and unwell. She had just received some unpleasant letters from her husband and these had added to her depression. 'I cannot tell you at present what they were,' Lady Elizabeth wrote to her son after leaving Ickworth, 'but most certainly he is a cruel man.' The Bishop's only reaction to the news of his wife's death was an expression of severe displeasure at certain passages in her will.

7

Time was beginning to run out for the Bishop as well, though he continued his feverish journeys as if trying always to keep one stage ahead of death. His health, never robust in spite of his immense nervous energy, caused him growing discomfort. In April 1801, writing from Rome, he complained to Lord Liverpool of an attack of 'gout' in his chest and stomach 'with excruciating pains and perpetual vomiting which terminated in a delirium and at last a total deprivation of sentiment and sensation'. His recovery from this serious attack was slow and it left him 'so reduced in strength as not to be able to dwell on very serious subjects'. By June he was well enough to go to Naples, returning to Rome for the winter, a pattern he was to follow in the succeeding year.

He had always had the strongest belief in the therapeutic value of the air of Naples and its immediate neighbourhood. From Castellammare he wrote, again to Lord Liverpool, in August 1802 boasting that the Neapolitan climate as well as bathing in 'certain acidulous waters deemed specific in all cases of obstructions', had converted his autumn into a summer. 'Above 300 persons of every rank and from almost every part of the kingdom pass the summer here in the recovery of their health,' he declared, 'and it is curious to observe the moral consequences arising from the removal of ventricular obstructions. Man, woman, and child seems to be regenerated by these ablutions, and those who arrived pale, languid and desponding return laughing, singing, and dancing.'

His day here, as described to Liverpool, certainly shows a

remarkable constitution in a man of seventy-two, despite all the ill-health he had suffered: 'I take my dip in the balmy invigorating sea-water – then to my usual breakfast of delicious coffee blunted of all its irritating particles by the yellow of an egg instead of cream and with 2 fresh eggs warm from the nest to prey on instead of the coats of my stomach. Then after helping "Hyperion to his Horse" I mount my horse and climb these beautiful mountains shaded by the broad-leaved chestnut tree for 3 hours regularly and then Home to a second breakfast copious as the first – yet such is the balmy aromatick salubrious quality of the atmosphere arising from various aromatick plants that it scarce supports the stomach until one o'clock – when all Castel a Mare rich and poor, old and young, native and foreigner sit down to dinner . . . then succeeds a tribute to the warmth of the climate – a long sleep of at least 3 hours – then fresh exercise according to our various faculties. Few sup – I cannot last till the morn, so a bottle of genuine Legitimate port wine with a few Potatos, at least as good and as mealy as your own Dutchy of Lancaster produces, supports my friend and me till the hour of Ten, when all Castel a Mare forget their cares, diseases or medicine – and so *da Capo*, my Lord, for at least 4 months together. Such a life is worth at least a debate in either House of Parliament, and its pleasures surpass even that of a Majority.'

In the last year of his life the Bishop had to contend with certain financial worries, largely due to delays in payment by his bankers in England who were alarmed at the rate of his expenditure. Lord Cloncurry, the Irish peer, who was in Rome in 1803, declared that Bristol received 'upwards of £5,000' each quarter which he spent immediately upon buying works of art. 'In this, as in most other cases, however, the proverb became true – wilful waste made woeful want,' he wrote, 'and towards the end of the quarter the noble prelate used to find his purse absolutely empty, and his credit so low as to be insufficient to procure him a bottle of Orvieto. There followed a dispursion of his collection as rapidly as it was gathered, but, as might be expected, at a heavy discount.'[19]

One must allow for a little exaggeration in Cloncurry's account, especially with regard to the Bishop's credit, which was always good in Rome; but there is no doubt that funds were not so plentiful as they had been. Bristol complained that his agents in

England and Ireland were keeping him on short commons, and Henry Bruce received many grumbling letters from his perplexed and anxious relation.

As far as the general public were concerned, however, the Earl-Bishop remained his extraordinary and eccentric self, unchanged apparently by time or circumstances and a cause of both amazement and embarrassment to his fellow countrymen when they encountered him in the streets of Rome or Naples.

It was in this light that he was seen by a certain Miss Catherine Wilmot, a young Irish girl, who witnessed the curious sight of the Earl of Bristol in Rome in April 1803, and must have been one of the last people to write an account of his strange appearance. 'Tho' he is one of the greatest curiosities alive,' she wrote in a letter home, 'yet such is his notorious character for profane conversation, and so great a reprobate is he in the unlicensed sense of the word, that the English do not esteem it a very creditable thing to be much in his society, excepting only where curiosity particularly prompts. I have often seen him riding and driving past our windows, and his appearance is so very singular that I must describe it to you. His figure is little, and his face very sharp and wicked; on his head he wore a purple velvet night cap with a tassel of gold dangling over his shoulders and a sort of mitre in the front; silk stockings and slippers of the same colour, and a short round petticoat, such as Bishops wear, fringed with gold about his knees. A loose dressing-gown of silk was then thrown over his shoulders. In this Merry Andrew trim he rode on horseback to the never-ending amusement of all Beholders! The last time I saw him he was sitting in his carriage between two Italian women, dress'd in white Bed-gown and Night-cap like a witch and giving himself the airs of an Adonis.'[20]

Within three months of appearing to Miss Wilmot in this strange garb the Bishop was dead. He died very suddenly from that complaint he had always referred to as 'gout in the stomach' which had so nearly proved fatal to him more than once before. On 8 July 1803, he was travelling from Albano to Rome when the attack seized him. The suffering man was taken into a peasant's cottage by the wayside, but when the occupants learnt that the person they were sheltering was a heretic bishop they were overcome with superstitious fear and refused to have him under their roof. So Lord Bristol was carried to an outhouse and there he died.

The Bishop had time before death claimed him to tear up a will in which, according to a letter from Lord Nelson to Lady Hamilton, he had left everything to 'those Italian devils about him'.[21] Lord Cloncurry claimed to have taken care of 'the wreck of his property in Rome' and saved it for his heirs, but in fact it was the Scottish prelate Cardinal Erskine who stepped in and rescued the Bishop's Roman effects, said to be valued at some £14,000, from the inevitable plunder that would otherwise have resulted from the absence of any relative on the spot to protect them.[22]

The fate of Lord Bristol's property in Italy has always been surrounded in mystery. The ultimate fate of his physical remains was somewhat grotesque but not out of character with the extraordinary life that had just come to an end.

It was decided that the Bishop should rest in the vault of the little church in the park at Ickworth where his ancestors are buried. It fell to the lot of Hugh Elliot, the new British Minister at Naples, to arrange for the body to be shipped home on board the man-of-war *Monmouth*, but in fulfilling this task he came up against the strong prejudice among sailors at having a corpse on board ship. In order to get round this difficulty Elliot ordered the coffin to be placed in a packing-case and labelled as an antique statue, and it was in this guise that the body of the Earl-Bishop came home. Soon a legend had grown up that the body had been lost at sea and a statue buried in its place.

To many people it must have seemed sad that the Bishop was not laid to rest in his Cathedral at Derry, for though he had neglected his See and spent the last eleven years away from it, he had always placed the interests of the Irish people first in the administration of his diocese. Though his political conduct there had been intemperate and hotheaded his ideas had been right and far in advance of any of his contemporaries in the Protestant ascendancy.

It is true that he deserted Ireland in the end, but he had tried genuinely to work in the interest of the whole community as long as he had lived there, and a tribute to this effect was made by the people of Derry after his death. An obelisk was erected to his memory on which it was recorded that during the thirty-five years that he presided over the See he had endeared himself to all denominations of Christians resident in the diocese. 'He was the friend and protector of them all . . .', the inscription read, 'and the hostile sects which had long entertained feelings of deep animosity towards each other were gradually softened and reconciled by his influence and example.' Among those who contributed to the cost of raising this memorial were the Roman Catholic Bishop and the Dissenting Minister.

This simple inscription proclaims Lord Bristol's one firm claim to fame and remembrance, for when all the follies and eccentricities and extravagances of his life are taken into account, it remains true that in Ireland at least, when he chose to live there, he was never unfaithful to that great article in his creed, the rights of humanity.

The obelisk to his memory stands in the park at Ickworth not far from the great house he was never destined to see. Many must regret that it does not stand in Derry.

Notes

I Men, Women, and Herveys

1. Hardy, F. *Memoirs of James Caufield, Earl of Charlemont*, vol. I, p. 103.
2. He was baptized 'Frederick' and not 'Frederick Augustus' as sometimes given.
3. Childe-Pemberton, W. S. *The Earl Bishop*, vol. I, p. 14.
4. Young, A. *Autobiography*, p. 103.
5. Falkiner, C. L. *Studies in Irish History and Biography*, p. 72.
6. *Memoirs of Lady Hamilton* (1815), pp. 114–5.
7. Cloncurry, Lord. *Personal Recollections*, p. 191.
8. Letter in the possession of Count Charles de Salis.
9. Belfast, P.R.O. of Northern Ireland, D. 1514/9/79.
10. *Memoirs of Lady Hamilton*, p. 113.
11. Wesley, J. *Journal*, vol. XVI, p. 170.
12. Falkiner, C. L. op. cit., p. 75.
13. Young, A. op. cit., p. 113.
14. Grosvenor, C. *The First Lady Wharncliffe and her Family*, vol. I, p. 12.
15. Foster, V. *The Two Duchesses*, pp. 118–19.

II Travels and Intrigues

1. Foster, V. *The Two Duchesses*, pp. 20–1.
2. Foster, V. op. cit., pp. 23–4.
3. Foster, V. op. cit., p. 38.
4. Foster, V. op. cit., pp. 48–9.
5. Morrison, A. *The Hamilton and Nelson Papers*, vol. I, Letter 82, p. 54.
6. Historical MSS Commission, 8th Report. Papers of Lord Emly. (Quoted by Childe-Pemberton, vol. I, pp. 206–11.)
7. Foster, V. op. cit., pp. 64–5.
8. Foster, V. op. cit., pp. 75–8.
9. Morrison. op. cit., vol. I, Letter 85, pp. 56–7.
10. Morrison, op. cit., vol. I, Letter 85.
11. Foster, V. op. cit., p. 68.
12. Jones, T. *Memoirs* (Walpole Society, vol. XXXII), p. 71.
13. Jones, T. op. cit., pp. 83, 88, and 121.

14. Cf. Childe-Pemberton, W. S. vol. I, p. 230, also Falkiner, C. L. *Studies in Irish History and Biography*, p. 79.
15. Walpole to Mann, 9 May 1779. (*Letters*, vol. VII, pp. 199–200.)
16. Franklin accused Hervey of hypocrisy in not extending the reforms he urged for Catholics to include Presbyterians as well, as this might result in loss of income. (Cf. Parton, J. *Life of Franklin*, vol. II, p. 510.)
17. Ayling, S. *George the Third*, p. 269.
18. Bentham, Jeremy. *Works*, vol. X, p. 108.
19. *The Irish Magazine and Monthly Asylum for Neglected Biography*, Nov. 1807, p. 60. (Quoted by Childe-Pemberton, vol. I, pp. 248–249.)

III Episcopal Volunteer

1. Falkiner, C. L. *Studies in Irish History and Biography*, p. 72.
2. Walpole to Cole, 27 December 1779.
3. Sprigge, T. L. S. *Correspondence of Jeremy Bentham*, vol. III, pp. 63 and 68.
4. Grosvenor, C. *The First Lady Wharncliffe and her Family*, vol. I, pp. 9–10.
5. Young, A. *Autobiography*, p. 103.
6. *Mrs. Carter's Letters to Mrs. Montague*, vol. II, p. 52.
7. Walpole to Mason, April 1782.
8. Walpole to Mann, December 1783. Walpole in fact underestimated the Earl-Bishop's income.
9. Childe-Pemberton, W. S. *The Earl Bishop*, vol. I, p. 291.
10. Foster, V. *The Two Duchesses*, p. 89.
11. Beckett, J. C. *The Making of Modern Ireland*, p. 230.
12. Hardy, F. *Memoirs of James Caulfield, Earl of Charlemont*, vol. II, pp. 105–6.
13. Barrington, Sir J. *Rise and Fall of the Irish Nation*, p. 293.
14. Sir Jonah Barrington then 'too young and too unimportant to have the honour of any acquaintance with that distinguished prelate' recalled these impressions in his old age.
15. Lecky, W. E. H. *Leaders of Public Opinion in Ireland*, vol. I, pp. 68–9 and 78.
16. Hardy, F. op. cit., vol. II, pp. 113–14.
17. Walpole to Mason, 8 November 1783.
18. Walpole to Mann, December 1783.
19. Young, A. op. cit., p. 131.
20. Lecky, W. E. H. op. cit., vol. I, pp. 70–3.

IV A Vagabond Star

1. Young, A. *Autobiography*, pp. 128–9.
2. Sackville Hamilton to the Duke of Rutland (cf. Childe-Pemberton, vol. II, p. 391.)
3. Foster, V. *The Two Duchesses*, p. 92.
4. Lady Louisa Hervey married Robert Banks Jenkinson (1770–1823), 2nd Earl of Liverpool, Prime Minister 1812–27.
5. Doran, J. *'Mann' and Manners at the Court of Florence*, vol. II, p. 418.
6. *Journal of Elizabeth, Lady Holland*, vol. I, p. 242.
7. Doran, J. op. cit., vol. II, pp. 418–19.
8. Grosvenor, C. *The First Lady Wharncliffe and her Family*, vol. I, p.21.
9. Grosvenor, C. op. cit., vol. I, p. 18.
10. Rankin, P. *Irish Building Ventures of the Earl Bishop of Derry*, p. 54.
11. Quoted by T. G. F. Paterson, 'The Edifying Bishop' (*Quarterly Bulletin of the Irish Georgian Society*, vol. IX, nos 3 and 4, pp. 79–80).
12. Grosvenor, C. op. cit., vol. I, p. 18. Also quoted by Childe-Pemberton, vol. II. pp. 414–15 with slight variants.
13. Cf. Childe-Pemberton, W. S. vol. II, p. 423, also M. Cheke, *The Cardinal de Bernis*, p. 285.
14. So described by Allan Cunningham.
15. Morrison, A. *The Hamilton and Nelson Papers*, vol. I, Letter 237, pp. 188–9.
16. Irwin, D. *English Neoclassical Art*, pp. 63–4.
17. *Journal of Elizabeth, Lady Holland*, vol. I, p. 141.
18. *Dublin Evening Post*, 25 November 1790.
19. Letter to Andrew Todd, 24 September 1785 (Quoted by Childe-Pemberton, vol. II, p. 391).
20. Letter dated 25 October 1770 in the possession of Count Charles de Salis.
21. Curtis, E. *A History of Ireland*, p. 330.
22. Morrison, A. op. cit., vol. I, Letter 194, pp. 154–5.
23. Morrison, A. op. cit., vol. I, Letter 200, p. 159. Lord Abercorn was one of the witnesses of Hamilton's marriage in London.

V The Anti-Revolutionary

1. Lord Bristol's will and the codicil he made at Aosta in 1794 are given in full in Childe-Pemberton, vol. II (Appendix, pp. 654–5).
2. Grosvenor, C. *The First Lady Wharncliffe and her Family*, vol. I, p. 20.
3. Christie's *Catalogue* for 24 March 1792. Lot 86.
4. Cf. Hussey, C. 'Ickworth House, Suffolk' in *Country Life*, 10 March 1955 (vol. CXVII, pp. 675–9).

5. Grosvenor, C. op. cit., vol. I, p. 34.
6. Goethe, *Converations and Encounters*, pp. 214–15. See also *Entretieurs de Goethe et d'Eckermann*, p. 266. Goethe recalled these events in 1797, but he gives the Bishop's age as 'about 63' so the events can be placed in 1793 when the Bishop was that age and in Jena.
7. Letter to John Beresford of Ballykelly, 3 September 1793. (Quoted by Childe-Pemberton, vol. II, p. 452.)
8. Fothergill, B. *Sir William Hamilton*, p. 258.
9. *Journal of Elizabeth, Lady Holland*, vol, I, p. 54.
10. Holland, Lord. *Memoirs of the Whig Party*, vol. I, pp. 56–7.
11. *Journal of Elizabeth, Lady Holland*, vol. I, pp. 115–16.
12. Morrison, A. *The Hamilton and Nelson Papers*, vol. I, Letter 232, p. 187.
13. It is unlikely that the picture reached its destination. Two portraits were painted by Angelica Kauffmann. One, described in the text, was done at Rome in 1790 and was later at Downhill; the second still hangs at Ickworth.
14. Crosland, M. *Louise of Stolberg*, p. 142.
15. Morrison, A. op. cit., vol. I, Letters 241 and 242, pp. 191–2.
16. Morrison, A. op. cit., vol. I, Letter 244, p. 193.
17. *Farington Diary*, vol. I, p. 81.
18. Morrison, A. op. cit., vol. I, Letter 248, pp. 195–6.
19. Robert Bradstreet to the Rev. N. Proby, quoted by Childe-Pemberton, vol. II, p. 467.
20. Morrison, A. op. cit., vol. I, Letter 250, p. 197.
21. *Letters of Lord Nelson to Lady Hamilton*, vol. I, pp. 255–6.
22. Ibid., vol. I, pp. 243–4.

VI The Adorable Friend

1. *Farington Diary*, vol. I, p. 152.
2. Foster, V. *The Two Duchesses*, pp. 116–17.
3. Cf. Childe-Pemberton, W. S. *The Earl Bishop*, vol. II, p. 478. It is possible, as this letter was sent to Derry, that it referred to Ballyscullion, then still unfinished, and not to Ickworth. On the other hand Joseph Sandys was already at Ickworth at this date.
4. Hussey, C. 'Ickworth Park, Suffolk', *Country Life*, vol. CXVII, pp. 678–81.
5. This letter from the Countess von Lichtenau's *Apologie* and subsequent letters from the Bishop to the Countess are in French in the original. (Cf. Childe-Pemberton, W. S. vol. II, pp. 418 et seq. who quotes from the French text.)
6. *Memoirs of Lady Hamilton*, pp. 117–18.
7. The Bishop's exact phrase is '*votre superbe théâtre*'.

8. *Journal of Elizabeth, Lady Holland*, vol. I, p. 138.
9. Cf. Trevelyan, R. 'Robert Fagan, an Irish Bohemian in Italy', (*Apollo*, vol. XCVI, no. 128, pp. 299 and 306).
10. *Letters of Lord Nelson to Lady Hamilton*, vol. I, p. 252.
11. *Journal of Elizabeth Lady Holland*, vol. I, p. 142.
12. Cf. Childe-Pemberton, W. S. vol. II, p. 496.
13. Morrison, A. *The Hamilton and Nelson Papers*, vol. I, Letter 281, p. 220.
14. Morrison, A. op. cit., vol. I, Letter 283, p. 221.
15. Foster, V. op. cit., pp. 140–2.
16. Cf. Childe-Pemberton, W. S. vol. II, pp. 523–4.
17. Morrison, A. op. cit., vol. I, Letter 298, p. 230.
18. Morrison, A. op. cit., vol. I, Letter 300, p. 230.

VII The End of the Journey

1. Falkiner, C. L. *Studies in Irish History and Biography*, p. 91.
2. Gordon, P. L. *Personal Memoirs*, vol. I, pp. 173–4.
3. Recounted by the traveller J. G. Seume of the painter Rheinhardt. Quoted by Childe-Pemberton, W. S. vol. II, pp. 607–9.
4. Morrison, A. *The Hamilton and Nelson Papers*, vol. I, Letters 293 and 294, p. 228.
5. Morrison, A. op. cit., vol. I, Letter 297, p. 229.
6. Morrison, A. op. cit., vol. I, Letter 300, p. 231.
7. Morrison, A. op. cit., vol. II, Letters 302 and 303, p. 1.
8. Morrison, A. op. cit., vol. II, Letter 305, pp. 2–3.
9. Morrison, A. op. cit., vol. II, Letter 308, p. 3.
10. Morrison, A. op. cit., vol. II, Letter 307, p. 3.
11. Foster, V. *The Two Duchesses*, pp. 152–3.
12. Cf. Childe-Pemberton, W. S. vol. II, pp. 576–7, quoted from the *Gentleman's Magazine*.
13. Morrison, A. op. cit., vol. II, Letter 383, p. 24.
14. *Journal of Elizabeth, Lady Holland*, vol. I, p. 219.
15. Cf. Childe-Pemberton, W. S. vol. II, pp. 591–2. (British Museum Add. MSS. 34911 f. 41.)
16. British Museum, Add. MSS. 41200 f. 105.
17. *Letters of Lord Nelson to Lady Hamilton*, vol. I, pp. 257–62.
18. Morrison, A. op. cit., vol. II, Letter 379, p. 39.
19. Cloncurry, Lord. *Personal Recollections*, p. 191.
20. Sadlier, T. (ed.) *An Irish Peer on the Continent*, p. 179.
21. Falkiner, C. L. op. cit., p. 95.
22. Cf. Cloncurry, Lord. op. cit., p. 191; Falkiner, C. L. op. cit., pp. 92–3.

NOTES

Quotations from letters or documents in the text, in particular the Bishop's letters to his two elder daughters and the letters to Lord Liverpool, when not indicated to the contrary in footnotes, are taken from *The Earl Bishop* by W. S. Childe-Pemberton, published in two volumes in 1924. This book is an indispensable source for any life of Lord Bristol and was based on papers in the possession of the Hervey family at Ickworth and the Bruce family at Downhill before its partial demolition.

Bibliography

Annual Register for 1803.

Ayling, S. *George the Third*, London, 1972.

Barrington, Sir Jonah. *Rise and Fall of the Irish Nation*, Paris, 1833.

Beckett, J. C. *The Making of Modern Ireland, 1603–1923*, London, 1966.

Childe-Pemberton, W. S. *The Earl Bishop*, 2 vols., London, 1924.

Cloncurry, Valentine, Lord. *Personal Recollections of his Life and Times*, Dublin, 1849.

Crosland, Margaret. *Louise of Stolberg, Countess of Albany*, Edinburgh, 1962.

Curtis, E. *A History of Ireland*, London, 1936.

D'Alton, E. A. *History of Ireland*, vol. III, London, 1910.

Doran, J. *'Mann' and Manners at the Court of Florence*, London, 1876.

Erskine, D. (ed.) *Augustus Hervey's Journal*, London, 1954.

Falkiner, C. L. *Studies in Irish History and Biography, Mainly of the Eighteenth Century*, London, 1902.

Farington, J. *The Farington Diary*, (ed. J. Grieg), vol. I, London, 1922.

Foster, Vere. *The Two Duchesses*, London, 1898.

Fothergill, B. *Sir William Hamilton*, London, 1969.

Froude, J. A. *The English in Ireland in the Eighteenth Century*, vol. II, London, 1874.

Gordon, P. L. *Personal Memoirs or Reminiscences of Men and Manners at Home and Abroad*, London, 1830.

Grosvenor, Caroline. (ed.) *The First Lady Wharncliffe and her Family*, vol 1. London, 1927.

Gwynn, S. *Henry Grattan and His Times*, London, 1938.

Hamilton, Lady. *Memoirs of Lady Hamilton*, London, 1815.

Hardy, F. *Memoirs of the Political and Private Life of James Caulfield, Earl of Charlmont*, 2 vols., London, 1812.

Holland, Lady. *The Journal of Elizabeth, Lady Holland*, (ed. by the Earl of Ilchester), vol. I, London, 1909.

Holland, Henry Richard, Lord. *Memoirs of the Whig Party during my Time*, vol. I, London, 1852.

Irwin, D. *English Neoclassical Art*, London, 1966.

Jacob, Rosamond. *The Rise of the United Irishmen*, London, 1939.

Johnston, Edith M. *Great Britain and Ireland, 1760–1800*, London, 1963.

Jones, T. *Memoirs of Thomas Jones*, Walpole Society, vol. XXXII, London, 1951.

Knight, Cornelia. *Autobiography*, 2 vols., London, 1861.

Le Brun, Mme Vigée. *Souvenirs*, London, 1879.

Lecky, W. E. H. *A History of Ireland in the Eighteenth Century*, vol. II, London, 1908.

Lecky, W. E. H. *Leaders of Public Opinion in Ireland*, 2 vols., London, 1903.

Luke, D. and Pick, R. (eds.). *Goethe: Conversations and Encounters*, London, 1966.

Morrison, A. *The Hamilton and Nelson Papers*, 2 vols., printed for private circulation, 1893–4.

Nelson, Lord. *Letters of Lord Nelson to Lady Hamilton with a Supplement of Interesting Letters by Distinguished Characters*, 2 vols., London, 1814.

Sherlock, M. *Letters from an English Traveller*, London, 1780.

Sherlock, M. *New Letters from an English Traveller*, London, 1781.

Sprigge, T. L. S. *The Correspondence of Jeremy Bentham*, vol. III, London, 1971.

Stuart, D. M. *Dearest Bess, the Life and Times of Lady Elizabeth Foster*, London, 1955.

Sykes, N. *Church and State in England in the Eighteenth Century*, Cambridge, 1934.

Tours, H. *Life and Letters of Lady Hamilton*, London, 1963.

Walpole, H. *Letters*, (ed. H. Cunningham), vols. VII and VIII, London, 1858.

White, T. H. *The Age of Scandal*, London, 1950.

Young, A. *Autobiography* (ed. M. Betham-Edwards), London, 1898.

Articles And Monographs

Hussey, C. 'Ickworth Park, Suffolk', *Country Life*, vol. CXVII, 10 March 1955, pp. 678–81.

Hussey, C. 'Ickworth, Suffolk'. *English Country Houses, Mid Georgian, 1760–1800* (*Country Life*, London, 1956).

Paterson, T. G. F. 'The Edifying Bishop', *Irish Georgian Society Quarterly Bulletin*, vol. IX, Nos. 3 and 4, July-Dec. 1966.

Rankin, P. 'Downhill, County Derry'. *Country Life*, vol. CL, Nos. 3865–6, 8 and 15 July 1971.

Rankin, P. *Irish Building Ventures of the Earl Bishop of Derry*, Ulster Architectural Heritage Society, 1972.

Trevelyan, R. 'Robert Fagan, An Irish Bohemian in Italy, *Apollo*, vol. XCVI, No. 128, October 1972.

Index

Books in National Trust Classics

The Earls of Creation
James Lees-Milne

The five Earls who are the subject of this book flourished at a time when the amateur exercised great influence over taste. Burlington, Pembroke, Leicester, Oxford and Bathurst created superb domains, most of which are still standing unaltered today.

Felbrigg, The Story of a House
R.W. Ketton-Cremer
Introduction by Wilhelmine Harrod

First published in 1962, this memoir is the history of a Norfolk country house from the seventeenth century until the 1960s, and the four families who have lived there. Written by one of the last members of the Wyndham family who bequeathed the house to the National Trust in 1969, the book pays tribute to this great house and its traditions.

First And Last Loves
John Betjeman
Illustrations by John Piper

An exuberant, convivial and affectionate collection of essays in which Betjeman writes very much as he was wont to speak, considering examples of architecture from Cheltenham to Leeds, London's railway stations to Ilfracombe's summer residences.

Gallipot Eyes
A Wiltshire Diary
Elspeth Huxley

An evocative diary of village life in a small Wiltshire community by the well-known author of *The Flame Trees of Thika.* Elspeth Huxley's diary records her everyday preoccupations, describes the people round her and notes the ever-changing patterns of existence.

Uppark and Its People
Margaret Meade-Fetherstonhaugh and Oliver Warner
Introduction by Martin Drury

An entertaining portrait of life over three centuries in the late 17th-century house of Uppark, built high on the Sussex Downs and now one of the National Trust's most highly regarded houses of its period.

A Hampshire Manor
Hinton Ampner
Ralph Dutton
Introduction by Lydia Greeves

The story of the delightful manor and garden at Hinton Ampner and of its owners, representative of the quiet country house in a secluded corner of England. Its celebrated garden attracts many visitors.

Pot-Pourri from a Surrey Garden
Mrs C.W. Earle
Introduction by Susan Campbell

This national and international bestseller started as advice for a friend, took shape into a personal, romantic, useful memoir about gardening, cookery, furnishing and education written in the form of a diary.